BARNEY BARNFATHER

BARNEY BARNFATHER

LIFE ON A SPITFIRE SQUADRON

ANGUS MANSFIELD

First published in the United Kingdom in 2008 by
The History Press
The Mill · Brimscombe Port · Stroud · Gloucestershire · GL5 2QG

British Library Cataloguing in Publication Data
A catalogue record for this book is available from the British Library.

Hardback ISBN 978-0-7509-4688-9

For Grandad – I wish I had listened some more

Typeset in Bembo and Syntax.
Typesetting and origination by
The History Press.
Printed and bound in the United Kingdom.

Contents

List of Illustrations

Foreword

FLT LT RODNEY SCRASE DFC,
NO. 72 (BASUTOLAND) SQUADRON

What do you remember of someone you last saw over sixty years ago? For me Barney was a dependable guy. Down at the flight line in Sicily, there he was in bush shirt and shorts, wearing his service cap with his reddish face around a bristly moustache. That was in Sicily during the summer of 1943. We had to contend with a hot climate with gusty winds, corned beef for meals, which melted off the plate, and living in tented accommodation with buckets of water to wash in; conditions in which it was not easy to keep smiling or to hear a snappy remark thrown in. But that was Barney, and that's the way we found him to be in his ten months with the Squadron.

In his five years' war-time service with the RAF, Barney would carry out three tours of operational flying in Britain, Malta, Sicily and Italy, interspersed with two tours of instructing, preparing new boys for their own tour of duty. Undoubtedly he found his time in 72 Squadron very fulfilling. In a unit in which there were air crew from most countries of the Empire, we all found him to be very much one of the boys and a competent pilot to whom one could look for guidance.

The man with whom he shared a nickname, Group Captain Barney Beresford OC 324 Wing, signed off Barney's log book in October 1945 with the assessment: 'Rated as exceptional as a fighter-bomber pilot and a flight commander.'

Acknowledgements

My first book has taken several years of research and I am indebted to a great many people for helping me. In addition to RAF and Squadron Records, my grandfather's Flying Log Book and those of others, personal diaries and first-hand anecdotes have been included as well as selected photographs from my grandfather's own collection. I thank the other pilots who willingly shared their memories, plus the US National Archive and Imperial War Museum Archive.

To anyone I have inadvertently omitted, may I apologise in advance, but I would in particular like to express my thanks to the following:

The RAF Ibsley Historical Group led by its Hon. Secretary Mrs Vera Smith, who put a request for information into its newsletter and also gave me permission to quote from her book on RAF Ibsley, *So Much Sadness So Much Fun*. She put me in touch with Keith Gamble, a former 234 Squadron pilot now living in Australia, who sent me photographs and his diary, and also with Foster Fisher, another former 234 Squadron pilot, who was shot down in April 1942 and became a POW. He now lives in Canada and gave me permission to quote from his recollections, which are also included in Vera's book about RAF Ibsley.

Bill Simpson, co-author of *603 Squadron – The Greatest Squadron of them All* with David Ross and Bruce Blanche, gave me permission to use information from their book about the squadron's time in Malta. He also put me in touch with Jack Rae, now living in New Zealand, who was able to recall his time on the island and in hospital, and in turn gave me permission to quote from his own book *Kiwi Spitfire Ace*.

Don Ross, now a retired USAF major general living in Nevada, learnt to fly at RAF Aston Down with 52 Operational Training Unit, near Stroud in Gloucestershire, at the same time that my grandfather was an instructor there. By his own admission he 'terrorised the pubs in Stroud', but was also willing to share his wartime diary and photographs.

Rodney Scrase has been good enough to write a foreword, share his memories and his log book and put me in touch with other 72 Squadron veterans such as Tom Hughes and its Membership Secretary Tom Docherty. Lloyd Snell, a Canadian radar mechanic with 43 Squadron, which formed part of 324 Wing alongside 72 Squadron in Sicily and Italy, was also willing to share his wartime diary and photos.

Chris Shores and Brian Cull have both written several books, and their advice and willingness to help an amateur like me is much appreciated.

The National Archive at Kew and the Imperial War Museum in Lambeth deserve a mention as they willingly help anyone attempting research even if they do not have all the answers.

Finally, this book would not have come to fruition without the help of Jonathan Falconer, who read and re-read the manuscript, made changes and suggestions and knocked it into the format you see now. Without him and everyone at The History Press, including Jane Hutchings and Abbie Wood, this book would not have been possible.

Abbreviations

ACM	Air Chief Marshal
AFC	Air Force Cross
AM	Air Marshal
AOC-in-C	Air Officer Commanding-in-Chief
ATA	Air Transport Auxiliary
AVM	Air Vice-Marshal
CFI	Chief Flying Instructor
DFC	Distinguished Flying Cross
DFM	Distinguished Flying Medal
DSO	Distinguished Service Medal
EAM	National Liberation Front (Greece)
EDES	National Republican Greek School
EFTS	Elementary Flying Training School
Flt Lt	Flight Lieutenant
Flg Off	Flying Officer
Flt Sgt	Flight Sergeant
Gp Capt	Group Captain
MO	Medical Officer
ORB	Operations Record Book
OTU	Operational Training Unit
Plt Off	Pilot Officer
RAAF	Royal Australian Air Force
RAFVR	Royal Air Force Volunteer Reserve
RCAF	Royal Canadian Air Force
RNZAF	Royal New Zealand Air Force
R/T	radio telephony
SAAF	South African Air Force
SFTS	Service Flying Training School
u/s	unserviceable
Sgt	Sergeant
Sqn Ldr	Squadron Leader
USAAF	United States Army Air Force
USAF	United States Air Force
VE Day	Victory in Europe Day
Wg Cdr	Wing Commander

Malta Under Siege

Experienced pilots from Malta had been sent back to Gibraltar to meet up with the aircraft carriers USS *Wasp* and HMS *Eagle* to guide the new batch of Spitfires into the beleaguered island. Squadron Leader Stan Grant from 249 Squadron would lead the first batch of sixteen. They were to fly along the north coast of Algeria and Tunisia as far as Cap Bon, then head south-east to skirt around the enemy-held island of Pantelleria in the Sicilian channel before heading for Malta.

On the morning of 9 May 1942 they were roused early. After eating breakfast and receiving a final briefing, they were ordered to their aircraft. They were only allowed to take the bare minimum of personal kit. With the engines roaring into life, the ground crew checked that the propellers were set to fine pitch. This had to be done because if the propellers had been left in coarse pitch, the Spitfires would not accelerate quickly enough to gain flying speed and would drop like stones off the bow of the huge aircraft carrier, USS *Wasp*. The deck officers waved their chequered flags and with full throttle applied, and emergency override to get the maximum speed out of the aircraft as they flew off the deck, the Spitfires began their historic journey to Malta.

Ray Hesselyn, a New Zealander, in his book *Spitfires over Malta* (jointly written with Australian, Paul Brennan, also with 249 Squadron, and author Henry Bateson) recalled the events of 9 May:

At dawn [Sqn Ldr] Gracie again addressed us. He stood on the roof of a utility truck with pilots, ground crew and soldiers lined up on the aerodrome in front of him. He spoke in the same strain as on the previous evening and wished everyone good luck. Oddly enough, on this crucial day the Ju88s had omitted their usual early morning raid and did not come over, nor did any Me109s. Between 9 and 10, four boys were scrambled, the rest of us knew they had gone up to cover the arrival of the new Spitfires. Everybody was happy and excited, keyed up with expectation.

In a few minutes the new boys started coming in over Imtarfa hill. At the same time the 109s arrived over Malta. The first bunch of Spits landed and I led an aircraft into my pen. The waiting ground crew pounced on it eagerly and began to rearm and refuel it. Its pilot, Pilot Officer Barnfather, an Englishman, climbed out of his cockpit and I handed him his written instructions. More Spits were coming over the hill and arrived in the circuit at the same time as a number of 109s. One of my erks, a big wild-looking fellow who had not shaved for three days, kept changing tools every few minutes. One minute he would have a rifle in his hands and [be] taking pot shots at the 109s and the next he would grab a tool and be undoing a panel or some screws on the Spits panel. Barnfather and I watched the Spits circling. That one will get it in a moment I remarked. It did. A Me109 blew a large piece out of the Spit's port side near the cockpit. The Spit made hurriedly for the aerodrome and after three attempts successfully force-landed. By this time there was a terrific din going on. The ground defences were engaging heavily and there was a lot of cannon fire between opposing aircraft. On the aerodrome, newly arrived Spits were being shepherded to their pens. They were refuelled and rearmed quickly and pilots clambered into their cockpits ready to take off immediately the order came. Within the 10 minutes of landing many of the new Spits were going up again.

It was a triumph of organisation and Barney had arrived in Malta.

CHAPTER 1

Early Life

Riversdale Robert Barnfather's arrival in the world at Yalding in Kent on 22 October 1917 was a little less spectacular than at Malta twenty-five years later. He was the third of three children who were born into a family of publicans. His mother and father, Thomas and Alice, ran The Engineer public house at Yalding. Confusingly, Riversdale would subsequently be known as 'Riv' to his family, 'Robert' at school, 'Barney' in his RAF career and 'Bob' at work and in later family life. For the sake of clarity, in this book we shall refer to him as 'Barney'. At the time of his birth, the First World War was three years old and Barney's father, Thomas, was serving with the Royal Engineers in France as a sergeant-major.

From 1930–4 Barney attended Latymer Upper School in Hammersmith, and it was on the sports field that he really excelled. He succeeded in getting his First XI caps in football and cricket and a cap in boxing. Indeed, he went on to represent the public school's First XI at outside half in football and his love of the game remained with him for the rest of his life.

From school Barney joined the firm of Gordian Strapping Ltd as a salesman, travelling the country selling their wares which included packs, pallet and strapping products. He would often stay in bed and breakfasts or pubs on his travels. It was on one such stop at a small town near Bristol called Keynsham that he met the Ollis family and, in particular, one of the daughters, Dorothy. She was 22 years old, highly impressionable and took a shine to the young travelling salesman with his own 'wheels'. Barney often stayed at Ivy Lodge opposite the Talbot Inn on the London Road; with his job as an area representative and salesman for Gordian Strapping, he became a familiar face around Keynsham.

The year 1939 arrived and with it the fear of another war with Germany. At 11.15 a.m. on 3 September, the Prime Minister Neville Chamberlain declared that 'this country is at war with Germany'. The Second World War had begun and by the end of September some 1½ million evacuees, mainly women and children, had been moved to areas of safety in the West Country, and the first British troops had been sent to France as part of the British Expeditionary Force to help defend the French border with Germany.

Despite the outbreak of war, the friendship between Barney and Dorothy blossomed, and Barney decided to volunteer for the Royal Air Force. He joined the RAF Volunteer Reserve (RAFVR) in August 1940 and soon after signing up he broke the news to the four people most immediately affected. Their reactions were almost the same in one respect, but quite different in others. His mother, he recalled, expressed no surprise, but she did betray a degree of anxiety; his father, whom he told over a pint in a pub at Purley, was also not surprised and seemed rather relieved that it was the RAF; neither was his brother in any way surprised. In fact, his brother's immediate response was to say that he too would be joining up. Barney's boss seemed to have been half expecting it, but Barney had the feeling that he was sorry he would be leaving.

Early in July he received a letter from the RAF Recruiting Centre asking him to report to the RAFVR Centre the following month. He was told to come prepared for immediate service and listed the various items that he would need.

Before he commenced his training, however, Barney had a far more important task and this was to get married. In view of his enlistment and because of the war, he had to obtain a special licence to marry Dorothy. And married they were, on 2 August 1940 at St John's Parish Church in Keynsham. Four days later he began his initial training and 'square-bashing' at No. 10 (Signals) Recruit Centre at Blackpool.

On completion of basic training, Barney's next move was in December 1940 to Babbacombe near Torquay in south Devon. Torquay and South Devon seemed far removed from all the action and consequently proved to be an attractive retreat. Those who could afford it chose to escape there from the larger urban areas which were under threat of bombing attacks.

In common with many other seaside resort towns, Torquay was also chosen by the RAF to establish a Reserve Wing, later to become an Initial Training Wing. Many of the local hotels were requisitioned for use as accommodation and for training purposes. New recruits continued their 'square-bashing' by the harbour side.

No. 1 Initial Training Wing (ITW) had been formed at Babbacombe in June 1940. Postings were made from Babbacombe to Elementary Flying Training Schools (EFTS) – including those overseas in Canada and Southern Rhodesia, now Zimbabwe – where they eventually qualified as pilots, observers, W/T operators and wireless operators/air gunners.

After passing simple examinations, those who were successful left for flying training elsewhere. Some of them went to the United States, while others were shared between two Elementary Flying Training Schools. Barney was posted to No. 14 EFTS at Elmdon, Birmingham, in April 1941.

The course at Elmdon lasted for about two months, at the end of which, in theory, a newly qualified pilot would be ready to join an operational squadron. After a few hours' dual flying Barney went solo on 30 April. By June, Barney was assessed as 'average' as a pilot and after a couple of weeks' leave it was confirmed that he was being recommended for fighters and was to report to No. 9 Service Flying Training School (SFTS) at Hullavington in Wiltshire, which was not that far by road from Keynsham.

By the end of May Barney had accumulated 13 hours dual and nearly 16 hours solo on the Miles Master and had completed several local cross-country navigation tests around Colerne, Hullavington and Babdown. By 6 August he was ready for his first flight in a front-line fighter, the Hawker Hurricane. The experience was exhilarating, the power impressed him and the flight was memorable. Formation flying and practice landings followed at different airfields, among them Aston Down near Stroud and Charmy Down at Swainswick, just outside Bath ('tricky due to the winds on the top of the hill'), where the airfield had been built overlooking the Georgian city and the beautiful valleys around Lansdown.

Barney learnt that the key to being a fighter pilot was to stick close to the leader, and that this would require immense concentration. He would need to remain alert and be adept at using the throttles, stick and rudder. With more practice it would become second nature and he would be able to take off and fly in formation, either in cloud or on landing.

The final examination proved straightforward and he was awarded his wings on 13 September 1941. His log book was endorsed with an overall proficiency as 'average' and an aptitude as a 'pilot/navigator'.

A couple of weeks later, Barney was posted to No. 57 Operational Training Unit (OTU) at Hawarden, a few miles from Chester, where he would learn to fly Spitfires. Before the Second World War, aircrew completed operational training on their squadrons. Once war had broken out, it became obvious that this could no longer be undertaken by operational units and by personnel actively engaged on operations. At first, squadrons were taken off operations and allocated to the task of preparing new pilots and crews, but before long these training squadrons were re-designated Operational Training Units (or OTUs).

Barney's first flight in a Spitfire was on 30 September 1941. It was a Mark I, powered by a 1,030hp Rolls-Royce Merlin II liquid-cooled engine, with a single-speed supercharger and a two-position, variable-pitch, three-bladed metal propeller, giving the aircraft a top speed of 362mph at 19,000ft and a service ceiling of 34,000ft. It was able to climb at 2,500ft per minute and could reach 20,000ft in 9 minutes.

He was shown the various cockpit instruments, the knobs and levers and the operation of the reflector gunsight, and the gun-firing mechanism with its 'fire-safe' switch. It was a vast array of instrumentation and Barney had to identify each dial and switch before he would be allowed to fly the Spitfire. After checking and re-checking, testing the controls, the radio, the oxygen and fuel states, practising rolling the perspex hood back and forth, switching on the gunsight and testing the range bar, he was ready. With the propeller in fine pitch, he primed the engine, switched on, and gave a nod to the airman by the external starter battery. He pressed the starter button and the Merlin engine burst into life. Recounting that moment years later, some aspects of that first flight were as vivid as if they had been the day before. Take-off was simple. Correcting the swing with the right rudder as the power built up, he bounced a few times on the grass and then he was up and clear of the airfield. The Spitfire climbed into the sky and once more Barney sensed the tremendous power of the engine. He practised aerobatics and medium and steep turns. The Spitfire responded to the slightest touch and the forward visibility was excellent. The only blind spot was behind the tail, but this was helped by a rear-view mirror mounted on the top of the windscreen.

One of the features of the Spitfire, he discovered, was the wonderful handling characteristic at low speeds and at high 'g' when close to the stall. With full power in a steep turn she would judder, but as long as she was handled correctly she would not spin. Some years later, Barney recalled coming in to land on that first flight. Returning to Hawarden, he put the airscrew into fine pitch, lowered the undercarriage, turned cross-wind, lowered the flaps and straightened out for a final approach before the Spitfire 'floated' down onto the grass airfield again. It was a description that many pilots would come to use about the Spitfire: she tended to 'float' because of her clean lines, which blessed her with a minimum of aerodynamic drag. She was an absolute delight to fly.

Over the next month Barney concentrated on his formation flying, practised dog-fighting, aerobatics and circuits and bumps, together with firing his guns and making practice interceptions. By 10 November he had completed the final leg of his training at 57 OTU and his course was finished. Again he was assessed as 'average', only this time he was posted on to an operational fighter unit – 234 Squadron based at Ibsley in Hampshire.

CHAPTER 2

Operational at Last

Ibsley and 234 Squadron, 1941

No. 234 Squadron was originally formed in August 1918 as a flying boat squadron. It flew anti–submarine patrols over the approaches to the English Channel until the armistice, but was disbanded on 15 May 1919. On 30 October 1939, it was reformed at Leconfield, Yorkshire, as a fighter squadron. Originally intended for shipping protection duties, it flew a mixture of Blenheims, Battles and Gauntlets until March 1940, when it began to receive Spitfires. The squadron became operational on 11 May and throughout the Battle of Britain it was based in southern England. In April 1941 it began sweeps over northern France from its base at Warmwell in Dorset.

During the latter stages of 1941 and early 1942, the RAF was given new orders to take the fight back to the enemy, across the Channel and into northern France.

The new Spitfire Mk VB, with which 234 Squadron was now equipped, was much improved when compared to the earlier marks, especially its rate of climb, and it had a better performance at height. It was proving to be a match for the latest Me109F, but it was to find the superb German Focke-Wulf Fw190 a tougher proposition. Attempts were made to increase the range of the Spitfire by using new long-range 'slipper tanks' which could be jettisoned once the fuel inside had been used. The additional fuel allowed aircraft to operate over the Brest peninsula or along the Dutch coast, but even so the Spitfires would be flying at the maximum range of their endurance and flying over an inhospitable English Channel.

The new fighter operations, called 'sweeps', were given codenames – Circus, Rodeo, Rhubarb and Ramrod, with the following meanings: Circus – consisting of a bomber force or fighter-bombers which would be escorted by fighters to draw up other enemy fighters into combat; Rodeo – fighter sweep without bombers; Rhubarb – small sections of fighters, mainly in pairs, would attack targets of opportunity such as trains, troops, road transport and airfields; Ramrod – bomber force with a fighter escort to attack a specific target.

Fighter squadrons based across southern England, and including those stationed at Ibsley, carried out operations such as these. No. 234 Squadron (which had moved to Ibsley in November), together with 118 and 501 Squadrons, formed what became known as the Ibsley Wing under the leadership of Wg Cdr Ian 'Widge' Gleed DFC. Gleed was tiny, standing only 5ft 2in tall, but he had earned the respect of everyone who served under him, having fought in the Battle for France and the Battle of Britain. No. 118 Squadron was commanded by Sqn Ldr J.C. Carver, RAFVR. No. 234 Squadron was commanded by Sqn Ldr M.V. Blake, a New Zealander and another pre-war pilot who had flown in the Battle of Britain; and No. 501 Squadron was commanded by Sqn Ldr C.F. Currant, inevitably known as 'Bunny'.

The airfield at Ibsley had been opened in 1941 as a satellite to Middle Wallop. It was situated to the west of the New Forest, near the village of Ringwood, and about 10 miles from Bournemouth. In November 1941 Ibsley had been honoured by a visit from HRH the Duke of Kent who also went into the Officers' Mess and witnessed the arrival of No. 234 (Madras Presidency) Squadron from Warmwell. They were equipped with Spitfire VBs, which carried the squadron code 'AZ'. At this time, daily operational life was pretty mundane as a look at a typical week from the 234 Squadron's Operations Record Book (ORB) reveals:

1 NOVEMBER

Four aircraft attacked the Beam station at Jo'burg, direct hits were observed by each aircraft on the main building, which was shattered. Two shipping reconnaissance carried out by eight aircraft. No shipping was sighted. A wireless station at Point du Saire was attacked by two aircraft but direct hits were not registered.

2 NOVEMBER

Four aircraft attacked wireless station at Audeville, hits registered on building but Plt Off Meyer developed engine trouble after the attack and is believed to have force-landed on Alderney. Convoy protection given during the morning.

3 NOVEMBER

Three shipping reconnaissance carried out over the Channel Islands by sections of aircraft. An 'E' Boat was attacked by Red Section [Flt Lt Mortimer Rose and Plt Off Bland] to the north of Sark. Further reconnaissance showed that this vessel had been sunk.

4 NOVEMBER

Local flying only.

5 NOVEMBER

Squadron left Warmwell for Ibsley.

6 NOVEMBER

Local flying. Escort given to Lysanders in search of missing Whirlwind.

7 NOVEMBER

Local flying. Convoy protection given until dusk.

December was also pretty quiet. The weather kept operations to a minimum, as the ORB records:

5 DECEMBER

Two aircraft [Sgt Walker and Plt Off Clarke] were sent on a shipping reconnaissance off the Cherbourg peninsula, from which they did not return. Subsequent searching by aircraft from Warmwell and six of our aircraft failed to find anything. It is presumed they penetrated the ten-mile limit of the French coast and were probably decoyed by enemy aircraft to fly over the peninsula, and were ultimately shot down by these bandits or by flak, which is known to be intense over the area.
   Local flying. Two sections scrambled base. Practice cannon firing and air testing. Convoy protection.

17 DECEMBER

Local flying, the squadron flew to Portreath, Cornwall, in the afternoon.

The presence of the German battle cruisers, *Scharnhorst* and *Gneisenau*, lying in Brest harbour posed a serious threat to the all-important convoys crossing the Atlantic. So much so that two large daylight bomber raids were specially mounted in December 1941. Again, the squadron ORB reports:

18 DECEMBER

The squadron, with eleven aircraft led by Sqn Ldr Blake DFC, acted as top cover for twelve Stirlings and offensive operations by Halifax and Manchester aircraft on Brest. They patrolled the area to the north of Brest outside the flak area to escort the Stirlings on their return flight. Several Me109s were sighted but they made no attempt to intercept. Plt Off Denville chased and engaged one of these enemy aircraft and registered hits on the fuselage, this claimed as damaged. The squadron returned to Ibsley in the afternoon.
   No Spitfires were lost and two Me109s were claimed as destroyed and two damaged by other squadrons, but the German battleships remained largely unscathed.

On the afternoon of Christmas Eve 1941, the squadron was ordered to Predannack. It was an easy time for the ground crews as the whole wing had flown off and did not return for several days. They had departed on another Ramrod operation against Brest and were expected back later that day. They needed to land at St Eval in Cornwall to refuel, but before they could take off again the weather worsened and they were grounded for a few days.

Back at Ibsley on Christmas morning there was egg, bacon and sausages for breakfast. The dining hall had been decorated with flags and bunting and the officers, NCOs and other pilots who had not made the trip, including Barney, served the other ranks. They had a full menu: soup followed by fish, with a main course of turkey, pork, stuffing, apple sauce and gravy with sprouts and baked potatoes. The traditional Christmas pudding and brandy sauce followed, and the meal was finished with beer, minerals, nuts and cigarettes. Considering that food rationing was in force, it was a grand affair.

During the meal the station orchestra, normally reserved for the Officers' Mess, played dance tunes and swing numbers. Later on in the afternoon, after a game of football, everyone had mince pies and two bottles of ale each. Activities were livened up by one of the 118 boys who took up a Tiger Moth and chased the ball around, flying at about 10ft off the ground. He nearly lost it after banking steeply when his wing-tip creased the grass. In the evening, professional performers in the RAF put on a polished and enjoyable performance so that everyone retired after a good day.

The squadron ORB recorded the following:

30 DECEMBER

The squadron operating from Predannack, Cornwall, gave escort to Halifax aircraft in an attack on the naval base at Brest. Sgt Joyce was posted missing from operation.

That morning the squadron had woken to a bright and frosty start and the wing had flown down to Predannack in Cornwall where, under Wg Cdr Ian Gleed and with Sqn Ldr Carver as his number two, they had taken off shortly after 1 p.m. on a Circus operation against Brest, Operation Veracity. The task of the wing was to escort the Halifax bombers and defend them against attack from enemy fighters. Some enemy fighters were seen and an aircraft that was lagging behind the main formation paid the price. The Spitfires escorted the bombers into the flak area and one Spitfire appeared to be hit by a bomb, which fortunately did not explode. The operation itself cost three fighters and three bombers. Sgt Pilot A.E. 'Teddy' Joyce was one of those lost. Apparently he had baled out from his plane, was wounded and taken prisoner of war. It was learned sometime later that he had been transferred to Stalag Luft III, the notorious prisoner-of-war camp at Sagen in eastern Poland.

CHAPTER 3

On the Offensive

234 Squadron, 1942

The squadron was released for New Year's Day and weather continued to hamper operations during the early part of the year.

8 JANUARY

Barney's Flying Log Book (Log Book): Swanage and Portland – nowt!!

Squadron ORB (ORB): Practice flying formation and cannon testing. Two bogey scrambles by four aircraft.

10 JANUARY

ORB: Local formation practice flights – one bogey scramble by two aircraft.
   Sergeant Campbell of 501 Squadron was lost when his Spitfire broke up in mid-air and crashed at Rockborne near Fordingbridge.
   Flying cancelled as the weather conditions poor. It wasn't just poor, the airfield was covered in snow and the runways had to be swept clear using bundles of heather gathered from Ibsley Common.

29 JANUARY

Log Book: Shipping recco – My first sight! Flight panic for 118 Sgt in drink.

ORB: Six a/c carried out search south-east of St Catherines point for missing pilot of 118 Squadron. Returned after one hour with nothing of interest to report. Sqn Ldr F.E.W. Birchfield took over command of squadron.

No. 118 Squadron's Commanding Officer was Johnny Carver and he, with Sgt Frank Brown, Plt Off Ted Ames and Sgt Hardy Kerr, had led a sweep attack on a distillery at Courselles sur Mer. It was on the return journey that Sgt Kerr was seen to be lagging when suddenly his aircraft shot into the air, turned on its back and crashed into the sea. Kerr was seen to bale out at 400ft with his parachute opening

before he hit the water, but a subsequent search by Coastal Command and his
fellow pilots proved useless and Kerr was presumed lost.

1–3 FEBRUARY

ORB: Weather cancelled all flying. Weather was bloody awful. No. 118 Squadron lost Plt
Off Ted Ames during a fight with several Me109s whilst on a 'Rhubarb' with Flt Lt Pete
Howard Williams, to whom he was flying No. 2. Williams managed to get one however
which dived into the sea, but he was then attacked by the other Me109s and had to
break off and take evasive action in and out of cloud to find his way home.

4–6 FEBRUARY

ORB: Local flying with practice formation and convoy protection.

7 FEBRUARY

ORB: Convoy protection, one bogey scramble, four aircraft carried out a shipping
reconnaissance of the Cherbourg peninsula but nothing of interest was sighted.

8 FEBRUARY

ORB: Four aircraft carried out another shipping reconnaissance of the Channel Islands at
08.40 a.m. Nothing sighted. Beat up searchlight positions.

9 FEBRUARY

ORB: Convoy patrol and exercise 'Thor' (Searchlight Co-op) carried out by the squadron.
One bogey scramble.

10 FEBRUARY

Log Book: German destroyer – made acquaintance of Herr Flak. With Hurribombers after
same, nothing doing.

ORB: Four aircraft carried out a shipping reconnaissance off the west of the Cherbourg
peninsula [Flt Lt Glaser, Plt Off Pike, Plt Off Cameron and Sgt Barnfather].
   An enemy destroyer was sighted, proceeding at speed due south of Alderney. Glaser
told them to keep wide and he would do a quick orbit to call for an emergency homing,
which they did. Our aircraft were fired upon without effect. Fire from shore batteries was
also experienced as the flight passed Flamanville on their return.

Sgt Keith Gamble of 234 Squadron recalled in his diary: 'Opened up with
everything and lucky to get back.' As soon as they landed, and following on from this
reconnaissance, four Hurricane bombers were escorted by eleven aircraft from the
squadron and twelve from 501 Squadron and were detailed to attack the destroyer.

The wing under Wg Cdr Gleed searched the area to the north of Jersey but failed to locate the destroyer. No enemy aircraft were sighted and no flak experienced.

Gamble again recalled: 'Went out with Hurribombers later on with 118 and 234. Twenty-seven planes altogether as Spike couldn't get off, never sighted it, must have been into port. Spent night at Mess looking at some photographs of Keith Buettel who was in England at Bradfield but had trained in Canada.'

ORB: At 1600 hours the squadron carried out a practice scramble followed by flight formation. Our twelve aircraft were airborne in 6 minutes and refuelled and rearmed in 22 minutes. Air-to-air firing was carried out. Convoy protection given by Black Section.

11 FEBRUARY

ORB: Practice flying. Four bogey scrambles by eight aircraft.

There was more bad luck for 118 Squadron when Sgt Pilot Tom Mathers and Sgt Pilot Keith Buettel RAAF, collided when at about 5,000ft over West Grinstead near Salisbury. Keith Gamble recalled with some sadness in his diary:

Flight formation and drogue firing in the morning, convoy with Mike Cameron afternoon, bit of activity and never got relieved for 2 hours. Drome cleared for me to come into land as very short of petrol, just cut out as I came over fence – pretty tinny! Barney and Wiggy [Barnfather and Webster] scrambled and off the ground in 1½ minutes, a record! Pictures at night, dinner at the Ritz at camp, still feeling pretty lousy. Keith Buettel and Tom Mathers killed today.

12 FEBRUARY

Log Book: After 'G' [Gneisenau] and 'S' [Scharnhorst] and others off Ostend. Plt Offs Pike and McLeod missing. Landed at Manston. Mac later confirmed as Plt Off W.

ORB: Four aircraft were scrambled at 0800 hours to intercept raiders that had attacked Warmwell and Exeter aerodromes. Several vectors were given but our aircraft failed to make any interceptions.

The squadron, together with 118 Squadron and 501 Squadron, were ordered to West Malling for Operation Fuller, to act as cover for the bombers of Bomber and Coastal Commands in the attack of the German cruisers *Scharnhorst*, *Gneisenau* and *Prinz Eugen*.

The three German capital ships had been trapped in Brest harbour for several months and had already been the subject of attacks by Bomber Command, escorted by fighters, including those based at Ibsley and including 234 Squadron. On the 12th however, in inclement weather, the German Navy attempted an audacious breakout from Brest, aiming to steam up the English Channel at speed to reach a safer port such as Wilhelmshaven. Heavy morning fog over southern England had prevented any RAF reconnaissance flights and the three German ships, heavily escorted by E-boats and flak ships, slipped out of Brest harbour undetected.

With the early morning reconnaissance cancelled, it was not until some hours later that the convoy was spotted, initially by two Spitfire pilots from Kenley, one of whom was Victor Beamish. By then, the German convoy had entered the Straits of Dover and it took some time to organise the attacks. The pilots of the Ibsley Wing were quickly alerted, as were many other squadrons in the south of England, and were sent to West Malling for refuelling and a briefing for what had become known as Operation Fuller. The plan was to fly from West Malling in an attempt to secure air superiority over the German ships, and give the RAF torpedo bombers a chance to execute their attack without being intercepted by German fighters.

By this time, however, there had been several attempted attacks against the ships. In one final attempt, Cdr Eugene Esmonde of the Fleet Air Arm and the crews of his Swordfish aircraft had made their almost suicidal attack; all six were either shot down by flak or by fighters. Esmonde died along with the rest of his crews and eleven other men, and was subsequently awarded a posthumous Victoria Cross. With the Ibsley Wing providing cover, Bristol Beaufort torpedo bombers made further attacks but they all failed and the weather, by then, was closing in and flying was becoming impossible.

All the fighter wings sent out were heavily engaged and apart from the Ibsley Wing, those at North Weald, Debden, Biggin Hill and Hornchurch were also highly involved from 11 and 12 Group. Widge Gleed and 501 Squadron came across several Me109s but mistook them for friendly so they slid into the murk without being chased. 234 and 118 joined in the battle shortly afterwards. Flt Lt D. McKay managed to get strikes on a Me109 which then collided with another and both fell into the sea, but these were the only victories and it came at a cost because 118 lost Stone, a New Zealander, while 234 lost Plt Offs Dennis Pike and McLeod.

The Germans had succeeded through a combination of bravery, poor weather, luck and a huge air screen over the convoy.

As stated above, the only success for the whole wing and 234 Squadron were the two Me109s that collided when fired upon by Flt Lt D.A.S. McKay DFM and Bar. His combat report recalls:

> I took off from West Malling at 1415 hours with my No. 2, and endeavoured to join up with the leading sections that had already taken off. They had already climbed above cloud so I could not see them. I lost Yellow 2, who was about 1,000yd behind so continued on a course of 090 degrees in cloud for another 20 minutes or so. On diving through cloud at about 2,500ft I could see the French coast about 5 miles away and on my right, approximately 1,000ft below, 3 Me109Fs. I got right behind them and attacked the starboard one of the three from about 250yd, closing to about 200yd. The right hand enemy aircraft reared up and dived sideways into the leader and both aircraft crashed into the sea locked together. I saw no sign of survivors and returned to West Malling at 1540 hours.

Sgt Pilot Don MacCleod made a forced landing in northern France only to be taken prisoner and spend the rest of the war as a POW at Stalag Luft III.

Keith Gamble recalled his recollections of the day:

What a day! On early morning readiness and while still dark we were scrambled to Portland, got vectored up and down coast, could see flashes of flak guns and bomb bursts at Warmwell but were not allowed to go in until guns had finished, plotting lousy and missed great opportunity of getting them, came back very disappointed and mad with controller. 118 and 501 called to readiness about 12 o'clock so we guessed something big on. 234 scrambled at 13.10 but again the plotting all to hell. Vectored up to West Malling, south of London, quick briefing by Wingco Gleed then Wing set out over North Sea. Horrible shambles as Wingco just buzzed off by himself and never gave the Wing half a chance to form up. Bags of activity, cruisers throwing up every imaginable kind of flak – shocking weather with cloud right down on deck, everybody split up, couldn't see whether you hit anything or not due to the clouds, everybody landed at different dromes.

234 lost Spike and MacCleod and 118 a couple. Altogether forty-two planes lost in the shambles. McKay got two certainties. Feeling pretty bad at night and went to bed early.

---

13 FEBRUARY

ORB: Convoy patrol the whole day. Practice local flying.

Keith Gamble's Diary: Rested during morning while maintenance squadron worked on kites, did a convoy during afternoon with 'Drink' and could just about walk when I got out of plane – reported to MO after coming off readiness and as temp was 101 was bunged straight into hospital, just five weeks since I was here and feeling pretty browned off at always having colds.

---

14 FEBRUARY

ORB: Air-to-sea firing. Height climb by two aircraft. Convoy protection given throughout the day.

Gamble was feeling a lot better but his throat was still sore. He wrote letters all day, and commented that it was 'great around here and [they] look after you very well – John came in and we jawed till about 22.45'.

---

15 FEBRUARY

ORB: Ship reconnaissance was ordered. Four aircraft from Red and Yellow Sections operated but the operation was abandoned as weather conditions were unsuitable. Air-to-sea firing carried out. Convoy protection was given throughout the afternoon. Four aircraft were scrambled to Portland but no interception was made. Two aircraft were scrambled to the Needles but this also proved to be a bogey.

Gamble's Diary: Not much sleep as throat very sore, doc called and said tonsils need removing, too much waste of time. John had a half day off so spent most of time with me, wrote letters.

16 FEBRUARY

ORB: Six aircraft carried out cannon firing. Squadron carried out a practice scramble followed by formation flying and four aircraft carried out air-to-air firing. Squadron released at 1702 hours.

Gamble's Diary: Doc came in the afternoon and let me go feeling a bit weak but glad to get out, spent night in the Mess writing letters and talking.

17 FEBRUARY

ORB: Convoy protection throughout the day. Four aircraft were scrambled to Worth Matravers but no interception was made. Three aircraft from Blue Section carried out a shipping reconnaissance of the western area of the Cherbourg peninsula but nothing of interest sighted.

Gamble's Diary: No flying yet, went into Salisbury with Johnny and saw *Sun Valley Serenade*, good show and went to supper afterwards, caught 21 bus to Fordingbridge and walked rest of way.

18 FEBRUARY

ORB: Squadron came to readiness at 0715 hours and gave protection to convoy until 1300 hours. Cannon firing carried out and Yellow Section was scrambled to Portland at 2,000ft but made no interception. Squadron was released at 1700 hours.

Gamble's Diary: On readiness this morning, nothing doing and weather too bad in afternoon, wrote home at night, pretty browned off at not being sent back home especially now that Singapore has fallen.

19 FEBRUARY

ORB: Squadron at '30 minutes' until coming to readiness at 1300 hours when the convoy was patrolled until release at 1712 hours. White Section was scrambled but again no interception was made. Red and Blue Sections carried out shipping reconnaissance off the Cherbourg peninsula, nothing of interest sighted.

20 FEBRUARY

ORB: Local practice flying. Air-to-air firing and shipping protection. Red and Blue Sections carried out a shipping reconnaissance off the Cherbourg peninsula, but again nothing of interest sighted.

Gamble's Diary: Readiness morning, convoy low-lying and camera to sea afternoon with Red Section. Long day, very browned off. Went into Ringwood with Red and Mac and had numerous whiskies and gins but couldn't get glow up! Caught 22.30 bus back to camp.

21 FEBRUARY

ORB: Air-to-sea firing and local practice flying. Protection was given to shipping, Red and Yellow Sections were scrambled followed by Blue, Green and Black Sections. Six bandits plotted south of Isle of Wight. Yellow Section [Plt Off Cameron and Sgt Cam] were vectored onto the position and carried out diving attacks on two aircraft, which they believed to be Me109s. Plt Off Cameron shot down one. Sgt Cam failed to register any hits.

Tragically it was found later that these aircraft were two Tomahawks from 268 Squadron who had been on a shipping recce with 501 Squadron. The Tomahawk shot down had been flown by Flt Lt C. Hawkins. He was killed when his aircraft hit a tree during an attempted forced landing near Corfe Castle. After further enquiries, it came to light that there had been bandits in the vicinity but that they had been above the friendly aircraft that had been attacked. Gamble also recalled the events of the day.

Gamble's Diary: Weather u/s in the morning but bags of action in the afternoon. 'A' Flight had two scrambles then we had a Flight scramble – all off in 2 minutes. I was No. 2 to Dave Glaser, got vectored all over Channel in and out of cloud with 64 about. Heard Yellow say he was going into attack, finally spent time looking for a pilot in the drink near French coast, finger well out. Up for 1.45 and only 10 gallons left when landed. Yellow 1 had shot down a Tomahawk in mistake for a Fw190 so poor old Cameron in hell of a fix.
   Went out with 'Drink' at 18.30 for last section on convoy and nearly got caught as weather closed in and couldn't find drome. Finally got in at about 19.30, very relieved to get down. Very tired and went to bed early.

22 FEBRUARY

ORB: Air-to-sea and cannon testing. Practice formation flying and convoy protection given.

Gamble's Diary: Early morning readiness, up at 0630 but never got a call till 1130 when Dave Glaser and self went out on convoy. Destroyer called us up and asked us to investigate surface craft south of them. Went out as far as French coast and finally picked it up mid-channel. Very disappointed as it turned out to be one of our boats on patrol. Practice flying with Red, Mac and Barry Denville in the afternoon – pretty rotten, can't fly with Denville and will punch him on the nose one day! Wrote to folks at night and listened to wireless. To bed at 2300.

23 FEBRUARY

ORB: Twelve aircraft led by Flt Lt McKay carried out a squadron 'Balbo'. Convoy patrolled until dusk.

Gamble's Diary: Squadron Balbo in the morning and had all the luck in the world as only about 5 minutes from the drome my aircraft put a big end through the sump, everybody thought I was on fire as smoke poured from the exhausts, but I managed to glide into the drome on a faltering motor and landed safely. I couldn't help thinking how St Christopher must have been looking over me as flying the same machine the day before, I had been at zero feet over the French coast. Convoy patrol during the afternoon and went to bed early as another early show due tomorrow.

24 FEBRUARY

ORB: Four aircraft carried out a shipping reconnaissance off the Cherbourg peninsula but returned with nothing of interest to report.

Gamble's Diary: Convoy protection given. Only practice flying in the morning as nothing happened on readiness. Had afternoon off and went into Bournemouth to get some photos and spent a couple of hours with Len and had a few drinks at the pavilion, early to bed again.

25 FEBRUARY

ORB: Convoy protection given.

Gamble's Diary: Quiet day, little flying, wrote letters at night and afterwards went to pictures at camp but felt pretty lousy again and couldn't keep awake so left half way through.

26 FEBRUARY

ORB: Shipping reconnaissance carried [out]. Three ships were sighted south of Alderney. A 'Roadstead' was subsequently carried out by four Hurricanes and twelve aircraft from 234 Squadron and twelve from 501 Squadron but they failed to find the target. Sgt Redfern was in collision with another of our aircraft and lost his tail and the aircraft crashed into the river at Ringwood. Sgt Redfern killed.

Gamble's Diary: Big day today, started off before dawn with Dave Glaser on convoy protection, came down about 0900 hours and after getting refuelled hopped off to France on a shipping recco without having breakfast. Wiggy [Webster] had Red for No. 2 and Dave flew No. 2 to me.

27 FEBRUARY

ORB: Convoy patrol throughout the day. Air-to-sea firing.

28 FEBRUARY

ORB: Twelve aircraft were detailed to act as cover for offensive operations on the French coast and were up from base at 0915 hours. They landed at Tangmere after an uneventful patrol and returned to Ibsley at 1200 hours. A further patrol was carried out by twelve aircraft, south of Selsey Bill, and gave cover to returning raiding forces. Scrambled four aircraft in the evening.

The first week of March saw the weather heavily curtail any operations and flying.

8 MARCH

Log Book: Through the 'rocks' 25,000ft and cheesy. Trying to scare some up! Don't think they saw us.

ORB: Practice 'beat up' of Blandford and Bridport. Shipping reconnaissance carried out by Blue and Green Sections off the Cherbourg peninsula but nothing of interest sighted. A diversion sweep carried out by the squadron off Cherbourg. This was uneventful, no enemy sighted and no flak encountered.

9 MARCH

ORB: 234 Squadron, with 118 and 501 operating from Redhill, as the Ibsley Wing, gave escort to six Bostons in a Ramrod attack on an oil storage depot at Mazingarbe near Bethune.

No. 234 Squadron was not engaged and returned to Redhill, then back to Ibsley in the evening. No. 501 Squadron saw Me109s and engaged, with Plt Off R.A. 'Dickie' Newberry claiming one destroyed and Sqn Ldr 'Bunny' Currant claiming a probable. 'Bunny' himself received hits but managed to get his plane back to crash-land at Lympne where his aircraft turned over and he was admitted to hospital with cuts and grazes.

No. 118 Squadron was engaged on the way back by Fw190s and Me109s, and Plt Off MacKenzie suffered hits to his fuselage and was also wounded. He made a gallant effort to get back, crossing the English coast, but he crash-landed on the Dover to Canterbury road and was killed.

10–12 MARCH

ORB: Weather cancelled all flying.

Keith Gamble's Diary: Still no flying, wrote letters and went to camp concert at night.

13 MARCH

ORB: Protection was given to shipping during the afternoon. No training in the morning due to weather conditions.

No. 118 Squadron lost their CO, Johnny Carver, who was shot down into the sea 5 miles west off the Casquettes after attacking two Ju88s. The French pilot with 118 Squadron, André Jubelin, scored hits on one Ju88, but Carver's aircraft was hit by return fire after he also attacked with Sgt V.K. Moody. There seemed little hope as he had been shot down so close to the French coast. The other Ju88 was attacked by 'Widge' Gleed and Plt Off R.C. Lynch from 501 Squadron and it was seen to pour black smoke, but then disappeared into cloud and could only be claimed as a probable.

Gleed's combat report for the day stated:

I was leading the cover squadron and in mid-Channel when I sent them home because of bad weather. I joined the close escort squadron and weaved. Having turned north after sighting Guernsey I saw a twin-engined aircraft that dived on to the port side of the formation. I immediately turned to attack having warned the rest of the formation on the R/T. The enemy aircraft turned towards me and climbed at full speed towards cloud cover. The enemy aircraft fired recognition signals. I identified it as a Ju88 and opened fire from dead astern at 400yd with short bursts of cannon and machine gun. The first two bursts seemed to miss and I experienced fairly accurate return fire from the top rear gunner. After the third burst all return fire ceased. From 250yd I gave several, half-second bursts of machine gun and cannon, one of which hit the port engine. This engine seemed to give off small explosions and flame. The enemy aircraft immediately levelled out and flew with one wing down. I then gave it another fairly long burst which finished my cannon ammunition. This attack had no result. Number two began attacking from astern so I broke away.

I then carried out a beam attack with machine guns only, giving a series of short bursts, and followed it up with a quarter attack. This last attack, during which I closed to 150yd, caused the nose of the enemy aircraft to dip suddenly, from which it recovered, and I saw it disappear in the rain in a very shallow dive with the usual smoke from the engines. During this last attack I heard Sqn Ldr Carver giving Mayday on his R/T. I tried to find him, but failed. All my ammunition was used.

Claim: One Ju88 probably destroyed.

Gamble's Diary: Camera gun in morning and called to readiness in the afternoon. No. 118 lost Sqn Ldr Carver when on the sweep, he tried to shoot down a Ju88 from the rear which is suicide. Drink Thomas posted overseas so we celebrated at Royal Oak. Wiggy, Barney and Mac tossed me around on way home, great fun and everybody in bed early.

14 MARCH

Log Book: Mid-Channel with Hudsons. Phooey!

ORB: Adverse weather again ruled out flying in the morning but the Squadron was brought to readiness at midday. Close escort given to two Hudson aircraft together with 501 and 118 Squadron. The wing carried out a sweep to the east of the Cherbourg peninsula but failed to locate the shipping target. Sgt Downing crashed an aircraft in taking off for local flying – pilot was uninjured.

Gamble's Diary: Called to readiness again, looks as if training is all a joke. Dave and self did a special convoy (American troops arriving) and put on a show for them for 2 hours. Recalled later and left with wing as escort for Hudsons pranging shipping off Le Havre. Pretty quiet show and not a success. Later caught 1600 hours bus and had tea at John's place, pictures at Bournemouth and a few drinks with Len at Sergeants' Mess. Back to Bath Hill, but with no bus in morning, Len lent me a bike to come back with.

15 MARCH

ORB: Practice formation flying for 20 minutes only, after which the weather closed down and cancelled all flying until the squadron was bought to readiness at 1230 hours. At 13.25 p.m., twelve aircraft led by Sqn Ldr Birchfield left to act as high cover to five Hudson aircraft in an attack on enemy shipping said to be in a position close to the September Islands. The shipping was not located, but two Me109s were found south-west of Guernsey on the outward flight and chased by Blue Section, but no interception was made.

An aircraft, later identified as a Beaufighter, but at first taken to be a Ju88, was attacked west of the September Islands, fortunately without results. Six Spitfires became detached from the wing on the return flight. They crossed the English coast at Dodman Point but the weather had closed down to about 50ft. The squadron leader took the Spits up to 3,000ft and then dived down and broke cloud at 1,000ft. Flt Lt Hogg crashed and was killed, Plt Off Locke (Canadian) crashed and was seriously injured, as was Sgt Gray, and although Plt Off Cameron also crashed, he was uninjured. All four aircraft crashed in the vicinity of Bodmin, Cornwall. The rest of the Spitfires landed in appalling weather, short of fuel at Exeter or at Bolt Head.

Gamble's Diary: Another show today, rode bike back from John's, 18 miles and nearly killed myself. Took off at 1400 hours with 118 and 501 and Hudsons. Dave Glaser sighted what he thought was a Ju88 and just fired but missed, Downing also fired and missed which turned out to be fortunate as the plane was a Beaufighter. Never saw the ships but came across 109s on the way back but couldn't catch them. Dave's section landed safely at Exeter but the other 8 tried to get above cloud to get a homing but were unsuccessful, tried coming down and after 3,000ft found themselves on top of mountains. CO and his four shot up into cloud again but Flt Lt Hogg and his three went straight in. Hogg was killed, Derek Gray and Bill Locke had both legs fractured and head injuries. Cameron got out OK. Poor show and Derek and Bill will be in hospital for many months. Poles from Exeter who came after us also had a bad day and up to the evening had lost three with ten others missing. Went to pictures at Ringwood at night with Fish and Mac and as usual went to sleep. Had a marvellous parcel from home for my birthday tomorrow, couldn't get over how funny it was arriving the day before the event.

16 MARCH

ORB: Training cancelled due to weather and the squadron was non-operational the whole day. Four officers and four sergeant pilots visited the Vickers Armstrong aircraft works at Eastleigh and Southampton.

Good news for 118 Squadron: its CO Johnny Carver had been picked up still floating in his dinghy a few miles off Portland. He had made about 70 miles and had been afloat for about 60 hours before being picked up by HMS *Tynedale*. The *Daily Mail* published the story of Carver's exploits on the 27th under the heading: 'RAF Men Told: Study this Story. Cool Head Carver Beat The Sea.' It went on to describe Carver's account of his ordeal. He had managed to survive on Horlicks tablets, benzedrine and a small amount of chocolate, and had collected rainwater to drink from the apron of his dinghy. Despite being afloat he had still managed to get sleep each night.

The rest of the month saw limited flying again because of the weather and boredom soon set in.

25–7 MARCH

Gambles Diary: Weather pretty shaky, same programme – flew the Maggie over to Ibsley, first flip in one and got a big kick out of it. Took old Finch over and scared hell out of him. Went into Weymouth with Barney and Wiggy and stayed at Bawdon, quite a nice place.

28 MARCH

ORB: Weather remained good, practice carried out at Warmwell.

No. 501 Squadron's Sgt Childs had a lucky escape. When on a practice interception he lost control of his aircraft and it spun into the ground near Burley in the New Forest, on the railway line at Brockenhurst. With the plane spiralling out of control he was thrown through the canopy and survived with nothing more than cuts and bruises.

IBSLEY, APRIL 1942

Much of early April was blighted by poor weather that restricted operations. A couple of Danes, Plt Offs Thalbitzer and Svendsen, were posted to the squadron and Flt Sgt Downing was posted to 130 Squadron. The Danish boys had a special delivery: three brand new Spitfires. These had been paid for by a group of Danish businessmen under the Danish Fighter Fund who had raised about £38,000 to buy the three Spits, and the money had been handed over to Winston Churchill at Downing Street with Joergen Thalbitzer and Axel Svendsen present. The idea was that the Danes would fly the Spits that had been paid for out of the funds raised.

Following the presentation the Danish Spits took off in close formation and beat up the airfield to impress the watching crowd. Each of the Spits had the Danish flag painted below the cockpit and was named after a Danish hero. The first was *Skagen Ind*, which meant 'homeward bound through the Skaw'; the second was *Neils Ebbesen*, a medieval Danish freedom fighter; and the third was *Valdemar Atterdag*, a medieval Danish King who had repelled the Germans from invading Denmark and in the process had reunited the Danish provinces.

---
14 APRIL

Log Book: Abandoned half way because of smoke trails.

ORB: Four aircraft left Ibsley at 0716 to carry out a shipping reconnaissance but this was abandoned after 20 minutes due to unsuitable weather conditions. Squadron then flew to Chippenham during the morning for Tactical Exercise 'Magnum'. Two bogey scrambles and convoy protection was given. Practice flying.

---
15 APRIL

Log Book: With Bostons [to] Cherbourg docks. Had a squirt at a 190 on Plt Off Boyle's tail. Flt Lt Mileham and Plt Off Simon missing.

ORB: Squadron gave close escort to nine Bostons in an attack on Cherbourg docks. Six of our aircraft were 'bounced' and attacked as they left the target by Me109s. Flt Lt D.E. Mileham and Plt Off M.L. Simon did not return and were posted missing. The search by our aircraft and a 'Lizzie' failed to report anything of interest.

---
16 APRIL

Log Book: With Hurribombers after Maupertus drome. Plt Off Bland missing. Plt Off Woolass missing from search.

ORB: Squadron gave high cover to six Hurricane fighter-bombers. Eight aircraft including Plt Off Bland became detached from the main formation and flew south to Rauville where they were attacked by eight plus Me109s from above and astern. Plt Off G.R.

Bland was posted missing. Squadron carried out a search and patrol in mid-Channel with six aircraft up at 1715 hours and carried out a patrol 30 miles north of Cap de la Hague. Several Me109s were sighted above our aircraft and at this point Plt Off R.S. Woolass was shot down near the Cap de la Hague. Remainder of aircraft landed at 1855 hours.

---

17 APRIL

Log Book: Over Cherbourg. 109s up and we got two. I landed Exeter. Maupertus drome again. 109s up again.

ORB: Squadron gave high cover escort to 118 and 501 Squadrons in an offensive sweep over the Cherbourg peninsula.

Sqn Ldr Birchfield, Sgt Webster and Plt Off Wydrowski engaged Me109s. Wydrowski claimed one enemy aircraft damaged. Squadron landed at 1035 hours with no casualties. At 1527 hours the squadron acted as close escort to six Bostons in an operation over the Cherbourg peninsula and harbour. The bombers were escorted into the target area where very little flak was encountered and no enemy aircraft got close to the bombers. After leaving the target area they turned north and 'Widge' Gleed with 118 Squadron spotted Me109s trying to gain height for an attack. One levelled out and attacked the Bostons but Gleed prevented the attack and claimed the Me109 as destroyed when the high cover Polish boys confirmed that the pilot had bailed out. The squadron brought them all safely back to the English coast at Christchurch and landed back at Ibsley with no casualties.

Gleed's Combat Report for the day: I was leading the Ibsley Wing with 118 Squadron on a sweep of the Cherbourg peninsula when I sighted three enemy aircraft coming towards us from beneath. I immediately turned right and started a diving attack. The enemy aircraft [Me109Fs] started a steep climbing turn and I failed to get within range. I ordered the medium cover squadron [501] to have a shot at them. The enemy aircraft started turning towards them so I climbed hard to close in to attack one of them. Two of the enemy aircraft dived away and were chased by 234 Squadron, the third enemy aircraft became completely surrounded by Spitfires. I saw one Spit on its tail firing from about 50yd. I fired a deflection shot of about 3 seconds from underneath, the aircraft flying through my sights as I fired. I observed hits on its belly around the centre section. The e/a appeared to stall and then went vertically downwards. I also saw strikes on the fuselage from the Spit on its tail. The e/a was followed down to 8,000ft by an aircraft of 501 Squadron when it was left diving vertically and smoking. I claim a share of probably destroying it. In my opinion the pilot was killed. The formation was followed back to within 10 miles of the English coast by several e/a. When I sighted the English coast I turned and started chasing an e/a. Although going at 12 boost, 3,000 revs, I could not close to under 600yd. The e/a appeared to have used his boost as well as black smoke was coming from it. As I did not want to chase it all the way to France I decided to have a shot at it. I opened fire from 600yd pulling my nose up and down allowing various degrees of bullet drop. No results observed, no hits claimed. I fired several long bursts until all my ammunition was finished. The e/a was last seen diving gently at about 2,000ft.

18 APRIL

Log Book: Cherbourg. 109s up and I had company on way home. Had a squirt but no good. Later confirmed an unclaimed 109 down in Channel.

ORB: An offensive sweep by 118, 501 and 234 Squadrons over the Cherbourg peninsula in an effort to draw up enemy fighters.

The wing returned without having made any interceptions. When the squadron was to the west of Ibsley at 7–8,000ft, Plt Off Cameron and Sgt Pilot Fairman collided. Cameron baled out and landed uninjured but Sgt Edward Fairman's aircraft crashed and he was killed.

24 APRIL

Log Book: Baque sur Mer!! and then to Gravelines. Six of us arrived and were jumped by 190s. 'Drink' Thomas and I got back. Flt Lt Watkins, Fisher, Svenson and Mac missing.

ORB: Squadron operated from Tangmere together with 501 and 118 and carried out a fighter sweep over the French coast at Berck-sur-Mer. Seven of our aircraft became separated from the main formation when they reached the French coast and were attacked from above and astern by twenty plus Fw190s. Black and Red Sections were badly 'bounced'. Flt Lt V.E. Watkins, an American, was shot down and killed. Flt Sgt F.C. Fisher, a Canadian, Plt Off Axel Svendsen, one of the Danes, who had recently taken delivery of brand new Spit and Sgt S. H. Machin, another Canadian, were all shot down and bailed out to become POWs.

Foster Fisher later recalled:

> The Ibsley wing crossed the French coast somewhere near Abbeville with 234 flying top cover for 501 and 118. Our squadron was at 26,000ft. I was acting as weaver flying about 200ft above and keeping an eye out for enemy aircraft. Near Aire the first group of Fw190s were detected coming from the south-east and making contrails at an altitude that I guessed would be about 5,000ft above us. Our wing commander called ground control station in England to see if they were plotting any enemy aircraft in their area. Ground control soon confirmed that they were plotting eighty plus in our immediate vicinity.
>
> By this time the Fw190s had circled around and started their attack from above and behind. I turned to see them and while I was in the turn I heard a loud bang and there was a bright flash in the cockpit and this must have been a cannon shell. The cockpit immediately filled with smoke and liquid and this must have been glycol. I opened the hood. When the cockpit cleared enough I could tell the aircraft was spinning. I initiated normal recovery procedure but there was no response to the stick so I assumed the control lines had been shot away by cannon fire. Smoke was still thick in the cockpit and I was afraid

that flames would start at any moment so decided that I had better get out fast. This was not a very easy task. The only safe way to get out of a Spitfire is to turn it upside down, push the stick forward and fall out. This would not work in my situation and I am still not sure how I got out. I was being held in by the force of the spin and couldn't get my body up. All I remember is that I got my elbows up on the sides of the cockpit and by using their leverage, while pushing with my legs, managed to ease my body up until my shoulders were out of the cockpit. The next thing I knew, I was free of the aircraft.

The trip down after I had deployed my parachute wasn't too bad. I was still very high and guess that I got out of the aircraft between 15 and 20,000ft. It was a clear day and I could see the Channel to the north and some towns down below. Two Fw190s were still flying around but all the other aircraft had disappeared. All was quiet except for the sound of these two aircraft and some gun firing in the distance. I was afraid that these two German aircraft were going to start shooting at me so I started to swing in my parachute, hoping it would present a more difficult target for them to hit. I need not have worried, for in a few moments they flew off and left me alone. About this time I noticed that the heel and side of the flying boot on my right foot had been shot away and blood was running out. Blood was also running down the side of my face and neck.

There was a strong wind blowing from the south, which was carrying me towards the coast and I thought I might drift all the way to the coast and come down in the Channel where I could be picked up and taken safely back to England. However I soon found I was going down faster than I was horizontal. As I got closer to the ground I could see some people running across a green field and I decided that these were French civilians who would rescue me and hide me from the Germans. This was not to be either. In another few minutes I could see that I was going to land in a military compound.

In fact he landed in the parade square of a German Army camp and was taken to a hospital in St Omer where he had an operation on his foot and shrapnel removed from his head. He spent three weeks there with about a dozen other pilots before he was transferred to another hospital at Frankfurt for interrogation, and then finally to a permanent prisoner-of-war camp, Stalag Luft III.

It was here that he met up with two former 234 Squadron pilots who were also POWs: A. E. 'Teddy' Joyce and Don MacCleod.

25 APRIL

Log Book: Mac and Fisher POW.

ORB: Convoy protection was given throughout the day and a search was carried out mid-Channel. 501 Squadron with eleven Spits carried out a sweep off Cherbourg but only six returned after encountering six Me109s who made the most of local cloud and cover to make repeated hit-and-run attacks on the squadron.

Flg Offs A. Palmer-Tomkinson and R. Wheldon disappeared without trace, Sgt K. Vrtis crashed into the sea and Sgt M. Rocovski plunged to his death when his parachute failed to deploy.

Gleed's Combat Report for the day: I was leading the Ibsley Wing of 118 and 501 Squadrons escorting six Boston bombers in an attack on Cherbourg docks. As we approached the target from the east, through the flak we saw twelve Me109s flying towards us from behind at high speed, about 1,000ft below us, themselves flying through flak. The close escort squadron, which I was leading, was flying by flights in pairs on either side of the bombers. I turned to attack the nearest enemy aircraft which was coming up towards the bombers, firing explosive shells. I gave a one-second burst deflection from above at above 150yd range, when several other Me109s overshot me and came between me and the bombers. The escort flight on the starboard side was with me and then, when the Me109s saw the escort flight on the port side turning to attack, they broke away and dived down to the south. Sgt Verrier, a rear gunner of one of the Boston bombers, saw a Me109 going down in an inverted dive just south of the coast with smoke pouring from it.

Claim: One Me109 claimed damaged.

---

27 APRIL

ORB: Squadron posted to Portreath, Cornwall, and arrived at 1945 hours after readiness at Ibsley. Plt Off Barnfather posted to Abbotsinch in Scotland pending a posting overseas.

The squadron had suffered badly in the past few weeks and the posting to Portreath was seen as an opportunity to recuperate. Its experience was typical of that encountered by squadrons of the RAF on the offensive at the time. Many believed that poor tactics were a contributory factor to such high losses, such as the basic formation flown by the RAF – three sections of four in line astern. It was almost impossible to keep a good lookout because the pilots continually had to keep a watch on the aircraft closest to them. No. 234 Squadron's experience was also not helped by the loss of experienced flight commanders, either over France due to enemy action or through posting to other units.

CHAPTER 4

Malta and the Struggle for Survival

For the Italians and the Germans, Malta was both a natural and vital target. Lying within 60–65 miles of the large Italian air bases in Sicily, the island dominated the key strategic centre of the Mediterranean. While Malta remained in British hands the Royal Navy could fight its way through the Mediterranean, but if Malta were to fall into enemy hands, the consequences would be unthinkable. Not only would the Mediterranean route be closed to British shipping, there would be no staging base for aircraft and troop movements to North Africa.

At one point, all that faced the might of Mussolini's air force in Sicily were some antiquated Sea Gladiator biplanes. They had been 'borrowed' from the Royal Navy and were being flown by RAF volunteers, none of whom had seen action before. The Gladiators had been sitting in crates at the navy yard at Kalafrana Bay, ready to be transferred to HMS *Glorious* when required. However, HMS *Glorious* was sunk off Norway in April 1940 so the transfer could not take place. The Gladiators were therefore 'borrowed' after Italy's declaration of war in June 1940, when it entered the war on the German side. In total there had been fifteen Gladiators, but three were sent to the Middle East, four more went to HMS *Eagle* and this left eight, some of which were used for spares. They became the Malta Fighter Flight and when reduced to three became known as Faith, Hope and Charity. The rest, as they say, was history.

For almost seventeen days the three ancient planes intercepted the Italian bomber formations. By increasing the number of their attacks they managed to convince the Italian intelligence that Malta had a substantial fighter force, and as a result the Italian High Command failed to bring forward their invasion plans. Malta, in reality, was at its most vulnerable.

In June and July 1940 Hurricanes began to arrive, some from HMS *Argus*, and they became the principal defence operating from Luqa overlooking Grand Harbour, Valetta. Throughout the late summer and autumn, the continuous bombing of the airfields and dockyards never deterred the Maltese inhabitants. In spite of the constant bombing of the convoys, escorted by the Royal Navy, supplies continued to get through, including food, ammunition and fuel. In August 1940 more Hurricanes were flown to the island from *Argus*, but then in November a similar attempt ended in tragic circumstances when fourteen Hurricanes took off into a strong headwind; nine ran out of fuel and were forced to ditch in the sea.

In the spring of 1941 Malta had a reprieve when most of the German Air Force based in Sicily was withdrawn for the proposed invasion of Greece and Crete. The harbours and airfields had remained operational, but only just. The civilian Maltese had put the shelters carved out of rock to good use and there were minimal casualties, but a worse ordeal was yet to come. The difficulty the British High Command faced in Malta centred around four main areas: maintaining the island's offensive role in the Mediterranean war, safeguarding and protecting the island against possible invasion, protection against the constant air attacks, and ensuring supplies reached the island to stave off starvation.

The vital west–east route from Gibraltar to Alexandria had to be kept open but as the British fleet was withdrawn, Malta remained the vital staging post for air traffic. Commander of the German Afrika Korps in North Africa, Field Marshal Rommel, had to rely on a supply route either by sea or air that passed close to Malta, particularly the route into Tripoli. If this supply chain could be hampered, or seriously impeded by air attack from Malta, or by submarines operating from the island, then Rommel's military capability in North Africa would be crippled. The strategy was not just to sink ships at sea or transport planes in flight, it was also to attack them in the Italian and Sicilian airfields and ports where they were based, and before they started their journey. Malta was also perfectly situated to keep watch on Axis movements of all kinds: it provided a forward base for reconnaissance and to ensure that the 8th Army in Egypt and North Africa were kept informed of changes in enemy tactics or movements of any kind. So seriously did Hitler take the threat of Malta to his North African campaign that, even when Moscow was threatened in the Russian campaign in the winter of 1941/2, he withdrew aircraft from the Russian Front to ensure that the Mediterranean supply route was kept open and Malta remained besieged. The Luftwaffe in Sicily was reinforced with Field Marshal Kesselring placed in charge again (he had commanded it in the Battle of Britain in 1940). The Luftwaffe arrived in enormous numbers with more than 600 modern front-line aircraft, so the siege of the island was about to enter a new phase.

Kesselring had orders to ensure a safe line of communication with the Afrika Korps in Libya and Cyrenaica and to neutralise Malta. The balance of power in the Mediterranean had shifted heavily in favour of the Axis forces. German submarines sank the British aircraft carrier HMS *Ark Royal*, several cruisers and the battleship HMS *Barham*. German attacks on the dockyards, harbour and airfields and the civilian population intensified. Valletta experienced a similar blitz to that experienced by London, the difference being that the bombs were concentrated in a very small area.

By early December 1941, attacks by Axis aircraft had intensified each week with only a few Hurricanes available to oppose them, then in early January 1942 Blenheim bombers attacked the Sicilian airfield of Castel Vetrano and destroyed large numbers of German and Italian bombers on the ground. Later that month a convoy steamed towards Malta under the protection of fighter cover from Malta. After the convoy's arrival, German attacks intensified, and during January and February 1942 the ability of Malta to strike back was severely hampered, so much so that not a single Axis ship was lost supplying North Africa. Gradually the life was being squeezed out of Malta and the number of aircraft able to fly was restricted by the damage being caused by the Axis attacks. Bomb craters on the airfields and runways in particular were a huge threat to operations and had to be constantly filled in, mainly by the army attached to the airfields.

Many miles of runway had to be repaired. The airfields of Luqa and Hal Far were linked by a narrow winding track which became known as the Safi strip, along which blast pens were constructed on both sides to protect the aircraft. The blast pens were built out of rock, sand and sand-filled fuel cans, and provided vital protection against shrapnel, splinter and bomb damage in order to keep the fighters operational and in the air. As the bombing intensified more aircraft were damaged and more were grounded. In March, Air Vice-Marshal Lloyd's request to have Spitfires sent to Malta was granted and on the 7th the first Spitfires bound for the island took off from HMS *Eagle* near Gibraltar. While they rallied the morale of the beleaguered population, there were not enough of them to make a critical difference and they remained hopelessly outnumbered. The convoy to supply Malta had failed to get through in February, and the next one in March from Alexandria ran into an Italian Battle Fleet and the Luftwaffe. Only two ships made the harbour at Valetta: the *Pampus* and the *Talabot*. Each carried vital oil and fuel. As soon as they docked they came under attack and the *Pampus* was hit, burnt and sunk; then the *Talabot* was hit. Only part of the cargo was saved. What was needed were more Spitfires and more supplies.

The Governor of Malta, General Dobbie, was concerned at what might happen if further supplies did not get through. Wheat, flour, fodder, oil, coal and ammunition were urgently required. As flour was in such short supply bread could not be made, and although hot meals were served by the victory kitchens each day, starvation and hunger were rife. Against this backdrop the bombing continued to be indiscriminate and wrecked houses, blocked roads and blew water mains. Many Maltese civilians were living almost permanently in the underground shelters or catacombs and it had now become a battle of existence. The deficiency in the diet began to lead to disease and the Governor warned that for all its resolve, the population of Malta was gradually starving and the island might fall. Dobbie was shortly to be replaced by Lord Gort VC, the decision being taken by Churchill and the War Cabinet who felt that Dobbie needed a rest.

A few days later His Majesty the King conferred the award of the George Cross on the garrison and people of Malta. The award could not have been made at a more grim moment and it was taken as a symbol of the King's trust in the will of the island to resist and to endure what was in store for them. The aerodromes and Grand Harbour continued to be bombed, but the bombing was indiscriminate, and many thousands of buildings were hit in Valetta and the surrounding towns and over 300 civilians were killed. On the airfields, where there was constant work to be done, the attacks indicated when it was time to go to the shelters, but the civilians spent most of their time in and out of the shelters. A vast number of people slept underground. Gas, water and electrical services continued to be hit and Valetta had to endure the constant attacks without any of these services for almost five months. Hot meals and hot drinks became more infrequent. Water reservoirs had been destroyed and there was so little oil that none could be spared for the pumps to draw the water from the underground shelters, so there was little for drinking or for sanitation. Food, and above all sleep, were in short supply. In the towns, tons of rock blocked streets and there were dozens of unexploded bombs hampering movement and clearance. It was often a scene of complete and utter devastation and a harsh and frightening existence.

The situation in Malta remained critical, with the population starving and the threat of invasion hanging over them. Churchill was insistent that more Spitfires needed to be sent, the question remained how to get them there. Of the aircraft carriers, HMS *Argus* was not available and HMS *Eagle* was being repaired and likely to be out of action for almost a month. Extremely urgent action was needed. Churchill appealed to the United States president, Franklin D. Roosevelt, asking whether their huge aircraft carrier the USS *Wasp* might be available to transport the urgently required Spitfires through the Straits of Gibraltar and allow them to fly off within range of Malta.

He cabled Roosevelt on the 1 April:

1. Air attack on Malta is very heavy. There are now in Sicily about 400 German and 200 Italian fighters and bombers. Malta can now muster only 20 or 30 serviceable fighters. We keep feeding Malta with Spitfires in packets of 16 loosed from HMS *Eagle* from about 600 miles west of Malta. This has worked a good many times quite well, but HMS *Eagle* is now laid up for a month by defects in her steering gear. There are no Spitfires in Egypt. HMS *Argus* is too small and too slow, and moreover she has to provide fighter cover for the carrier launching the spitfires and for the escorting force. We would use HMS *Victorious*, but unfortunately the lifts are too small for the Spitfires. Therefore there will be a whole month without any Spitfire reinforcements.

2. It seems likely, from extraordinary enemy concentration on Malta, that they hope to exterminate our air defence in time to reinforce either Libya or their Russian offensive. This would mean that Malta would be at the best powerless to interfere with reinforcements of armour and supplies to Rommel and our chances of resuming the offensive against him at an early date ruined.

3. Would you be willing to allow your carrier *Wasp* to do one of these trips provided details are satisfactorily agreed between the naval staffs? With her broad lifts, capacity and length, we estimate that *Wasp* could take 50 or more Spitfires. Unless it were necessary for her to fuel, *Wasp* could proceed through the Straits of Gibraltar without calling at Gibraltar until the return journey, as the Spitfires would be embarked in the Clyde.

4. Thus instead of not being able to give Malta any further Spitfires during April, a powerful Spitfire force could be flown into Malta at a stroke and

give us a chance of inflicting a very severe and possibly decisive check on the enemy. Operations might take place during the third week of April.

Roosevelt agreed and the USS *Wasp* was made ready at Glasgow to receive the modified Spitfires of 601 (County of London) Squadron and 603 (City of Edinburgh) Squadron. Both were notable Auxiliary Air Force units which had been heavily involved in the Battle of Britain in 1940 but were now building up to full strength again. Many of the pilots were inexperienced and some had never even flown on operations before. Sqn Ldr David Douglas-Hamilton commanded 603 Squadron.

Here is an extract from a letter to Air Marshal Sir Sholto Douglas from Air Chief Marshal Sir Charles Portal, dated 29 March 1942 and marked 'Secret':

As you know we are now preparing to send in by carrier another 32 Spitfires for which you are selecting pilots from your command. I should like you to send in the best pilots from two complete Spitfire squadrons since I am convinced that this is the only way of overcoming the disadvantages inherent in the lack of team spirit. I think it would have a very good effect on the morale of the RAF at Malta and the people of the island to learn that their defence has been taken up by the pilots of two crack squadrons from Fighter Command with all the experience of operations in this country behind them. The Luftwaffe should also get a salutary surprise. Would you go ahead with the selection of personnel on these lines.

It was vital that experienced pilots were sent to the cauldron of fighting over Malta, but it became clear later that the experience of the pilots from the two squadrons selected left much to be desired. Some had not even seen combat.

Having survived the first half of April, the inhabitants and personnel within the garrison of Malta had to carry on the good work until the 20th when the strong reinforcement of Spitfires was expected. It was considered by some to be a race between the arrival of the reinforcements and the potential arrival of enemy gliders from Sicily. Intelligence reports had confirmed that the glider airfields were ready and the threat of invasion hung over the island. With the constant bombing there was a risk that the airfields could not stay operational with the tonnage of bombs that was being dropped. The problem was whether or not the airfields would be fit to receive the incoming Spitfires, and even if they were, would there be enough equipment left to operate them?

The task of keeping the airfields operational fell mainly on the army, but it was not just a case of clearing the shambles left after one bombing attack, it had to be done day in day out and night after night. Aircraft pens had to be rebuilt after they had been bombed and at a time when there was still a risk of further bombing attacks and still a possibility of further casualties. Thousands of tons of stone and earth had to be used to fill the bomb craters and the constant movement of the stone and earth seemed never-ending. Steamrollers worked constantly, and the army worked tirelessly to keep the airfields in use.

USS *Wasp* left Glasgow on 13 April carrying forty-seven Spitfires for the reinforcement of Malta and was escorted by HMS *Renown* and six destroyers. The pilots did not know where they were being posted but were briefed by Wg Cdr Maclean. He told them that they were to be taken into the Mediterranean, just north of Algiers, and there, out of range of the Luftwaffe, the Spitfires would be flown off the flight deck to Malta, keeping close to the African coast. It would be the largest reinforcement of Spitfires to fly into Malta. On the 19th they passed through the Straits of Gibraltar and met up with two further cruisers and destroyers to bolster the escort. They were taking no chances – the Spitfires had to get through. It was planned that they would take off the following morning in four groups led by Sqn Ldr Gracie, who had been in Malta already but had returned to England to argue the cause for more reinforcements.

Early the following morning they started to take off. Gracie nearly made a mistake by flying towards Gibraltar instead of Malta and apart from one American defection, who flew to Algeria and claimed to be a lost civilian pilot, all of the Spitfires arrived successfully in Malta after a flight that took nearly 3½ hours. Their journey had taken them along the French African coast, past Tunis, the German-held island of Pantelleria and then to Malta. No. 601 Squadron flew into Luqa and 603 Squadron into Takali.

The pilots were taken to the Officers' Mess. On the way it became evident how much of a pounding Malta had experienced. There were parts of burnt-out aircraft everywhere – Spitfires, Hurricanes, Beaufighters, Marylands and a few German planes which had been shot down near the airfield. Everywhere there were bomb holes, craters, wreckage and battered buildings, and buildings reduced to piles of rubble. The arrival of the Spitfires had not gone unnoticed by the Germans and it was not long before the first air-raid sirens were sounded. All of the airfields came under attack; Takali was hit first, then Luqa, Hal Far and then Grand Harbour. The spectacle of witnessing such a staggering attack so shortly after arriving on the island was awesome. Many of the pilots had never heard the whistle of a bomb before and some had not seen enemy aircraft. It was an incredible spectacle, and it was repeated later that afternoon and early evening.

The Air Officer Commanding, Air Marshal Sir Hugh Pugh Lloyd, went to Takali with the Sector Commander, Gp Capt Woodhall, to welcome the new pilots and also witness the raids. By the end of the day about 300 German and Italian bombers had been sent to Malta, mainly to destroy the newly arrived Spitfires. Many of the Spitfires were still being serviced before they could be flown again. Lloyd and Woodhall addressed the new pilots that evening; many of the pilots were speechless and had never seen anything like it. Welcome to Malta.

The following morning the stark realisation of the ferocity of the attacks became apparent. Most of the Spitfires had been damaged and were unserviceable, some of the protective blast pens had collapsed under the weight of the bomb explosions and the planes had suffered shrapnel damage or been destroyed altogether. The bomb craters had been largely filled in overnight but they could only find six serviceable aircraft. Almost all of those flown in from the *Wasp* had been damaged or destroyed.

The following day, 22 April, Air Chief Marshal Tedder sent a telegram to the Chief of Air Staff. It confirmed that after the arrival of the Spitfires from the *Wasp*, the Luftwaffe had attacked within 90 minutes and within 3 days had dropped over 500 tons of bombs on the airfields of Takali and Luqa. The German intention was to bring Malta to submission by air blockade, destroying the airfields, aircraft and equipment and the harbour facilities to prevent a convoy unloading. The defence of the island still only had six to eight Spitfires for each sortie, since nine had been destroyed on the ground and another twenty-nine had been rendered unserviceable by bomb damage in their blast pens. A further eight had been destroyed in combat and most of the rest had been damaged in the aerial fighting. Further damage to the small number remaining was likely from taking off and landing among the bomb holes. The telegram ended by adding that it would not be possible to run a convoy to bring the vital supplies needed before the air situation was satisfactory, as it would be destroyed en route or in harbour. Malta needed 100 Spitfires a month: abundance was necessary to hold the island, and after landing they must be put back in the air before the next raid arrived, or else face destruction on the ground.

Churchill again acted on the information and sent another message to President Roosevelt:

I am deeply anxious about Malta under the increasing bombardment of 450 first-line German Aircraft. If the island is to hold out until the June convoy – the earliest possible, it must have a continued flow of Spitfires. The last flying off from *Wasp* was the most successful although the enemy attacks broke up many after they had landed. We are using HMS *Eagle* to send in 15 or so at a time. I shall be grateful if you will allow *Wasp* to do a second trip. Without this I fear Malta will be pounded to bits.

Roosevelt responded as Churchill had hoped on 25 April and confirmed that *Wasp* could be made available for a second trip with Spitfires to Malta.

Churchill wrote to the Chief of Air Staff the same day: 'Now that the president has agreed about *Wasp* let me know the programme for feeding Malta with Spitfires, week by week, during the next eight weeks.' On completion of its first delivery of Spitfires the USS *Wasp*, after a brief stop in Gibraltar, arrived back in the Clyde on 26 April. The codename given to the second operation to deliver further Spitfires to Malta was Operation Bowery. It was clear that after the farce of the first delivery, the reception arrangements for the second batch of planes had to be improved. It was also evident that experienced pilots were required.

On 25 April, ACM Tedder had sent on to the Air Ministry in Whitehall a message received from Hugh Pugh Lloyd in Malta. It read:

Regret the quality of Spitfire pilots from Operation Calendar is not up to that of previous operations. In 601 Squadron, seven out of the thirty-three pilots have had no operational experience and a further four have had less than 25 hours flying on Spitfires. In 603 Squadron, twelve out of the twenty-three pilots have never fired their guns in anger. The officer commanding

603 Squadron, David Douglas-Hamilton, reports that seven of his most experienced pilots were posted away from their squadron before they left. Only fully experienced pilots must come here. It is no place for beginners. Fully appreciate the shortage of experienced pilots at home and will absorb inexperienced surplus here. Hope however that Malta can be treated as a special case.

On 26 April the Air Ministry responded to Air Marshal Sir Sholto Douglas:

My Dear Sholto
You will remember that on the 29th March Chief of Air Staff wrote to you emphasising the necessity to select the best and most experienced Spitfire pilots for Malta. I attach a signal from C in C Middle East which speaks for itself. I understand that 601 Squadron have not been operational since October '41 and they were equipped with Airacobras until the middle of March '42 at which time they started to get their first Spitfires. The Squadron Commander had therefore only fourteen days in which to get the squadron used to the Spitfires and out of this period he had to allow overseas leave to his pilots. Only eight out of his squadron have had at that time any operational experience whatsoever and the majority of them had never flown Spitfires.

As regards 603, the squadron was taken out of the line at the end of December. They were not at that time fit to undertake any operation, but before they received orders for Operation Calendar they had lost twelve of their best pilots. Seven more including two Poles and two Australians had to be given up before they sailed so that by the time the squadron embarked, the Commanding Officer reports that he had only five pilots who had any operational experience at all. Fortunately we ordered fifty-five pilots to be sent to Glasgow for this operation and only forty-seven planes were embarked. The Squadron Commanders were thus able to draw on the reserve pilots, several of whom had adequate experience.
Yours Wilfred Freeman

With the *Wasp* back on the Clyde by 26 April, plans continued for Operation Bowery and the second delivery of Spitfires to Malta. Apart from the requirement for experienced pilots, plans were made to get experienced ground crews and spares through to the island by using the fast minelayer HMS *Welshman*.

27 APRIL

Barney received news of his immediate posting to 603 Squadron and travelled by train overnight to Glasgow Central station, but needless to say the train arrived late. He remembered having to carry heavy kit which would have included a parachute bag, parachute, an emergency dinghy, a yellow Mae West life jacket, a flying helmet, goggles and a steel helmet. Orders had come through so quickly that there was no time for official embarkation leave. He was transferred by bus to Renfrew airfield next to the Clyde, not really knowing what to expect or where he was to be posted.

Embarkation arrangements remained chaotic. The *Wasp* had moved into George V dock next to Renfrew. It was clear that on loading the first of the forty-seven Spitfires aboard, the long-range tanks which had been fitted still leaked, so the captain ordered loading to cease until they could be made good. Only after some of the fuel tanks had been repaired could loading continue.

The crew of the *Wasp* continued the repairs to the long-range tanks themselves. They sailed to Scapa Flow and then finally set sail for the Mediterranean on 3 May with an escort of American destroyers *Lang* and *Skerrett*, the English battlecruiser *Renown* and cruiser *Charybdis* and English destroyers *Echo* and *Intrepid*.

'Very much at Sea.' Many in the squadron were very surprised to learn that American ships were 'dry' but coca cola and fruit drinks were plentiful and any amount of American magazines were available. Officers were accommodated two to a cabin, most of which had air conditioning; aircraft occupied the hangar floor and were lashed to the ceiling. The Spitfire undercarriage wheels were steadied by wooden blocks, their wing-tips lashed to the deck by ropes and cables and more were suspended from the roof girders, slung there by canvas loops which swayed gently as the big aircraft carrier rolled in the swell.

Pilots assembled and were told they were going to Malta. Many of them were not sure what to expect and it resulted in a certain amount of panic-buying from the ship's stores, which were fortunately well-stocked. In order to get into the Mediterranean without being seen by enemy agents on the shores of Spain or North Africa, the force was going to have to run through the Straits of Gibraltar in the dead of night. The Spitfires would be launched from a position off the coast of Algiers. With the extra 90 gallons of fuel in the drop tanks the Spitfire V still had a range of 950 miles if the tank was carried to the destination, or 1,050 miles if the tank was dropped when empty. Since the distance to Malta was approximately 660 miles, it left a fair margin in case of unexpected headwinds or if they had to fight their way through to reach the island. The extra tank and the 90 gallons of fuel together weighed about 770lb and this meant that the Spitfires were taking off already overloaded. There would be little margin for safety and no unnecessary weight could be carried. Two of the four cannons were left unloaded and only

60 rounds of ammunition were loaded in each of the other two. The pilots were instructed to take a minimum of personal kit and what was to be carried had to be packed in such a way that the Spitfires could still fight if required. The rest of the pilot's kit would be flown to Malta by courier aircraft later.

The pilots were briefed on the take-off from the carrier, an exercise in itself as none of them had been trained for such an event. The technique was to rev up to 3,000rpm on the brakes, then release the brakes and select emergency boost override. After take-off the Spitfires were to come together in four formations, each formation departing when ready.

Preparations in Malta for the arrival of the Spitfires continued after the debacle following the arrival of the first batch. Every effort would be made to fly off the Spitfires early on in the day, preferably before midday, so that they could make their way to Malta and land before dark thereby reducing the risk of running into unseen bomb craters and holes in the gloom when they arrived. Secondly, and almost too obviously, but of the utmost importance was that the Spitfires were serviceable in every respect before they were flown off the aircraft carrier, and would be ready to go into action immediately after landing on Malta and once they had been refuelled. Some of the Spitfires that had arrived on 20 April had apparently been in such a poor state of repair, that even though personnel worked on them through the night they remained unserviceable the following morning. Guns were dirty and had not been synchronised, most of them had not been fired since they had been installed and the radios often did not work. With aircraft in such short supply, it was ridiculous that newly arrived aircraft were kept on the ground for two or three days while they were being made serviceable.

The organisation on landing was also capable of improvement following the arrival of the first batch on 20 April. Provided they arrived serviceable and in daylight, it was considered possible that the Spitfires could be put back into the air within 10 minutes of landing. To achieve this, five men were to be placed in each aircraft pen with an experienced pilot. This pilot would be used to the fighting conditions over Malta, would have to be ready to jump into the cockpit when the Spitfire had been quickly serviced and turned around and then stay there at readiness for take-off. It was also the pilot's job to ensure each member of his team knew what he had to do to ensure this quick turn around. The petrol was to be kept in 5-gallon tanks or tins especially protected by sand bags outside each aircraft pen because there were insufficient petrol bowsers. Each aircraft pen contained all the necessary equipment and personnel to rearm, refuel and therefore service each aircraft. The long-distance tanks, if they had been retained, would have to be removed. It would be equally essential to ensure a minimum delay between the landing of the Spitfire and its arrival at its allotted aircraft pen where the experienced Malta-based pilot would take over. Each aircraft would be allocated a number on landing that corresponded to the aircraft pen it was assigned to. The aerodrome control officer would shout the number and a member of the ground crew would jump on the wing and direct him to the appropriate aircraft pen. For it all to work, however, practice was needed, right down to the last detail. Nothing would be left to chance.

---

7 MAY

During the night Force W, as the convoy had become known, was joined by HMS *Eagle* which had been repaired and still had on board seventeen more Spitfires which had not been delivered on earlier runs into the Mediterranean. HMS *Eagle* had sailed from Gibraltar with an escort of HMS *Ithuriel, Partridge, Westcott, Wishart, Wrestler, Antelope, Salisbury, Georgetown* and *Vidette.* Following Force W was the fast minelayer HMS *Welshman* with her consignment of stores, medical supplies, aircraft engines and further ground crews for the Spitfires that were shortly to take off from USS *Wasp* and HMS *Eagle.* Once dark had fallen the crew of HMS *Welshman* began to disguise their vessel, fitting plywood bulkheads to her superstructure and smoke cowls on her three funnels. The intention was to confuse the Germans and Italians into thinking that she was the large French destroyer *Leopard,* in the hope that she could get through to Malta with her vital supplies.

---

8 MAY

On Malta, preparations were made for the second batch of Spitfires that were expected the following day. Readiness was at dawn for all the pilots of 603 Squadron and a practice for the arrival of the reinforcements. Every pilot was allocated a pen and stayed there until lunch.

ORB: Raid by Ju87s and a few Ju88s at 10 a.m. and they bombed Hal Far and Luqa. Five were destroyed and several probably damaged. Two Hurricanes were damaged, one with a glycol leak landed wheels-up at Takali. Further raid on Takali at 1400 hours by Ju87s, which was the first raid on Takali for over a week. Most of 603 Squadron at the time were in trenches or given posts where they were able to fire off rifles. Bombs fell all around them but no damage was caused.

On board the *Wasp* the pilots of the reinforcement force received a further briefing from their US Navy Air Commander for their take-off the following day. They would get weather reports from Malta, but would not be launched unless clear skies were forecast over their entire route. This would be important because the only navigational equipment they were going to carry were maps, compasses and watches. For the final part of the journey they would get radio bearings from Malta.

The US Navy Air Commander instructed them on procedures for take-off. During the launching operation the carrier would be committed to sailing a straight course in broad daylight within easy reach of enemy airfields, so the sooner the pilots were away after the launch had begun, the shorter the time the *Wasp* would be exposed to enemy attack. Later that afternoon the first twelve Spitfires would be taken up on the flight deck and arranged aft to leave room in the hangar to lower the aircraft suspended from the ceiling. At first light the following morning the carrier would turn into wind, and its own squadron of Wildcat fighters would take off to provide air cover for the Spitfires to take off. As the last aircraft began its take-off run, the Spitfire in the hangar nearest the lift would start its engine, and the lift would then go down to pick it up and take it to the flight deck. The pilot would need to taxi forwards so that the lift could go down for the next Spitfire, which had in the meantime also started its engine. The whole operation would be complicated and the pilot instructions were minute and detailed. Above all else they had to follow the deck crew instructions implicitly.

---

9 MAY

Log Book: Spitfire VC – Code BR345/3-Z – Algiers to Malta 0330 hours. From USS *Wasp* – Good trip but lost a few en route.

Experienced pilots from Malta had been sent back to Gibraltar to meet up with the fleet and guide the new batch of Spitfires into Malta. Sqn Ldr Stan Grant from 249 Squadron would lead the first batch of sixteen. They were to fly along the north coast of Algeria and Tunisia as far as Cap Bon, then head south-east to skirt around the enemy-held island of Pantelleria in the Sicilian channel before heading for Malta. On the morning of the 9th they were roused early and, after breakfast and a final briefing, allowed to their aircraft. They were only allowed to take the bear minimum of personal kit. With the engines roaring into life, the ground crew had to check that the propeller was set in fine pitch. This had to be done because if the propeller was left in coarse pitch, the Spitfire would not accelerate quickly enough to gain flying speed and would drop like a stone off the bow of the huge aircraft carrier. The deck officers waved their checkered flags and with full throttle applied, and emergency override to get the maximum out of the aircraft off the deck of the carrier, the Spitfires began their historic journey to Malta.

Once off the aircraft carrier the trick would be to retract the undercarriage quickly and push the stick forward to build up speed to be able to climb away. Nerve-racking but exhilarating! Only one failed to get away: Sgt R.D. Sherrington, who had left his propeller in coarse pitch – exactly what was supposed to have been checked. Another pilot, Canadian Plt Off Jerry Smith, got airborne but found the long-range drop tank to be faulty. Against orders and to everyone's surprise on the *Wasp*, he turned back after ditching the drop tank and, following an aborted attempt, made a successful landing back on the *Wasp*.

Once the sixteen Spitfires had formed up under Sqn Ldr Grant, they had to turn due east towards Malta. When they reached their cruising altitude of 10,000ft they had to throttle back to 2,050rpm to get the most out of each gallon of fuel. The skies were clear to the south and they could make out the reddish brown peaks of the mountain range, the Monts de la Medjerda, which ran along the Algerian coast. The sun was incredibly bright and gradually the ground haze began to obscure the mountains which had been a useful navigational aid. Eventually out to port was the Italian-held island of Pantelleria, which gave them their next navigational fix. From near here, Sqn Ldr Grant advised Malta of the flight's imminent arrival and within half an hour they were over Takali covered by Spitfires from 603 Squadron already based there.

ORB: Squadron at readiness – Six pilots were scrambled at 1000 hours to cover reinforcement Spitfires coming in from two carriers. 109s about and one was shot down. John Buckstone followed one down and was either shot up or followed it too far and in the haze went into the sea with it. Fifty-nine Spitfires arrived at 1100 hours with twenty-three landing at Takali. Sixty-four had taken off originally from the *Eagle* and American *Wasp*. One had gone into the drink on take-off, another had engine trouble but landed successfully. One was shot down by Me109s and two more were missing, probably in the drink, short of petrol. 249 Squadron scrambled again within 15 minutes of arrival of Spitfires. Jolly good effort. 603 as a Squadron was equipped with twelve aircraft. CO Sqn Ldr David Douglas-Hamilton split them into three sections of four aircraft. He led Red Section with Neville King, Richard Mitchell, a new arrival, and Sgt Webster. White Section was led by Bill Douglas with Paul Forster, Jack Slade and finally Sgt Brown. Blue Section was led by Flt Lt Lester Sanders with Tony Holland, H. 'Bert' Mitchell and Johnny Hurst.

Blue Section scrambled again at 1200 hours, but no luck. 603 Squadron scrambled again in the early afternoon after stand to. Most pilots kept out of the cockpit. At 25,000ft attacked bombers coming in. R/T was bad on new aircraft so position of bombers could not be heard. Squadron dived down on Takali but they were bombing Luqa and there was no interception. Me109s circled the aerodrome for some time before the Spits could land. Italian raid at 1830 hours. Scrambled in error on white Verey light, which most thought was a green – their signal for a scramble. Climbed to 12,000ft but saw nothing but Spitfires. Got down just before another raid for which White and Blue Sections were scrambled. Ju88s bombed Takali with Red Section still in slit trenches. Bill Douglas dived to attack but got mixed up with the 109s, one of which he shot down and Jack Slade damaged another.

Ray Hesselyn, a New Zealander who went on to have 21½ credited kills, and had arrived in Malta in March having flown from HMS *Eagle*, was posted to 249 Squadron and recalled the events of the 9 May in his book, *Spitfires over Malta*:

> At dawn Gracie again addressed us. He stood on the roof of a utility truck with pilots, ground crew and soldiers lined up on the aerodrome in front of him. He spoke in the same strain as on the previous evening and wished everyone good luck. Oddly enough, on this crucial day the Ju88s had omitted their usual early morning raid and did not come over, nor did any Me109s. Between 9 and 10, four boys were scrambled, the rest of us knew they had gone up to cover the arrival of the new Spitfires. Everybody was happy and excited, keyed up with expectation.

By 1055 hours eleven of the new Spitfires had taken off, flown by 249 Squadron pilots and lead by Sqn Ldr Stan Grant who had just arrived. Eventually all the

Spitfires were down, the only casualty being Flt Lt Ray Sly, another Australian, who had been with Paddy Finucane and 452 Squadron in the UK. He misjudged his approach at Hal Far and crashed into the top of a dispersal pen and his Spitfire blew up. Sly was dragged from the wreckage but died later the same afternoon.

The day had been the success so thoroughly planned for. A total of sixty-one Spitfires had arrived safely, although three had been lost with all the pilots killed, one had been damaged in combat and a further six damaged on the ground. Nevertheless, with the remaining Spitfires on the island its defense had never been in better shape. The last raid had ended at about 6 p.m. but it was not until about 9.30 p.m. that the pilots, new and old hands, were able to leave the airfield, dog-tired and covered in dust.

Despite the loss of several of the Spitfires en route, and with John Buckstone covering their arrival in the morning, the day had been a resounding success both for 603 Squadron and for the air defence of Malta itself.

10 MAY

Early in the morning of the 10th, HMS *Welshman*, the fast minelaying cruiser had made an unescorted run from Gibraltar and had crept into Grand Harbour. Its cargo included quantities of anti-aircraft ammunition, smoke canisters, aircraft engines, powdered milk, canned meat and dehydrated foods together with 100 RAF technicians to help service the batch of Spitfires on the island. Unloading HMS *Welshman* started almost immediately under cover of the smokescreen now available, and the newly arrived Spitfires.

ORB: 603 Squadron readiness at dawn with CO David Douglas-Hamilton and ten pilots at stand to. Three pilots scrambled at 0800 hours to try and intercept the early morning reconnaissance flights but nothing seen. The first air-raid warning sirens sounded at around 1100 hours when about ten Ju88s and twenty Ju87s with a large fighter escort attacked the harbour. They were met by an incredible barrage from the anti-aircraft guns. 603 Squadron scrambled again from Takali from where the barrage over the harbour looked like a giant black umbrella. Into this smokescreen the Germans dived, followed by the Spitfires. There seemed to be planes everywhere, twisting, turning, and trying to get into position, and with the reinforcements now available the Spitfires were having notable successes. In the confusion claims afterwards became exaggerated.

From the ground, thousands of civilians could see the spectacular air battle developing over Grand Harbour and they cheered each time a German plane crashed. The spectacle was witnessed by the ground crews at the airfields, who threw their tools, hats, rifles and anything else they could lay their hands on into the air when they saw any German crash or go up in flames. Soon the returning Spitfires were coming in to land. Plt Off Tony Holland, who had flown into Malta from USS *Wasp* on the first reinforcement on 20 April, claimed three Me109s as damaged, and a Ju87. Two other pilots who had also flown in with the first reinforcement on 20 April also had claims. Sgt Johnny Hurst claimed a Ju87 destroyed and another damaged and Flt Lt Bill Douglas claimed two Ju87s as probables.

ORB: Stand to again at 1400 hours but no scramble, though there was another raid with about thirty Me109s escorting Ju88s again heading for *Welshman* in the harbour. With 603 Squadron held in reserve, Spitfires from 126, 249 and 601 Squadrons were scrambled to meet the raid though it was only 249 Squadron who reported engaging the enemy. They had climbed into the sun with Gp Capt A.B. Woodhall (Woody) advising them to get as much height (Angels) as possible. At 25,000ft he told them that there was a big plot of Ju88s coming in with plenty of small jobs up high. Sqn Ldr Stan Grant was leading the Spitfires and spotted them first below them. In the ensuing action Grant claimed one bomber destroyed, Flg Off Buck Buchanan and Plt Off Les Watts added two more as probable and Sgt Hesseln a further probable Me109.

As evening approached at around 1700 hours another raid began to build up on the radar screens and this time it was the turn of the Italians with a large escort of Me109s. 601 Squadron and 126 Squadron were scrambled to meet this raid and one Italian was shot down in flames and while one of the crew bailed out, he was killed when his parachute failed to open. Three more were claimed as damaged. A second wave included more Ju87s. 603 Squadron again scrambled shortly afterwards. Red Section and Blue Section returned to land but scrambled again along with 126, 185, and 249 Squadrons.

Plt Off J.G. Mejor, a Belgian, was shot down as he came in to land, though he baled out unhurt south of Valetta. The squadron diary records the Spitfires were airborne for about one hour. Ju87s again attacked *Welshman* in the harbour but the anti-aircraft barrage put them off. Their aim was wild and failed to damage the ship. It would appear that half the Luftwaffe baled out into the barrage – the CO saw about twenty parachutists. Later they were told they were airborne mines sent up by the ground defences.

That night Rome Radio tried to claim that forty-seven Spitfires had been destroyed and a strong force had been attacked in the harbour. In fact only three Spitfires had been lost and two of the pilots were safe; the strong force in the harbour was just HMS *Welshman* and it had again left under cover of darkness. The RAF, with the reinforcements flown in from the USS *Wasp*, had recovered air superiority and 10 May could justifiably be claimed as a major turning point in the air battle for Malta.

Thousands of Maltese had witnessed the air battles and Paul Brennan later wrote: 'When evening came the Maltese knew we had won a great victory and the gloom and depression which had hung over Malta for so long had been lifted and vanished.'

11 MAY

On the following day the headline and columns in the *Times of Malta* read:

BATTLE OF MALTA: AXIS HEAVY LOSSES.
SPITIFIRES SLAUGHTER STUKAS.
Sixty-three enemy aircraft destroyed or damaged over Malta yesterday.

The last two days have seen a metamorphosis in the Battle of Malta. After two days of the fiercest air combat that has ever taken place over the Island, the Luftwaffe has taken the most formidable beating since the Battle of Britain two-and-a-half years ago. Teamwork has been the watchword during all these weary months of taking a pounding, with very little else but to grin and bear it. For months on end the gunners have hurled steel and defence at the enemy. They have been subjected to probably the most diabolical bombing the gunners have ever known, they have been ceaselessly machine-gunned, they have suffered casualties but others have taken their places and never once have they faltered. The people of Malta owe them a debt of gratitude, which is incalculable. Since the beginning of April this Island has been pounded without ceasing but yesterday the boot was on the other foot. The Hun set out to liquidate our aircraft on their aerodromes but instead he got a shattering shock. Instead of being on the ground our fighters were in the air waiting for his blood. During the afternoon raids the sky looked like some fantastic wasps' nest with aircraft milling about in a breathless hectic rough house.

In spite of their overwhelming numbers the victory in the air battles on the 10th had knocked the Luftwaffe and Italian pilots off balance. The arrival of the new pilots from the reinforcements from USS *Wasp* allowed the CO to split the squadron into more familiar 'A' and 'B' Flights. These were: A Flight – Flt Lt Douglas, Plt Offs Forster, Slade, McLean, Barnfather and Northcott, 2/Lt Swales, Flt Sgts Boyle, Irwin, Johnson and Otto and Sgts Webster and Barlow; B Flight – Flt Lt Lester Sanders, Flg Offs Richard Mitchell and Holland, Plt Offs H. 'Bert' Mitchell, Barlow, Dicks-Sherwood and King, WO Rae and Flt Sgts Brown, Hurst, Bye, Haggas and Sgt Buckley.

Log Book: Scramble. 1/3rd 109 destroyed. Collided with Flt Lt Douglas. Both brollied down OK. Shared 109 with Douglas and Forster.

ORB: Dawn readiness. Squadron scrambled at 1100 hours. Bandits reported approaching but only one turned up and was promptly shot down. 603 saw only a few 109s. 603 Squadron again at readiness at 1230 hours. Earlier in the morning 249 Squadron went over to Sicily to show the flag. One pilot got separated and got mixed up with about twenty Macchi 202s at sea level. He flew head-on at one and frightened it into the water.

Squadron scrambled at 1700 hours. Three Ju88s bombed Luqa. Three 603 pilots destroyed a 109. Although the raids were small by comparison to the previous day, 603 Squadron still encountered Me109s over the island. Three Ju88s were attacking Hal Far and Luqa with an accompanying force of Me109s and a force of about twenty-one Spitfires was scrambled to meet them at about 1700 hours.

Bill Douglas was seen chasing one of the Me109s, opening fire on it. He reported seeing some strikes with the Me109 streaming glycol and smoke, and some of the others went in to finish it off, zooming in from different directions. They were over eager. Suddenly two of them were in collision (Barney and Douglas) and both aircraft disintegrated. It was a bad crash and both pilots baled out at a fairly low altitude; both got away with it. Douglas had a sprained ankle. Barney recalled later: 'I was just about to fire again at the Me109 when suddenly I found myself in the air with no aeroplane around me so I just pulled the ripcord.'

Such was the force of the collision that the pilots did not need to unstrap themselves. They baled out straps and all. Barney landed with his Sutton harness still around him. In the distance the Me109 was seen to crash. This was the only time that Spitfires collided with each other over Malta. Douglas and Barney both had severe bruising and were taken to hospital at Imtarfa suffering from shock. Their CO, Sqn Ldr David Douglas-Hamilton might have been expected to be critical about the loss of two Spitfires, but the most he wrote about their attack on the Me109 was 'lads were too keen to finish him off'.

It was an incident that would be remembered by pilots in Malta because it had happened at fairly low level and in view of several watching pilots who were keen to see the developing air battle. In another account of the incident, contained in *Diary of a Malta Pilot*, it is also described:

> Luck was also on our side. Two pilots from 603 Squadron [Douglas and Barney] intent on killing the same Me109 failed to see each other and collided heavily at about 5,000ft, both machines disintegrated and the pilots, who still had no idea what had happened, suddenly found themselves in fresh air with no aircraft. Barney was still sitting in his seat and had to take the locking pin out of the harness to jettison it before he could open his parachute.

Ray Hesselyn, who had been visiting his good friend Paul Brennan in the hospital at Imtarfa near Takali, had also witnessed the collision. There were several other pilots who were also at the hospital at this time and Hesselyn had been obliged to see them, too. There was Sgt John 'Junior' Tayleur, an Englishman who had flown off HMS *Eagle* with Paul Brennan and others back on 7 March during one of the first ferry missions to the island; Flt Sgt Jack Rae, another New Zealander who had been among the first batch of pilots to fly off USS *Wasp* under Operation Calendar back on 20 April and who was one of the squadron's more experienced pilots; Flt Lt W.C. 'Bud' Connell, a Canadian who had taken command of A Flight in 126 Squadron following his arrival on 21 February in a Short Sunderland from Gibraltar; Plt Off R.W. 'Jimmie' James, a Rhodesian from 249 Squadron; Flt Sgt E.A. 'Junior' Crist, a Canadian who had flown off *Eagle* under Operation Picket on 29 March and a couple of the 'Hurriboys' who were anxious to find out how the Spits were doing. Brennan and 'Hess' were sitting talking quietly when the sirens went. Everyone including nurses, orderlies, outpatients and visitors lined the verandahs and pathways to watch the air battle develop. No one could have imagined that shortly two of its participants would end up in hospital with them.

In hospital Barney and Douglas joined the same ward as Flt Lt Johnny Johnston from 126 Squadron, who had been shot down on 6 May and was still recovering from burns he had sustained. He had been attacking some Me109s who had themselves been attacking some Hurricanes coming in to land at Hal Far when his Spitfire was hit by cannon shells and caught fire. He either blacked out or was knocked unconscious and had come round to find his plane enveloped in flames. He managed to bail out but his face and arms were severely burnt and he had been rushed to hospital where he had an operation. The 90th General Hospital at Imtarfa was at the northern end of the island and at one of the highest points on Malta. It had been a regular military hospital in peacetime and had taken casualties from the blitz and attacks by the Germans, both civilian and military. The 45th General Hospital, a second-line hospital, was established as well to take naval casualties and Maltese gunners. The Maltese had regiments of heavy ack-ack batteries as well as the KOMR (Kings Own Malta Regiment). Imtarfa had good facilities including – crucially for the x-ray department – lifts to the first and second floors.

Bill Douglas made light of the incident in a letter to his family the following day: 'At the moment I am in hospital with nothing worse than a sprained ankle and some skin off my knees. I'm really very lucky as I collided with another Spit and had to bale out. Neither of us is hurt, I sprained my ankle landing. We've been having terrific fun here and I'm fed up being out of the battle for such a miserable reason.'

12 MAY

ORB: Dawn readiness. Eight aircraft scrambled at 1100 hours, and two returned early leaving six to tackle the Me109s. Bert Mitchell's Spitfire was lost when it went into a steep dive and into the sea. It was reported that he called the controller, Gp Capt Woodhall over the R/T: 'Goodbye Woody I've had it.' One pilot had a shell in his wings while attacking a 109. One pilot missing. Apparently he was shot up and wounded and again shot up by a 109 when landing in the water in his dinghy. 1500 hours – A Flight took over. 1600 hours – three pilots did a reconnaissance up the coast of Sicily to entice up fighters and so upset the normal 1700 hours raid. Climbed to 30,000ft and squadron was airborne for an hour and was just in time to catch some Italian bombers over their target area. Two were claimed shot down, the first by Plt Off Dicks-Sherwood and the second jointly by Flt Lt Sanders and Flg Off R.A. Mitchell.

Sanders had flown in from the USS *Wasp* on 20 April with Operation Calendar. Dicks-Sherwood and Mitchell (not to be confused with Bert Mitchell of the RNZAF lost earlier in the day) had both flown in from the *Wasp* with Barney a couple of days beforehand under Operation Bowery.

ORB: Raid by three Ju88s followed shortly after while refuelling unfortunately. Bombs damaged two Spitfires and a petrol tanker at Takali.

13 MAY

ORB: Five aircraft available from 603 B Flight and five pilots at readiness. Scrambled at 1230 hours. Raid by twelve Ju87s on Hal Far, 249 Squadron also scrambled. Many Me109s overhead and attempted to strafe them as they took off, without success. One Ju87 was claimed as damaged by Flt Sgt Brown. 603 Squadron again at readiness at 1300 hours.

Raids in the afternoon, with small groups of Me109s coming in and a reconnaissance Ju88 in the evening. Two pairs scrambled at different times but saw nothing each time.

14 MAY

ORB: Dawn readiness. Squadron who had been on cannon test patrolled and tried to intercept another lone reconnaissance Ju88 at 17,000ft. Climbed to 21,000ft in the sun but had no luck spotting the raider which dropped bombs on Sliema killing eight civilians and injured nine others. First air raid of the day occurred at about 1000 hours and scramble order came through when bombers and their Me109 escort were already over Takali. They badly damaged CO's aircraft, but four pilots took off. Trouble with 109s, one pilot firing a burst but with no known results. 249 Squadron destroyed two and damaged a third.

The next alert sounded just after midday with three more Ju88s making for Takali. CO in slit trench saw one after another shot down in flames. One Ju88 was shot down after a burst of machine-gun fire from Flt Sgt Johnny Hurst got the petrol tank and he had to jettison his bomb load. He came down out of control losing one of his engines on the way. The aircraft burned merrily and we plainly saw one of the crew at the front of the wreckage.

Another raid by Ju88s at 1700 hours on Luqa. One was hit by the anti-aircraft gunners, though two of the crew baled out while the aircraft spun down into the sea, and was claimed by Flt Lt Sanders and Flg Off Mitchell. Plt Off Dicks-Sherwood also claimed another Ju88 with Sgt Tim Goldsmith from 126 Squadron.

It was later claimed that seven Ju88s had been destroyed with one damaged from the ten that had originally attacked and with four Me109s also claimed as destroyed – a very good day.

15 MAY

ORB: B Flight at readiness. Scrambled at 0800 hours to meet a raid over St Paul's Bay from the Italians. Three Italian S.84bis escorted by about thirty MC202s approached the northern end of the island and dropped bombs. Flg Off Mitchell attacked one enemy aircraft and claimed damage after firing a long burst into it.

Another air raid, this time a fighter sweep at 1100 hours though 603 not scrambled, and at 1500 hours A flight came to readiness and was scrambled at 1540 hours to meet another lone reconnaissance Ju88 escorted by Me109s. Squadron climbed to 25,000ft and stooged around at that height for about half an hour. Very cold and one or two pilots had frost bite! The Me109s were engaged over Hal Far and the CO, David Douglas-Hamilton, attacked head-on with himself and a Me109 both firing, He reported that his fire had appeared to cause the port wing of the aircraft to break off and did about five flick rolls before crashing into the ground near Paola Hill. The pilot Lt Herbert Soukop bailed out with his arm smashed by a cannon shell. Sgt W.R. Irwin also claimed hits on another 109 which was last seen going out to sea emitting smoke, and he was credited with a probable. No damage was incurred to the squadron. Raid by Ju88s on Takali but again no damage done.

16 MAY

ORB: A Flight at dawn readiness but not used until 1000 hours when four pilots including the CO scrambled to meet escorting Me109s. CO got one long burst and saw strikes and claimed one damaged and Plt Off G.W. Northcott also claimed another damaged. On returning to land Sgt F.R. Johnson was shot up by cannon shells and landed wheels-up at Takali. CO was beaten up by Me109s when he landed but they missed completely. Italians in meantime had bombed Takali and hit and destroyed a Spitfire and killed three men and wounded another. B Flight took over at lunchtime. Further raid at 1515 hours met by 249 Squadron. Managed to reach a 'century' score since being on the island when Pete Nash and Johnny Plagis were credited with a Me109 over Kalafrana Bay. Three pilots posted to Luqa and 125 and 601 Squadrons who were down with dysentery and therefore short on pilots.

603 scrambled at 1800 hours and airborne over the island at 17,000ft under the impression that a 'six plus' raid was approaching which turned out to be a German observation aircraft, a Dornier 24 with its Me109 escort. Section vectored to the scene of operations and first sign was fluorescence on the water. Section ordered to attack. Flt Lt Sanders and Flt Sgt Hurst each claimed a Me109 destroyed and Flg Off Mitchell one damaged. The Dornier 24 was also attacked but no strikes were seen as the sun was glinting on the hull and it escaped back towards Sicily. Section landed after about 50 minutes, the latter part of the evening proved uneventful.

The squadron's injured pilots, including Barney and Bill Douglas, were visited by David Douglas-Hamilton, who had also called to see the German pilot he had himself shot down a few hours earlier. The German pilot was on the same ward as Barney and Douglas and Tim Johnston. His left arm, shattered by cannon shells, was in plaster. Evidently he was fairly small, quite muscular and blonde and only about 21 years old. He could not speak English so when the CO tried to explain that he had been the pilot who had shot him down, he appeared extremely excited and wanted to shake his hand. When he had bailed out he had landed on the roof of a house with his parachute dangling him just out of reach of an angry Maltese crowd who had been anxious to finish him off. He had to be rescued by soldiers.

There was some discussion among them about German pilots who were rumoured to be machine-gunning pilots who had bailed out and were either on parachutes or in dinghies, or who had been rescued by the motor launches. The German would not accept that this had happened but several instances were quoted and he evidently was embarrassed about the possibility of such actions being taken by his compatriots.

17 MAY

ORB: 603 scrambled but had no luck and saw nothing. Later in the morning at 1200 hours six pilots were again scrambled on the approach of Me109s escorting another Dornier 24 rescue plane searching for downed pilots. Plt Off Barlow and Flt Sgt J. Hurst claimed the Dornier damaged but were jumped themselves by the Me109s, and in the ensuing fight Plt Off King claimed one Me109 damaged. Also reported the loss of Plt Off Pete Nash DFC from 249 Squadron who shot down a Me109 but was then shot down himself and crashed near Dingli; the loss of this popular pilot with 11½ credited kills was a great loss to all of us. 603 Squadron did not do much for the rest of the afternoon.

In the evening the last of the long-serving Hurricane boys who were tour-expired, and a number of the inexperienced pilots from the last reinforcement flight from the *Wasp*, were sent back to the UK aboard an American Curtiss Wright. Meanwhile, in Gibraltar a further delivery of Spitfires was being planned under the codename Operation LB. Force H, with HMS *Argus* and HMS *Eagle* accompanied by HMS *Charybdis* and six destroyers, left Gibraltar with *Argus* providing the air cover. *Eagle* was to launch another seventeen Spitfires to Malta the following day to replace those already damaged and lost.

---
18 MAY

ORB: Only one scramble by 603 but saw nothing. Large German fighter sweep to attack our air–sea rescue launches in reply to our attack on their rescue flying boat. B Flight on in the afternoon but only one scramble at 1800 hours when we were acting as cover for a further arrival of seventeen Spitfires from HMS *Eagle*. These were the backlog of fighters remaining at Gibraltar during the recent reinforcement flights and had now been made serviceable. They were led in by Flt Lt Laddie Lucas and Flg Off Daddo-Langlois, both of whom had been flown back to Gibraltar for the purpose. Eight landed at Takali and the new pilots allocated to 603 included Plt Offs Eddie Glazebrook, Owen Berkeley-Hill and Dudley Newman.

The days that followed fell into a pattern. Two flights each took it in turns to be at readiness, one at dawn until early afternoon and the other for the afternoon and evening. The pilots saw little routine however and ate, drank, slept and flew when they could – it was pot luck if and when they could, though.

---
19 MAY

ORB: A Flight on duty at dawn with B Flight off duty at dawn. At 1100 hours 603 Squadron airborne to meet a fighter sweep by Me109s but they kept their distance. A Flight back on duty at 1300 hours. Italian raid in early afternoon but 603 Squadron not scrambled, but were later at 1900 hours to meet Me109s escorting bombers. Squadron climbed to 6,000ft but saw nothing. About four Ju88s attacked Takali at dusk and one Spitfire was damaged and burnt out.

---
20 MAY

ORB: A Flight on duty at dawn again. 603 Squadron did some practice flying from 0800 hours to 0900 hours. No enemy aircraft sighted. Scrambled again at 1100 hours. Bounced two Me109s and bursts at long range and chased enemy aircraft about 20 miles to the south but could not get close. Fighter sweep again at 1400 hours but 603 Squadron not scrambled. 249 Squadron on practice flight but pancaked at 1600 hours because of 109s approaching. 109s followed them and bounced them over Takali but did no damage. Dusk scramble by the CO on the approach of three raiders at 2000 hours.

---

21 MAY

ORB: Dawn readiness by B Flight. One scramble by two pilots but no luck. A Flight on duty at lunchtime. Scrambled again at 1900 hours with the CO and three other pilots airborne but the plot faded. One Me109 shot down by Flt Lt Barnham from 601 Squadron and the aircraft was seen to crash near Filfla.

---

22 MAY

ORB: A Flight on at dawn and scrambled at 0800 hours by Red Section. A few Me109s about but went away before we could get up to them about 20 miles west of Gozo. B Flight on duty in the afternoon and scrambled again at 1800 hours when a few Me109s were about but not many came in. One Spitfire [Plt Off Barlow] got shot up by another with cannon shells – a very bad show.

---

23 MAY

ORB: All Takali stood down at 1300 hours to give everyone a rest, in particular the ground crews. Air Marshal Ludlow-Hewitt visited Takali and Medina and had lunch there. An excellent lunch with Gozo wine and with CO present. A Flight on duty in the afternoon led by Bill Douglas who was operational again following his collision with Barney on 11 May. They were scrambled but without luck. Scrambled again but raiders only approached to within 25 miles of the island.

---

24 MAY

ORB: A Flight on duty at dawn. Found an unexploded bomb in middle of runway and two more near the western dispersal points and had to evacuate them. Three aircraft were on practice flight when Me109s came in but they made off before we could get near them. Red Section also scrambled but saw nothing. Scrambled again later in the morning but CO had to land again owing to R/T trouble. Four pilots had a long-range burst but claimed nothing.

A Flight on in the afternoon and three patrolling Spitfires of 603 [Plt Offs Barlow, Glazebrook and Dicks-Sherwood] encountered three Italian fighters; two were claimed by Plt Off Barlow and a further one by Plt Off Dicks-Sherwood. Dusk raid by about six Ju88s and while 126 Squadron was airborne but saw nothing. Some bombing in the night and runway hit.

---

25 MAY

ORB: Nothing of note, stood down again to give everyone a rest.

---
26 MAY

ORB: One section scrambled in the morning but no luck. A fighter sweep by Italians was met at 1430 hours by eight aircraft from 603 Squadron and others from 185 and 249 Squadrons. Bounced the Italians from 28,000ft. Flg Off Mitchell and Barlow each claimed one shot down, their aircraft being seen to crash in flames and Flt Lt Sanders damaged another after another tough dogfight. Pilots said performance and turning ability of the Italian fighters about the same as that of our Spitfires, though they also commented that the Italians got panic-stricken when bounced from above and half-rolled in all directions. Raid by Me109s on Luqa at about 1900 hours but 603 Squadron not scrambled.

The decision was taken to evacuate some of the battle-fatigued wounded and sick pilots because sufficient numbers of acceptable replacements were now available and more were on their way. In addition to the stresses and strains of operations and constant attacks, the flies were now becoming a problem in the summer heat and made living conditions intolerable. The sandflies were making the men ill and there were still restrictions on the drinking water.

---
27 MAY

ORB: Relatively quiet day. Four small formations of Me109s reported over the island but no interceptions were achieved. Owing to illness many pilots were off duty including the CO and Barney. There were just enough pilots to keep flight routine going. Eight is now the accepted number the squadron requires to keep the squadron operational since the last reinforcements arrived. That number can be kept constant during the present lull but it is clear that each squadron can only just provide sufficient pilots, what with the sickness and inexperience. One pilot has already been sent home due to a crash and another due to inexperience.

---
28 MAY

ORB: Little activity over Malta, one scramble in the morning by Red Section against Me109s with one pilot getting a long-range burst without success. No scrambles in the afternoon although Me109s attacked Luqa at about 1700 hours.

---
29 MAY

ORB: Even quieter than the previous day. There was no activity all morning. Practice flying by Red Section in the afternoon. Blue and Red Sections scrambled against Me109s at about 1730 hours after they had bombed Hal Far, and although they climbed to 25,000ft and saw a couple of Me109s could not catch them as they were going too fast.

---
30 MAY

ORB: Stood down as there was no activity.

A lull in enemy air activity continued but the supply situation was becoming critical as there had been no convoy to Malta since March, even before 603 Squadron had arrived on Malta. Fuel and ammunition for the aircraft was being brought in by submarines but a substantial convoy was required if the island was to survive. While the general situation in the air had eased, Me109s still swept in to draw up the Spitfires. In general the squadrons were well equipped and organised with a surplus of pilots, which meant that the duty rota allowed periods of rest every few days. Usually the men tried to relax away from the airfield, and bearing in mind they were mostly in their early twenties, if they had been in 'Blighty' they would have been chasing women and drinking. On Malta, there were no servicewomen and alcohol was in short supply, although it was available if you looked for it. Brandy and port were recommended for Malta Dog [diarrhoea], but pilots had to be wary of suffering a hangover if they were on duty the following morning, despite the rumoured cure that oxygen provided. Other than walking, relaxation was found by swimming, often at St Paul's Bay, away from the airfields. The water was beautifully blue and clear with the temperature warm enough to stay in for long periods.

1 JUNE

ORB: A Flight at dawn, scrambled at 0900 hours for 109 sweep but saw nothing. Blue Section on duty in the afternoon. Scrambled again but saw nothing. 109s swooped again. No. 185 got a 109 destroyed and one damaged in the morning. No bombs all day but one was dropped at dusk on Luqa. One pilot fired a burst but no results. Another raid on Luqa at midnight, bombs all over the place.

2 JUNE

Log Book: Practice flying.

ORB: Stood down all day. Raid by Italians on Hal Far. CO and six pilots took the opportunity of a bathe. Transport of course was the difficulty but they were taken to the beach and collected in the evening. Two sea mines were found on the beach. New pens for the Spitfires had been built and four new pilots posted to 603: Plt Offs A.A. Glen, H.W. McLeod, G. Carlet and WO Gray.

3 JUNE

ORB: Squadron paraded at 0500 hours for inspection by the Station Commander.

The squadron was now in three sections and awaited the arrival of the new Spitfires that were to be flown in from HMS *Eagle* under the codename Operation Style. By 0915 hours thirteen had arrived, one crashed on landing with another two lost en route. No. 249 Squadron was allocated four new Spitfires and 603 eight. The new fighters had hydromatic airscrews which were a big improvement and gave them a better rate of climb.

The number of serviceable aircraft was up to twenty, but later reduced to twelve (which allowed one squadron to be stood down and one to be at one-hour readiness each day). The minimum number of Spitfires to be operational on the island was thirty-six – or five squadrons – that meant three on and two off. There was a scramble at 1400 hours by Red and Blue Sections but nothing was seen. Me109s attacked Gozo followed by another raid at 1800 hours, but 603 did not get airborne. Plt Offs McLean, Berkeley-Hill and WO Rae were posted to 249 Squadron.

---

4 JUNE

Log Book: Scramble. Jack Slade and I bounced by 109s. Spun off turn and lost Jack, the Huns and bags of height.

Barney and Plt Off Jack Slade, as part of B Flight, were scrambled to meet a small fighter sweep from Sicily.

ORB: B Flight airborne at dawn. One raid swept the north of the island and had come in from Sicily. All three Sections scrambled at 1040 hours but again with no luck. One or two pilots fired shots but did no damage. Red Section scrambled in the afternoon to cover an approaching raid but it did not come in. Another attack in the evening, with four pilots airborne but again no contact.

---

5 JUNE

Log Book: Practice. 20 minutes 'W'.

ORB: 603 on one-hour readiness all day but no action.

---

6 JUNE

Log Book: Practice. 20 minutes 'W' and then scramble late on.

ORB: On duty at dawn with CO airborne with Red Section scrambled against Ju88s. Further scramble at 0700 hours against the Italians. Climbed to 24,000ft about 20 miles east of Malta with the Italians coming in at about 18,000ft. There were only five of them but they were escorted by about thirty-six Italian fighters. The CO fired shots and saw strikes but Plt Off McLeod's Spit was hit by return fire from one of the bombers so he had to break off and dive away but was followed down by an Italian fighter from their escort which was then chased off by one of our boys [Plt Off Glazebrook].

Shortly after Red Section had been scrambled, Blue and White Sections were scrambled again. Blue Section intercepted the bombers about 25 miles out to sea. Plt Off Glazebrook fired a burst from a beam attack and then, west of them, Blue Section also reported contact and Mitchell and King both claimed probables after seeing glycol streaming from two aircraft. The ground crew reported that two enemy aircraft came down with two parachutists also down east of the harbour from one of the enemy aircraft.

Another scramble at about noon against a fighter sweep of 109s which turned out to be [Reggiane] Re2001's looking for ditched Italian aircrew from the previous raid. A Flight took over readiness at 1300 hours and soon after Red Section was again scrambled but it turned out to be a PR Spit coming into Luqa. The Flight went to 15 minutes readiness for about an hour-and-a-half, but with only twenty-three serviceable pilots, some had to do more than their fair share.

Towards evening, Blue and White Sections scrambled to 22,000ft north of Gozo, but two pilots returned. Plt Off Northcott with oxygen trouble and Plt Off King with a faulty radio, leaving just Jack Slade and Barney. With White Section they made contact with four Me109s and attacked, but after a bit of a scrimmage they pushed off. Last scramble of day at 2030 hours by Douglas and Forster with a report of an incoming raid at about 14,000ft to the north, and while there were contacts, they lost the intruders in the darkness and haze. Landed safely, with one enemy aircraft claimed to be burning in the sea, hit by anti-aircraft fire.

The station band was in full swing in the Mess in the evening, so with 603 stood down the following day, an enjoyable evening.

7 JUNE

ORB: Station photograph arranged for 0900 hours in the Mess but everybody was late as the 'daily routine orders' of yesterday had not gone off until the afternoon. Squadron given an almighty rollicking by the Station Commander who insisted that dress was to be regulation at all times even in the Mess in future!

Raid at 0600 hours from 88s and 109s with anti-personnel mines aimed at Takali with slight damage to three Spits. Various raids by fighters and crackers, and bombs dropped around Luqa. The crackers are a new departure, they are released in large containers which then descend and burst open scattering hundreds of grenades about the size of a cigarette case which explode when they hit the ground. They are very sensitive and can go off when picked up or shaken and one Maltese killed himself and injured several others when he played around with one at Takali. Takali rendered inoperable because the grenades scattered everywhere, but runway okay.

8 JUNE

ORB: One more hour of summertime, but that means we get up one hour earlier. B Flight on duty at dawn. Whole squadron scrambled at 1100 hours against a fighter sweep. Two pilots from White Section were bounced by the 109s, Plt Off Dicks-Sherwood and Flg Off Barlow, with Barlow missing presumed killed after he crashed into the sea. The others searched for him after they had seen a splash but found nothing. Squadron strength reduced to twenty-two with sickness and losses so got permission to keep ten instead of twelve, otherwise one pilot would have to be on all day.

9 JUNE

Log Book: Scramble. New Spit arrivals but 109s in afterwards.

ORB: Early morning patrol but saw nothing.

New delivery of Spitfires expected from HMS *Eagle* under Operation Salient. The same basic procedures for the previous deliveries was to be followed and they started to land about 1000 hours.

Red Section scrambled at 1100 hours with Blue Section shortly after, and patrolled just off Gozo. Blue and White Sections [Plt Off Jack Slade, Barney, Plt Off Geoff Northcott and Plt Off Dudley Newman] climbed to 20,000ft but saw nothing. Red Section was bounced at 14,000ft and several times after that, but chased some 109s down to sea level off Grand Harbour but could not catch them, so climbed up again before they were bounced again. Sgt Webster claimed hits on one bomber. In the meantime thirty Spits all got safely in with sixteen landing at Takali, one overshot and hit a pen and one landed without a tail-wheel.

B Flight took over at 1315 hours and were on 15-minute readiness for a couple of hours until at about 1800 hours, Red Section was scrambled and 5 minutes later Blue Section, against a plot showing twenty plus bandits. Glazebrook had to land quickly again because his undercarriage would not retract. White and Red Sections did not make contact but Blue Section did, with Hurst claiming a damaged [Fiat] Br20. The rest of the Section fired bursts without effect and were then bounced by 109s. Red Section made a pass at the 109s at about 24,000ft but were unable to engage and then chased the Italians off. All Sections landed safely after about an hour. B Flight stood down at 2130 hours.

Some bombing in the night and several 'delayed action' bombs dropped. Italians bombed Takali and burnt and damaged a Spit.

---

10 JUNE

ORB: 603 were kept at one-hour readiness. Italian bombers over in the morning near Luqa caused some damage. A few fighter sweeps and more bombs and crackers in night. The crackers are officially called 'butterfly' bombs. Beaufighters shot down a Ju88 in flames after dark.

---

11 JUNE

ORB: A Flight on at dawn. Practice flights by White and Blue Sections to try our new pilots. Scramble at 1115 hours by both White and Blue Sections, with White patrolling minesweepers in Grand Harbour. Blue Section 'stooge' around at 18,000ft for 45 mins and then climbed to 24,000ft to intercept 109s reported at 22,000ft over the island. Pilots did not observe enemy aircraft. B Flight on duty in the afternoon but they were not scrambled. A few bombs fell during the night.

---

12 JUNE

ORB: 603 Squadron stood down all day. Seven bombers came over at dusk and bombed Takali and the Officers' Mess was straddled with bombs, although no bomb damage to the Mess, some pilots had burns.

13 JUNE

ORB: One scramble by B Flight but no enemy seen. There were no scrambles by A Flight in the afternoon. Talk by Station CO about the pending arrival of another convoy, split from the west and east under the codenames Operation Harpoon and Operation Julius.

14 JUNE

ORB: A Flight on duty at dawn, and sixteen pilots now available. Other squadrons stood down while being fitted with long-range tanks. A few odd scrambles but nothing came over all day. One pilot did a sweep over Sicily and sighted a destroyer. Talk by AOC to all the pilots in the evening. Two convoys were coming, one from the east due at dawn and one from the west due the following afternoon, with both under heavy escort.

15 JUNE

ORB: Sixteen aeroplanes on readiness increased to twenty during the day. Each of the five Sections were scrambled at least twice as the convoy got closer to Malta.

0955: Eight up with CO but found nothing. On landing CO's undercarriage collapsed but he was unhurt.

1125: Four up to provide protection for four Fleet Air Arm Albacores returning from attack on Italian cruisers that had been approaching convoy.

1210: Four up and scrambled but no contact despite smoke being seen.

1405: Four up looking for pilot forced to ditch, and acted as a guide for ASR launch which picked him up.

Late afternoon further patrol by 603 and spotted the convoy about 15 miles east of Lampedusa with HMS *Welshman* approaching as well. Although no action for 603, there had been fierce battles all day and one of the ships sunk was HMS *Kentucky*. Fifty-five hours flown but no bursts fired all day. No. 249 Squadron experienced pretty much the same.

Only two of the convoy under Operation Harpoon reached the safety of Grand Harbour with HMS *Welshman*. Sadly, the personal effects and baggage for the squadron were lost in one of the ships that went down. Supplies brought in were vital but were not enough to break the siege. It meant the island could survive for a little longer, though things were still pretty desperate.

16 JUNE

ORB: Many rumours floating around, it seems that four of our six merchantmen were sunk: two sunk yesterday, two the day before, with one destroyer and two cruisers damaged. One of the merchantmen was a tanker. Rumours of enemy losses and ships are very contradictory and probably won't be settled for a while. Enemy aircraft claimed destroyed yesterday: thirteen and seven probable. We apparently lost four Spitfires, but three of the pilots are safe, one Beaufighter and two gunboats. B Flight on duty at dawn. Raid by three Ju88s on convoy in harbour at about 0700 hours, no contact made. Ju88s on eastern convoy have turned back. Sixteen pilots from 603 on again, four patrolled several ships off the island during the Ju88 raid but after that no fun all day. One Ju88 approached island at midday but no strike; it turned back before reaching the coast. One or two scrambles by 603 but pilots made no contacts. Ju88 raid on convoy, two destroyers and a light vessel sunk, though the convoy reports twenty-three enemy aircraft destroyed. Convoy from the west heavily attacked and turned back after running out of ammunition.

17 JUNE

ORB: Ten aircraft on stand-by at dawn. One Section at one-hour's readiness but later reduced to twelve aircraft. Two scrambles all day but in each case the plots faded. A Ju88 over in the morning on reconnaissance so 249 was scrambled, but too late to contact it. Fighter sweep in the afternoon but no luck. More information on the convoy with tanker sunk. From now on all transport is stopped except for essential services like repairs and aerodrome work etc. Station CO was thinking of getting a horse. Pilots now have to walk a good mile to dispersal and back. Two other ships carrying high octane fuel were sunk but the ones that got in carried some as well as the spares, flour and cigarettes.

18 JUNE

ORB: A 'sirocco' wind blew up in the night, haze and stifling heat all day. Twelve aircraft available for duty but this was reduced to eight in the afternoon. At 2100 hours squadron stood down and 249 Squadron took over.

19 JUNE

ORB: 603 on all day, A Flight on in the morning. One scramble of one Section but no contact made. Warning at 0700 hours but no enemy aircraft arrived. B Flight on in the afternoon, two scrambles but no contacts made.

20 JUNE

ORB: B Flight on at dawn, one Section scrambled and saw six Italian fighters off St Paul's Bay and chased them back to Sicily and though they were catching them, they were not fast enough. At 1600 hours scramble by all three Sections, one 109 was seen but no contact made.

21 JUNE

ORB: One Ju88 shot down last night. A Flight on at dawn but nothing doing as one scramble took off. B Flight on duty in the evening and one scramble but too late for any action. 185 Squadron shot down two 109s at Takali, one pilot being injured. At 2300 hours about twelve Ju88s dropped incendiaries and cracker bombs. Beaufort made strike against two motor torpedo boats and one escort ship. Three Beauforts missing and one escort ship. 601 Squadron attacked further east.

---

22 JUNE

ORB: Raid at 0300 hours last night, bombs dropped all over the place and widely scattered. B Flight on at dawn, but nothing doing. Later raid with cracker bombs dropped. Fighter sweep at teatime. More raids at 2300 hours with flares, explosives and cracker bombs.

---

23 JUNE

Log Book: Stood down owing to 'twitch sickness' still persisting.

The common symptoms of fatigue are irritability and insomnia, but the most obvious sign in a fighter pilot was what became known as 'twitch' or 'twitch sickness'. This was particularly so when a man remained on operations for too long without a break. It manifested itself in an involuntary muscle contraction, usually of the head, sometimes an upper or lower limb, but in Barney's case it was a facial 'twitch' – hence 'twitch sickness'. It was hardly surprising that Barney needed to rest after his collision with Bill Douglas on 9 May and after he and Jack Slade had been bounced by Me109s on 4 June. He had also been on operations constantly since November 1941. He recalled later that he had tried to hide it but it was soon spotted and he was stood down. He also recalled that sometimes it was personal behaviour that made them stand out once 'twitch' had got a hold, and it could take two extremes: you did not want to fly any longer but would not acknowledge it and found minor faults with your aircraft so as not to fly; or you became completely nonchalant and adopted a 'couldn't care less' attitude. Either way a fatigued pilot was stood down.

ORB: A Flight on at dawn. Scramble at 0800 hours by all three Sections, each met with 109s and some bursts were fired all at long range. One Section [Slade and Glen] chased enemy aircraft back to Sicily. At 1100 Red Section was to escort Beaufighters out on a strike, they were vectored but saw nothing. 601 Squadron departed for Egypt. B Flight was on in the afternoon and scrambled at 1800 hours against an Italian raid. Three bombers arrived over Malta. 603's Blue Section [Plt Offs McLeod and Dicks-Sherwood] got two Macchi 100s and McLeod followed another down to the deck and saw strikes on the Macchi which flew into the sea. Red Section shared an enemy aircraft destroyed with Blue Section. Flg Off Mitchell was caught by return fire and had to bale out over the sea but was picked up unhurt. Squadron attacked an Italian convoy sinking one motor vessel. Three out of twelve Beauforts were lost. Italians tried to bomb Takali but hit Luqa instead at about 2300 hours with flares and bombs dropped all over the place.

---

24 JUNE

ORB: 603 Squadron stood down all day. Hitch-hiked to bathe at St Paul's Bay. Nothing doing in the way of raids. Beaufighters attacked Ju88s last night.

25 JUNE

ORB: No raids last night. Beaufighters got three enemy aircraft, one Ju87 and two Ju88. A Flight on at dawn, though no scrambles in the morning. One pilot of 185 Squadron awarded a DFC Bar having destroyed eleven enemy aircraft. Scramble by S Flight to cover convoy due in. 249 Squadron destroyed two Me109s but one Spitfire crashed on the aerodrome having been hit in the glycol tank with the pilot killed. Raid in night at 0300 hours. Many flares, explosive bombs and cracker bombs, mainly around Luqa. The Italian shot down three days ago and who had baled out and was captured had said, 'Spitfires always above us and we always get bounced'.

26 JUNE

ORB: B Flight on at dawn, one scramble but no contact. A Flight on in the afternoon and scrambled at 1800 hours. Italians bombed Grand Harbour, ten aircraft scrambled. CO and one pilot went down ill.

All aircraft attacked by 109s and could not reform as someone's transmitter had been left on. Several managed to get in among the bombers and damage them though none were claimed as destroyed. Sgt Stamble on his first operational sortie got a burst at a bomber but saw no results. He 'pranged' on landing and damaged a wing-tip. Another scramble by Red Section to cover the minesweepers but no action.

27 JUNE

ORB: A Flight on at dawn. Two scrambles to intercept 20 miles out but no contact, though 249 Squadron shot down three Italians. Two scrambles by B Flight in the afternoon but nothing doing. Bombing around Luqa about 0100 hours with a full moon. One or two delayed action bombs went off later in the afternoon.

28 JUNE

ORB: 603 Squadron stood down all day. What remains of 601 Squadron is coming to Takali and this means some redistribution of pens. 249 Squadron went on night readiness at Luqa all night. Two scrambles but no contact.

29 JUNE

ORB: Raid on Hal Far about an hour before dawn. Hal Far made unserviceable by enemy action, though Beaufighters shot down four raiders. CO and three pilots [Barlow, Swales and Stamble] scrambled in pairs at 0900 hours, though Swales returned with R/T trouble and this delayed the rest and prevented them from gaining enough height. Eight Me109s came over and were above the section's usual 24,000ft. After a while two enemy aircraft detached themselves and bounced the Section and Plt Off Barlow was shot up and had to bale out. He came down in the sea near Grand Harbour and was picked up unhurt. Scramble later in the morning, one pair from Blue Section but the plot faded. Scramble again in the afternoon by White Section of B Flight and tried to trace a plot at 27,000ft. This turned out to be fighters but they went back to the coast off Sicily and they only got a brief sight of them, no joy.

---

30 JUNE

ORB: Early stand to by B Flight at 0530 hours but there was no action in the morning. A Flight came on duty in the afternoon but not scrambled. Four raiders came over at 2300 hours and bombed the Luqa neighbourhood and Hal Far. Spitfires not scrambled because the moon was not yet up. One unlucky bomb hit the fighter control transmitting station. The station was out of service for 3 hours. Beaufighters were up but no contact.

At 0350 hours, scramble by two Spitfires for an Italian raid coming in, though the Spits were not used to the transmissions. Climbed to 15,000ft 20 miles north of the island, then over Gozo and Hal Far as they [had seen] bombs being dropped there but [when they got there] saw nothing. One pilot saw a Ju87 but lost him again and a Beaufighter may have destroyed a Ju88 as the plot faded and the CO then saw a mark in the water 3 miles out from Gozo.

Towards the end of June a simple ceremony marked the apparent victory over the German and Italian forces based in Sicily that had been pounding Malta. It also marked the successful arrival of the two ships under Operations Harpoon and Julius. It seemed that these big events warranted a display with Lord Gort holding an investiture and decorating some of the pilots who had fought so valiantly. It also meant that the garrison and the Maltese people could see and acclaim their heroes. There was some concern over the safety of the crowd from bombing attacks because they would need to assemble in front of the Castille, facing the square in Valletta, to witness the ceremony. But it went ahead nevertheless.

Facing Lord Gort were ranks of pilots, soldiers, and sailors with thousands of Maltese and the garrison there to witness the event. It was left to Sir Hugh Pugh Lloyd to read the citations for each award given to the airmen: 'Four enemy aircraft destroyed for one, eight for another, rescuing a crew from a burning plane, refuelling aircraft under fire, sinking two merchant ships,' and so on. Each pilot, soldier and sailor was acclaimed and applauded as they climbed the steps to collect their awards.

It was also signifcant that pilots from every corner of the Commonwealth and the USA featured in the ceremony. Men such as James, Legge and Buchanan had come from Rhodesia; Middlemiss, Verrol, Jones, Williams, Buerling, Linton and MacNair from Canada; Yarra, Brennan, Copp, Mayall and Tweedale from Australia; Rae, Dickson and Hesselyn from New Zealand; and Peck, Tilly, Coffin, Junior, and MacLeod from the USA.

There were others: MacQueen, McNamara and Allardyce, who had been lost in the fighting; Bisdee and Delara, who had been pulled from the sea; Turner, Tayleur, Lee, Sluggett, Smith, Berkeley-Hill and the squadron CO, David

Douglas-Hamilton; Gilbert, Shaw, Barnham, Ferraby, Allen, Hurst, Lloyd, Graves, West, Lucas, Goldsmith, Andrews, Lawrence, Stenberg and Reid; Watts, Johnson, Grant, Cormack and 'Timber' Wood; Barnfather, Daddo-Langlois 'Daddy Longlegs', Holdsworth and Slade; Heppel, who had been shot down coming into land and whose parachute had only just deployed before he hit the ground, and Reid, Mayer, Mitchell, Hutchison, Noble and Hetherington.

With so many names and so many awards it was both a poignant and moving ceremony, notable also for those no longer there or still fighting and protecting the island from further attacks.

It was also clear that the German and Italian forces were building an intense new offensive.

---

1 JULY

ORB: A Flight on at dawn, scrambled in search of motor vessels believed to be 40 miles SE but nothing seen. Scramble later by two Sections to intercept 109s and saw them at 10,000ft but 109s at 20,000ft. No engagement.

Enemy aircraft kept going round Luqa all morning but their bombing was innacurate, though some incendiaries fell on Luqa. No damage resulted from last night's raids. Orders came through from the Station Commander that night fighting by Spitfires would cease. He does not consider that it pays and is a waste of petrol.

A Flight on again in the afternoon and as usual got all the fun. A lone Ju88 came over with twenty fighters at 1400 hours and dropped one big bomb near the GGI Station. Only one Section scrambled but no interception. Later Blue Section also scrambled but nothing doing.

At 1800 hours an Italian raid came over, two bombers with about twenty fighters as escort, so all three Sections were scrambled. Blue Section behind the others and Red and White Sections engaged a mixture of Italian and German fighters first at about 28,000ft. Italians were not on same level and half-rolled and went down trying to entice our fighters after them while the German 109s followed them firing all the time. Flt Sgt Ballantyne was shot up and glycol hit so had to bale out after getting one Me109 destroyed and another probable. Blue Section attacked the bombers still escorted by about fifteen fighters. Johnny Hurst fired about 150 rounds into one bomber and damaged it but he was hit in the radiator and had to force-land on the airfield. Plt Off Eddie Glazebrook fired a burst at the other bomber but with no visible results, while Parkinson claimed an Italian fighter destroyed. All pilots fired bursts and engaged the bombers which were apparently heading for Takali, and made them jettison their bombs NW of Imtarfa.

During the action cannon shells exploded around Rabat just in front of the Officers' Mess. A fool of an airman blew three fingers off his hand in trying to mess about with the detonation of an unexploded one. Altogether a successful action considering how greatly outnumbered we were.

Scramble again before dusk but made to land just before six enemy aircraft came in after dusk to bomb. Cracker bombs dropped at Krendi Mess. Beaufighter fired bursts off shore then a small glow indicating a Hun flare. The new Beaufighters are doing very well. This was the ninth brought down by one pilot. 603 Squadron now have six pilots who have distinguished themselves by parachute on Malta. Afraid if this happens much more we will be made into a 'parachute-dropping squadron'! Another raid by Ju88s at 0100 hours with bombs dropped all over the place. A big fire at Luqa with seven airmen killed and fourteen injured by bombs. Some more bombs dropped on Mdina, though those that fell near the Sergeants' Mess were all duds. Mess had to be evacuated though at about 0300 hours.

2 JULY

ORB: B Flight on at dawn, scrambled at 0830 hours against a raid of ten fighters at 28,000ft with more fighters above them. Flg Off Mitchell fired a burst and damaged one, another fired but saw no results. Plt Off Johnny Hurst DFC did not return and nobody knows what happened to him, presumably his aeroplane crashed into the sea. Whatever the cause, he would be missed as he was one of the pilots who seemed to be coping well with the pressure. Scrambled again at 0945 hours for a plot of between fifteen to twenty coming in. Raid was Italian this time. Red Section, five pilots, and White Section, four pilots, tried desperately to get to a maximum height before they could cross the coast. Fortunately the bombers spent a few minutes out to sea before coming in and this enabled both Sections to get to 26,500ft. With White Section in the lead, they sighted the bombers and escort first and for once had a height advantage and were 'up sun'. Before the escorting fighters could bounce them they attacked the five Italian Cants, Flg Off Mitchell made a beam attack and saw strikes on the fuselage and the port engine catch fire. Plt Off Newman followed closely behind and also saw strikes and then Plt Off Johnson finished the queue with a long burst from 90 degrees astern. Red Section got bounced by 109s before getting into the bombers and had a tussle to extricate themselves. Plt Offs King and Glazebrook both got hit in glycol but both force-landed okay at Takali. Plt Off Smith engaged a 109 after the bombers had gone and followed it out and destroyed it, 15 miles north of Grand Harbour.

A Flight on duty in the afternoon. No scrambles, although three Ju88s came over at 1400 hours over Luqa at high level for once. One was destroyed by 249 Squadron and another damaged. Later two Italian Cants came over at about 1900 hours. 249 Squadron again scrambled when 603 should have been and while they got into a good position to attack down-sun, were bounced by 109s. Three rescue searches carried out for one pilot up to 20 miles east of Hal Far. One parachute was rumoured to be in the water, but no luck. He had been with 603 since December 1940. Heavy blitz at night at 0100 hours. Bombs dropped all over the place and several crackers on Mdina. HE cracked a looking glass in the CO's room. Bad luck to the Hun. Another strike by Beaufighters followed by Beauforts at dawn. Evidently a big convoy is being keyed up. At least twenty-five raiders.

3 JULY

ORB: 603 stood down all day. Raid at 0900 hours – twenty enemy aircraft. No bombers seen. Two aircraft down in the sea with supposed engine failures. One pilot baled out. Italian bombers over again at 1400 hours. One Me109 shot down at 1800 hours. Further raid by Huns at 0100 hours mostly around Luqa. Bombs on Takali. A Beaufighter took off and the flare path on the runway could have attracted the German bomber. The

Beaufighter got two, one without firing a shot. It flew lower and lower until it hit the ground in flames and was seen clearly from Mdina. Beauforts and others out on strike and apparently pranged the rest to Rommel's convoy.

4 JULY

ORB: B Flight on at dawn. Red Section off at 0800 hours to look for Beaufort crew which had come down on a bearing of 100 degrees. Unfortunately no fix had been obtained and search was fruitless. Scramble by 249 Squadron at 0845 hours for an Italian raid, with 603 stood to but again not scrambled. Italians made for Luqa and 249 got all three of them. CO got one and Plt Off Rae, formerly of 603, got another. The three were in flames and several crew baled out. One crashed near Luqa, the others into the sea. Scramble by Red Section for a fighter sweep following this raid, and Plt Off King got jumped and ended up with a few bullet holes in his plane, but landed okay. A Flight on duty in the afternoon. Italian raid dropped sticks just beyond the eastern dispersal at 1900 hours and set a Beaufighter on fire with thick black smoke. 249 was airborne but no contact made and 603 Squadron was not scrambled until dusk. Flt Lt Douglas and Plt Off Slade airborne. About eight enemy aircraft came in just after dark and made a dead set for Takali. Two Beaufighters up as well. Spitfires landed at 2300 hours when it was quite dark without having seen anything. A small wave of raiders came in after they had landed and dropped bombs on Imtarfa. Spitfires up in the dark despite orders to the contrary!

5 JULY

ORB: Big raid at 0200 hours, more attacks around Takali. A Flight on at dawn. Raid by three Ju88s at 0730 hours again at Takali. Three sticks of bombs and one load of crackers around the western dispersal point and damaged a Spitfire. Two Sections of 603 Squadron, Red and Blue airborne but three returned, two with their R/Ts out of service and one from 185 Squadron also had to return – sounds almost like sabotage? Five under Flight Commander met about six Me109s and a dogfight ensued, with a few short bursts on either side but with no damage, most unsatisfactory. They should have scrambled the whole squadron. Hun seemed to be making a dead set at Takali now after yesterday's Italian failure.

B Flight on in the afternoon. Raid at 1700 hours by twenty, including three Ju88s which bombed Takali. Diving down to 1,000ft they burned out one Spitfire. All 603 was airborne and climbed to 27,000ft and eventually saw the Ju88s going out on the deck. Much too high as Ju88s never come in above 17,000ft. Did get near some Me109s and Macchis going out at high speed. Several bursts ensued and Plt Off McLeod got a Me109 damaged. 185 Squadron got a Ju88 and two Me109s. Scrambled again at 1800 hours and again one had to return with R/T trouble. A thirty plus raid came within 25 miles but turned back. Squadron scrambled again at 1930 hours for a raid of twenty plus again. Ju88s bombed Takali with high explosive crackers on southern dispersal and around the eastern pens. Fortunately all spare aircraft had been taken over to Luqa in anticipation. No damage was done. Flg Off Mitchell had to return again with R/T trouble and there was rather a mix up over the vectoring with the squadron over Luqa while the bombers were over Takali. One or two bursts with inconclusive results. Four night-fighter aircraft were sent over to Luqa for night-fighter duties.

6 JULY

ORB: Raid by seven Ju88s at 0100 hours. Bombed Takali and scattered loads of crackers around western dispersal point, an infernal nuisance. Many did not go off and lay in front of pens. One Spitfire damaged. Twelve Spitfires of 603 scrambled, climbed up to 22,000ft and saw the bombers but did not engage them because of the fighters. Brush up with 109s and Macchis. Flt Sgt Parkinson damaged and got black smoke. Raid by Italians at 0930 hours and aircraft scrambled to keep them safe from bombing. Bombed Luqa. Red and Blue scrambled but both were too late and saw the enemy aircraft above them at 15,000ft. A Flight on at lunch time. Scrambled at 1600 hours for a Ju88 raid. Blue Section also scrambled. Climbed to 9,000ft over Luqa and dived on five Ju88s bombing Hal Far. Attacked by Me109s at 5,000ft. Plt Offs Glen and Carlet managed to go on and destroy two Ju88s on the way home. Pinkie got hit by return fire but had the best of the dogfight with the Me109s. Bill Douglas was shot up and had to crash-land without flaps but was unhurt. Plt Off Irwin shot up that Me109 and probably destroyed it. He too had a couple of bullets in his aircraft. Jack Slade was shot up and had to land on Luqa, wheels down but unhurt. Squadron airborne 13 minutes, several aircraft out of action for this raid. Scrambled again at 1830 hours for an Italian raid which bombed nowhere in particular. Red and Blue Sections scrambled, though one did not get off due to engine cutting. Climbed to 20,000ft into the sun over to the NW of the island. Intercepted four bombers at 17,000ft going out NNE of Grand Harbour. Guy Carlet damaged a Macchi and destroyed another and Bill Douglas damaged a further Macchi. Four other pilots [CO Douglas-Hamilton, Swales, Pinney and Glen] each damaged bombers then returned to the island. Airborne 50 minutes, then scrambled again with five aircraft after a further argument with Ops at 2030 hours to target three Ju88s north of the island. Climbed to 20,000ft north of Takali. Red and Blue Sections were between Luqa and Takali when the Ju88s were sighted coming in from the NE. A few bursts were fired head on, and they then followed them down. CO's guns jammed after a few rounds. 2/Lt Swales got a long burst in on a Ju88 and this was later confirmed destroyed. Plt Off Glen shot the wings off one and made it burn and then got a Me109 over Grand Harbour. Plt Offs Carlet and Irwin also fired bursts at another Ju88 and it in turn was destroyed so all three were downed. Plt Off Turlington was shot up in the engine by cannon fire but put up a good show landing wheels down at Hal Far. Plt Off Carlet got strikes on his aircraft but no damage. A good day for 603, the best we have had so far in Malta. A Flight in luck for once. Raids shortly after by nine plus bombers with one stick south of Takali. No luck with Beaufighters who were having jamming trouble.

7 JULY

ORB: 603 Squadron stood down all day. Lent three aircraft to 249 Squadron to make up an eight for them. Raid of three Ju88s on Luqa where one or two bombs and many crackers were dropped. The Ju88s did not dive much and did not come below 10,000ft.

They were weaving a lot and a bit scared after yesterday. Saw one hit by anti-aircraft fire over Takali and it came down in flames and blew up. Saw three or four parachutes come out. Two came down very fast and only one seemed to land properly. A few bombs were dropped over Luqa. Twelve enemy aircraft in total were destroyed, one by flak. Seven Spitfires lost but five pilots okay.

8 JULY

ORB: For once no bombs last night. Beaufighters shot down a single raider. B Flight on at dawn with aircraft at readiness, but short of aircraft now. Scrambled for raid by two Ju88s which bombed Luqa. 603 Squadron climbed to 25,000ft and though they were scrambled when the plot first appeared, it was an hour before it started to come in. They were getting short of petrol but engaged and dived on the Ju88s. Flt Lt Sanders fired and damaged one, fired at another and his guns jammed. Plt Off King also hit one and saw black smoke coming from it, then chased the Ju88s, fired another burst but saw nothing. Sanders was hit by return fire, one bullet in his windscreen which did not penetrate. He had been joined by Plt Off King again whose Spitfire crashed into the sea and broke up. Flt Lt Sanders was then attacked by more Me109s west of Gozo, one on each side of him and he was badly shot up and had to crash-land at sea off shore by Gozo. He was picked up okay apart from a cut over his eye. The loss of Plt Off Neville King, who was killed when his Spitfire hit the water, was also keenly felt. Two dinghies found at Hal Far, one was empty, the other containing a Hun. The other did a decent landing and was picked up by a fishing boat. Raid by seven Ju88s at 1230 hours and bombed Luqa with some heavy stuff and crackers but they overshot badly. Saw Spitfires getting into the Ju88s but also saw Spitfires being bounced by Me109s. One Ju88 went down on fire and a further one was destroyed. One pilot was bounced by 249 Squadron and apparently both were killed. Flg Off Ray Hesselyn of 249 Squadron got two, his score now up to thirteen destroyed.

A Flight on duty in the afternoon. Raid by five Ju88s on Hal Far dropped a lot of crackers and delayed actions. Aerodrome out of service so had to land on Takali. 603 and 249 not scrambled. No interceptions were made and no damage to the Huns. Spitfire of 185 Squadron overshot and pranged at Takali. CO of 249 Squadron, Sqn Ldr Lucas, awarded the DFC, very well deserved as he came out with the Hurricanes in February.

9 JULY

ORB: Some bombs and crackers dropped at 0500 hours. One stick near Takali. Scramble by eight aircraft against a raid of seven Ju88s. Climbed to 14,000ft – raid came in from north and bombed Takali. Dived on them at once, and bombing was most erratic presumably because they were being shot at. Flt Sgt Bye got a burst head-on just as the Ju88s began their dive. Sgt Webster hit one with a beam attack, the rest chased them and were just getting keyed up to fire when in came the Me109s and they had to break. Some of them were fired on at long range by the Me109s to frighten them off the bombers. Raid by six Ju88s on Hal Far at 1300 hours. Again airborne. Two pilots from A Flight flew with Red Section and climbed to 20,000ft. Flt Lt Douglas had an oxygen leak and felt a bit dopey, passing out as they went for the fighters. Plt Off Turlington knocked pieces off one of the Me109s and Plt Off Carlet made a burst but made no claim. Mixed up with Me109s a bit with Carlet missing. 249 Squadron got two Ju88s which bombed Luqa and destroyed two aircraft. 249 also got a fighter. B Flight on in the afternoon. Raid by five Ju88s on Takali and hit eastern dispersal point with heavy high explosive. Many bursts heard from Mdina. One of the Ju88s was seen to go out smoking. 603 Squadron scrambled quite late, climbed to 10,000ft and came in on the bombers. Excellent cooperation given by 249 Squadron who attacked and split up fighter escorts and left two Me109s to defend the bombers.Flg Off Mitchell fired a burst at a Ju88 which later went down into the sea, Flt Sgt Parkinson got a Me109. Another Ju88 was hit by flak and he helped it down with an accurate burst. Plt Off Ballantyne was shot up by a Me109 in spite of a warning by 249 Squadron and had to bale out. Got into dinghy okay but he capsized the dinghy and climbed in again. He was picked up and left in the evening for Luqa. Raid at 1145 hours by a lone Ju88 which dropped no bombs and was illuminated by searchlights. Probably an intruder night fighter.

10 JULY

ORB: Raid at 0700 hours by eleven Ju88s. Heavy high incendiary dropped on Takali at eastern dispersal point on aerodrome which was covered by heavy fog and a pall of smoke. There were also crackers dropped at western dispersal point. Pilots were scrambled but late and none got higher than 7,000ft. Seven aircraft from 603 airborne, one u/s. Plt Off Dicks-Sherwood destroyed a Ju88 with two 4-second bursts and Flt Sgt Parkinson damaged another. Four Me109s destroyed by 126 and 249 Squadrons. Takali was out of service due to heavy haze and bombs so had to land at Luqa, but they returned to Takali before too long. We were reduced to four serviceable aircraft at readiness. Raid at 1145 hours by six Ju88s on Hal Far strip, and did high-level bombing in loose formation so were probably Italians. Some were seen to break away for a time and then join up. Four aircraft of 603 Squadron airborne, climbed to 28,000ft and bounced some fighters. Flg Off Mitchell fired at a Macchi and saw the pilot bale out. Scramble again in the afternoon at 1700 hours by B Flight but we could only manage two Sections. One had to return due to R/T failure leaving only two in the Section. Climbed to 20,000ft and then to 23,000ft to meet a twenty plus raid which came within 20 miles but then the plot disappeared, apparently not coming in. The squadron was in a good position to bounce them out of the sun.

11 JULY

ORB: No bombs last night. A Flight on duty at dawn. Fog over island and flying was impossible. A reconnaissance enemy aircraft came within 5 miles of the island at 0800 hours and a twenty plus raid with Ju88s came in at 0830 hours. No. 249 Squadron were airborne and 603 was scrambled shortly after, but cancelled before they were off due to the bad weather. Raid on western strip so all 603 pilots had to shelter. High explosive and crackers dropped, some of which fell on Luqa and killed two horses. Two or three strips fell across the aerodrome and destroyed a petrol bowser. One bomb fell very close to a shelter and shook up a pilot quite a bit. Ju88s were bombing from high level again.

249 damaged one and destroyed a Me109 without loss. Another high level raid at 1500 hours, this time on Hal Far. 603 Squadron scrambled, but too late to catch them. Squadron only at 7,000ft when enemy aircraft were at 17,000ft. Raid by twelve Ju88s at 1845 hours on Takali. 603 Squadron had just landed after being first off and scrambled for an attack on Sicily and had been up for 1–2 hours so could have stayed up for another half an hour. Three of our aircraft were damaged by the bombs and some petrol burned. Serviceable aircraft were now reduced to five. More dive-bombers with crackers, some fell on aerodrome. Hun tried to fox us and it is clear that squadrons must be scrambled as early as possible so clocks put back one hour.

12 JULY

ORB: Another very hot day. Raid at 1000 hours by eight Ju88s on Takali. 603 Squadron airborne. Some bombs around but none on the aerodrome this time. High-level bombing again. Squadron climbed to 20,000ft to attack but owing to a haze, enemy aircraft chased out to sea. Returned later to bomb Takali but no damage. Just after our aircraft landed, one Spitfire was slightly damaged by a delayed action across the pen. Further raid by Ju88s at 1600 hours. 603 Squadron not scrambled and three of our aircraft were damaged in consequence. One bomb landed slap on a dispersal hut and burned some flying kit and one pilot had a narrow shave. Another DA [delayed action] bomb landed near a pen, but fortunately the aircraft was out patrolling some ships, otherwise it too would have been hit. In future all aircraft on the island during a raid will be scrambled. Damn poor show by Ops and everybody feels browned off that in the past two days, 603 Squadron has been bombed four times on the ground.

13 JULY

ORB: A Flight on at dawn. Squadron scrambled at 0730 hours. CO and two pilots climbed to 20,000ft. Attacked out of the sun. Found ourselves on the same level as bombers. Nine enemy aircraft carried out high-level bombing on Luqa, which was ineffective. 603 got in some bursts and damaged one or two, but return fire was quite strong. 2/Lt Swales was shot up by three Me109s but managed to land at Hal Far okay. Scrambled again at 1100 hours and climbed to 17,000ft to meet the bombers, Ju88s which were bombing Luqa. Several pilots fired bursts. Plt Off Irwin hit a Ju88 bombing Takali at 17.00 hours. Thank goodness that 249 and 603 were airborne. 603 Squadron attacked the bombers again and many bursts left the engine of one enemy aircraft smoking. Blue Section was detached to deal with the others. Plt Off McLeod was wounded but landed without power and although he overshot his aircraft wasn't seriously damaged. A good show.

14 JULY

ORB: Raid by Ju88s on Luqa at 10.00 hours. Both 249 and 603 Squadrons were airborne. Went 30 miles out and split up fighters at 24,000ft but some Macchis were higher up. Two pilots were shot up but unhurt. Flt Sgt Parkinson jumped a Me109 and shot it down, and succeeded in diverting the fighters. Two Ju88s at least shot down. Fighter sweep at 1200 hours, but 603 not airborne. No bombs and no more raids all day. Spitfire reinforcements arriving tomorrow. Hun may be saving up for moonlight blitzes, anyway the Hun seem to be short of aircrew. Sgt Les Colquhoun awarded the DFM. Sixteen pilots standing by from dawn. New Spitfires arriving about 0930 hours. Eight aircraft from 603 Squadron scrambled to cover approach of second party, but two had to return with R/T failure. All Spitfires arrived safely on island, though one had pranged on taking off from the carrier. Seven aircraft allocated to 603 with six new pilots who seem pretty inexperienced. For once no interception by Huns on the reinforcements. No raids all day except on fighter sweep at 1600 hours. 603 was airborne but only got to 15,000ft when bounced several times [eight aircraft of B Flight]. No one shot up and one pilot had a burst. In the evening news came in that HMS *Welshman* was bound for Malta again and was being heavily bombed. Possibility of sending out long-range Spitfires to cover it in the morning.

---

15 JULY

ORB: HMS *Welshman* safely in in the morning. B Flight on at dawn. One scramble against six plus fighter sweep. No contact made due to late scramble. A Flight on duty in the afternoon. Two scrambles for small raids by enemy fighters, but again not scrambled early enough to gain enough height so nothing seen. A few bombs on Luqa shortly after dusk.

Finally, on 15 July Barney was flown out of Malta in a Lockheed Hudson with Gp Capt A.B. Woodhall, Malta's outstanding fighter controller, who was also long overdue a rest, bound for Gibraltar. Much of his last few days on the island were spent 'in a drunken state brought about by accompanying "Woody" on a terrific round of farewell drinks and visits'. Gp Capt Woodhall had been absolutely tireless and had always considered the pilots first. During practically every raid on the island since the beginning of February he had controlled the fighters from the control room. It had been a miracle how he had stood up to the strain, but every pilot had been extremely grateful that he had and nothing was better calculated to inspire confidence during an air battle than 'Woody' giving his instructions over the R/T in his calm friendly voice.

The final entry in Barney's log for July 1942 reads: '. . . and so to bed, the nicest trip ever and we all sat near the windows for our first sight of blighty.'

The first sight of Blighty was to be RAF Perranporth, built high on the Cornish clifftops above the town of Perranporth and about 320ft above sea level, close to the village of Trevellas, by which it was known locally. The bleak and exposed location made flying conditions hazardous but it, and Portreath slightly futher up the coast, were the first airfields in Cornwall accessible to planes coming in from the Middle East that were routed out and around the Bay of Biscay, Spain and Portugal to avoid the Luftwaffe over German-occupied France. The purple and yellow heather, abundant on the clifftops in Cornwall at that time of year, would have never looked so welcoming. The author went there himself sixty-two years later, almost to the day, and he knows how Barney must have felt.

Little did Barney know, but less than a year later he would return to Malta – only this time on the offensive for the invasion of Sicily.

CHAPTER 5

No. 52 OTU, Aston Down

The impact of the war in Gloucestershire can be summed up in two words: aircraft and evacuees. The county was home to some of the world's best-known aero-manufacturers. Local factories became the workhorse for the air war and the RAF arrived in force, changing the local landscape. The area also became home to thousands of children escaping the bombing raids on London, Birmingham and the cities of the Midlands.

The factories of Gloucester, Cheltenham and the Stroud valleys were vital in equipping Britain for war. Tens of thousands of local workers, many of them women, developed and produced the hardware that eventually led to victory. The list included everything from Churchill tanks and Bailey bridges built at the Gloucester Wagon Works, to the military uniforms made with cloth from the Stroud valley mills. The best-known firms, such as the Gloster Aircraft Company (GAC) and the Bristol Aeroplane Company at Filton, were geared up for war production long before the outbreak of hostilities. They were complemented by specialist work carried out at firms such as Rotol Airscrews, Dowty and even the Morelands Match Factory, which switched to the production of special igniting devices. The output of these firms played a crucial role in Britain's defence and the eventual defeat of Hitler. For instance, GAC built 2,750 Hurricanes and more than 3,000 Typhoon fighters during the war. It meant women employees had to work a five-and-a-half day week with compulsory overtime.

The air war did not just affect life in the factories and workshops. Outside the towns, the RAF and the USAAF were visible throughout the county. Personnel were based at RAF Innsworth, 7 Maintenance Unit (MU) at Quedgeley, as well as the many airfields and bases in the county including Moreton-in-Marsh, South Cerney, Bibury, Down Ampney, Fairford, Long Newnton, Aston Down, Babdown Farm, Moreton Valence and Little Rissington. In fact, by the time construction ended in 1944, there were twenty-three new airfields in Gloucestershire.

When it opened in 1938, the airfield at Aston Down included within its boundaries the former First World War airfield at Minchinhampton, and several of the First World War buildings were adapted and revamped for the new enlarged base. But it was the requisitioned farm at its southern end, Aston Farm, from which it took its name. There had already been an operational training unit (OTU) at the airfield in 1940 when 5 OTU was re-designated 55 OTU, and remained a fighter training unit until it departed, being replaced by 9 Ferry Pool, which was staffed by the Air Transport Auxiliary (ATA). No. 52 OTU arrived at Aston Down in August 1941 and was equipped with Spitfires, Hurricanes and Miles Master trainers. Flying accidents unfortunately became more regular, but were the result of the necessity to train more pilots. No. 52 OTU's ORB records that:

There have been a good many new instructors posted in during August [1942] and are glad to welcome Flt Lt Daddo-Langlois, an ex-pupil, Flg Off Graves, Plt Off Barnfather and Plt Off Brennan, and Flt Sgt Sim DFM and Sgt Tayleur, all of whom have recently returned from Malta. Flt Lt Barraclough has been posted overseas during the month putting in much conscientious work on this unit.

Barney was in illustrious company among the instructors. Raoul Daddo-Langlois, known as 'Daddy Longlegs', had been posted to Malta earlier in 1942, joining 185 Squadron on Hurricanes and was then posted to 249 Squadron on Spits in March after the first delivery from an aircraft carrier. While on Malta he had managed to shoot down several Germans and had been awarded the DFC and promoted to flight lieutenant before he left Malta in July.

Michael Graves had also been posted to Malta earlier in the year, flying from HMS *Eagle* to join 126 Squadron in March, but was injured in a bombing raid and had to spend the next month in hospital, at the same time as Barney, at Imtarfa. He returned to duty and achieved further successes before his tour ended in July and he was posted back to England for a rest and to join 52 OTU at Aston Down.

Paul Brennan, an Australian, had been on Malta since March and flown with 249 Squadron. He had also achieved several victories and by June had been awarded the DFM and commissioned. His last victory, his tenth, had been on the island in July before he too was posted back to England for a rest and to instruct at 52 OTU.

Bob Sim, a New Zealander, had flown to Malta from HMS *Eagle* in March and served with 185 Squadron on Hurricanes before the arrival of the Spitfires in May, when the squadron was re-equipped with them. He served on Malta until July when he too was posted back for a rest. Following his return to England he was commissioned.

Sgt 'Junior' Tayleur had also been on Malta with 249 Squadron before he was injured in April when trying to shoot down a Me109, and his cockpit hood had been shattered by cannon shells. He had suffered injuries which meant he had been hospitalised at the same time as Barney before he too was posted back for a rest and to instruct.

One trainee pilot who recalled his time at Aston Down, where he was based at the same time as Barney and the other instructors recently returned from Malta, was an American named Don Ross. He recalls:

I arrived at Aston Down in early July of 1942 as an 18-year-old sergeant pilot just out of Watton AFU up near Norwich. I had come to England in April after completing a short flying refresher program for the RAF in the States which started in December of 1941 (I had been flying while in high school and soloed at 16). While at Aston Down I was assigned to a training squadron as Course No. 21 under Sqn Ldr Sunderland-Cooper. We flew Mk I and II

Spits and progressed through all the thrills and chills of becoming fighter pilots. I left Aston Down upon completion of my training the first week in October '42 and transferred to the USAAF in London as a second lieutenant and joined an *Eagle* squadron as part of the 4th Fighter Group; the 335th Fighter Squadron.

I had a lot of fun at Aston Down. We terrorised the pubs in Stroud and all along the road to town. On a couple of occasions I flew under the bridge over the River Severn not far from there. I think the main reason for doing it was that they made a big point of warning everyone not to do it, and suggested that there were probably cables dangling down to discourage the practice. The only fighter (of our own) I ever damaged was in a forced landing of a Spit at a base near Cirencester. I was landing in bad weather and caught my right gear in a recently dug trench which resulted in a complete belly-in. The Spit was fixable and I was okay. As I recall, I really hated it that I had damaged that fine little airplane.

---

4 AUGUST, 1942

Ross's Diary: I have kicked around quite a bit in the last few days. Last Saturday night I had an awful walk, I walked until 4 a.m. after walking a girl home, it was really awful over hill and dale, got lost and eventually tried to sleep in a haystack. Plenty of spiders, did not make base again until daylight after leaving the dance at midnight.

We flew all day Sunday and the afternoon Monday, formation flying. Last night went into Stroud and met a couple of girls at an inn. This morning I flew 1.15 [hours] doing aerobatics. I had a lot of fun, hedge-hopping, dogfighting and all of that. I like to go down the River Severn along the banks, real low. I flew over Bristol this morning and 'shot up' the barrage balloons, practice shooting only. I had a lot of fun. We had lectures on escaping from Germany this morning.

---

5 AUGUST

Ross's Diary: I flew 1.05 this afternoon out to the Bristol Channel and saw Cardiff. I 'shot up' ships, barrage balloons and just about everything. I got into a stiff dogfight, too, with an instructor. He jumped me but I shook him off my tail, actually got on his and stayed there. He had a Mk II Spitfire with cannons and a bigger engine. I stayed on his tail about 15 minutes through valleys, up, down, upside down, every manoeuvre in the book. I got on his tail by doing a vertical reverse in a tight turn, I sailed round and he went flashing by, then I got him. Later today I flew with Flt Lt Barraclough. I flew the best I have ever done, through all the manoeuvres. The other guy as No. 3 (Plt Off Lao, a Burmese pupil) was all over the sky. I flew as No. 2. I stayed with my wing-tip right on No. 1's roundel, almost touching.

When we landed he told the other guy, Plt Off Lao, what he did wrong, and just grinned at me and said that was excellent. He took me inside and we sat down and smoked a cigarette. He told me I flew good and asked me about my past. He said 'you are pretty keen on flying aren't you?' I told him I was and how I got started and all. He sure is a swell guy, I like him and he seems to like me. We did have a hot formation going. Lao the other guy was around once in a while! When we broke up I peeled over and did a slow roll over the field and landed. I need sleep tonight. Last night I stayed in Stroud. I met some gal in a pub. We kicked around town a while and I walked her home, only 3 miles each way, that was nothing, I am getting used to worse than that. I came to camp on an early bus this morning.

6 AUGUST

Ross's Diary: I got to bed at 9 p.m. last night and slept well. I got up early and went over to the Flight and took some pictures. I put in 1.15 in the Link Trainer but didn't fly. Around noon today Flt Lt Barraclough and Jack Ludlow started up on a formation flight. Barraclough was taking off first and Jack, though he was off and gave his ship the juice right behind him (Spit pilots are fairly blind straight ahead when the nose is up and just off the ground), Barraclough's glycol cap was leaking so he hadn't taken off, he had stopped on the runway. Jack hadn't seen him and as he went tearing off the ground he felt a terrific crash. He went on climbing but could not get his landing gear locked up or down. He came in and landed and his gear collapsed and he went up on his nose. Barraclough's prop had torn a big hole in the belly of Jack's fuselage and severed his brake cables and all. Jack had torn the antenna off Barraclough's Spitfire, about 6in from Barrcalough's head. Neither of them was hurt. After looking at the damage caused, they were two of the luckiest guys I ever saw.

After ground school this afternoon I hitched a ride to Stroud to get my pictures out of the shop, but they were closed. I got back for PT at 7 p.m. I showed Yi my album tonight. This morning I showed Barraclough my class book. It was a nice day today, I now have 18 hours on Spitfires, and I fly again tomorrow afternoon.

7 AUGUST

Ross's Diary: Today was rainy so no one flew. After ground school this morning I went over to the Flight and took a few pictures. Later Roach and I went down town and saw a movie, *Meet John Doe*. I hitched a ride back to the base as it was raining. Early to bed. We fly all day tomorrow and then have Sunday off.

9 AUGUST

Ross's Diary: It was so rainy yesterday that flying was called off. Jack and I decided to go to London. We got all ready and called a taxi down the hill to pick us up at 12 noon. Well he never showed up so we hailed an army lorry driven by an ATS girl and told her to open it up to Brimscombe, where our train was to be. We were a minute late by then. We broke all speed records and got to the station ahead of the train; luckily it was late. We got our tickets and all at once I had a hunch I shouldn't go. I cashed my ticket and let Jack go on with Jock, a Scottish guy. I hitched a ride into Stroud and after walking around a while I got hungry and decided to go the limit on some fruit. The grapes cost 10 shillings a pound ($2 roughly) so I bought a half pound and two nectarines at 2s 6d each. I went to the movies and saw *Meet John Doe* again since this was the only movie house open of the two.

Around 4 p.m. I got my film prints from the shop and booked a room at the Clifton House and went up and read a book I had bought called *Spitfire*. Around 6 p.m. I had supper and went over to the Imperial House bar and had a few drinks and ran into the girl I was out with last Tuesday night. We went to a little village dance about 4 miles from Stroud and had quite a bit of fun. At around midnight I arranged to get a ride down near Stroud with an army searchlight crew that had furnished the band for the dance. We all piled into the lorry and headed out. The skies were clear, star-studded now, really black. All the soldiers were talking and kidding about this and that girl they had danced with and how she kissed etc. They were having a big time. They dropped me off about 2 miles from Stroud and I walked on to the hotel and hit the hay, turning my watch back an hour for new time. About an hour later Warren and Bennett, two New Zealand sergeant pilot friends of mine from our barracks, came barging into our room which had four beds in it. All of them were full, so I let Warren sleep with me.

This morning, after a good breakfast, I hitched a ride on an army motorcycle to Chalford, just a mile down the hill from our aerodrome, then another ride on an RAF truck hauling aeroplane motors up to the drome. I'm now back in the barracks, it's a nice day but the wind is bringing more clouds in off the sea. I didn't fly today. By the way, Jerry was over yesterday afternoon, bombing Gloucester, out of low clouds. It is only about 15 miles from here, so our sirens sounded.

10 AUGUST

Ross's Diary: Today wasn't too eventful. I flew the Link in the morning but didn't get to fly. The weather is still terrible, windy and rainy. This morning Jack, Joe and I went to see the adjutant, then the wing commander, about our commissions. He said that he was doing all he could, so we asked to see the group captain (colonel – station commander). They said they would call us later. We went to station headquarters and were escorted by a wing commander in to see the group captain. We told him the whole sad story (of our class of volunteers from Aero Centre and the fact that half were made pilot officers and the other half were made sergeant pilots) of how much we deserved commissions and he said he would help us. We are to see him again in a week.

Later I went down to Stroud on a bus and got my pictures from the hotel where I left them, then hitched a ride back on a motorcycle. Tonight I learned that a guy sleeping in the next room got killed this afternoon, crashed in a Spitfire. No one knows how. I watched his buddy go through his suitcase, it sort of got me, such a meagre little bit left to show for the poor fellow's life. Jack Ludlow came in tonight and swiped the dead fellow's sheets; someone [else] had gotten Jacks'. Jack liked his bed better so he grabbed it too. I helped him and felt like a grave robber.

11 AUGUST

Ross's Diary: It is 10 a.m. We had a test in the intelligence room this morning but it is starting to cloud up again so we may not get to fly this afternoon. I haven't flown since last Wednesday. It is now 8 p.m. and I flew 1.10 this afternoon. I was supposed to do map reading but I just couldn't. I hadn't flown for a week so I went up and let off steam. I hunted for dogfights, shot up one Spit, really gave a Wellington bomber all I had. I dived down between two big clouds and for the first time clocked 400mph. I was at 10,000ft so I must have been doing a true airspeed of nearly 440mph. Then I did some low flying down the River Severn, diving along the railroad tracks and everything I saw. I had a swell time, was really happy to be in the air again. I flew in and out of rain squalls as the weather was pretty bad. There was a 40mph wind and mountains of clouds. I hit such bumps at times that the engine would cough – Spitfires have gravity feed carbs with no fuel injection so they cut out in negative G situations. I made a good landing. It is raining outside again now. I feel cozy in my little room. Jack has gone out on a date this evening. I have just finished writing three letters. I fly tomorrow morning if it is clear enough. Just lately the weather has been terrible. I have a little over 19 hours on Spitfires now.

12 AUGUST

Ross's Diary: I flew 1.40 this morning on a cross-country with the squadron leader. We flew about 200 miles. I flew later in the evening, was supposed to go on another cross-country in a Spit but things just didn't work out. (I couldn't get orientated on the compass and was afraid to leave the base area because I was sure I would become lost.) The sky was full of clouds and it was raining under every other one. Half the time I was going blind, the gyro wouldn't stay accurate and the damned compass was about 40 degrees off. To make it worse I had to pump the damned gear up and down, the automatic hyrdaulic would not work. I was so mad I could not see straight. I just stuck my maps in my boots and came down over the drome in a dive and landed (not my greatest day). Retired to my room with extra chocolate rations.

13 AUGUST

Ross's Diary: I guess we are through with ground school now. For the last two days we have spent the whole day at the Flight. I flew 4 hours today. The first flight was a cross-country to Reading, Cranfield and then back. I got on my course and hit Reading okay, but I got my compass course wrong going to Cranfield and ended up over a strange town. I straightened out my maps and pinpointed myself directly over Oxford as I could see the railroad patterns and the colleges. I then picked out the right railroad track and flew down the old 'iron beam' to Cranfield. (Not what we were supposed to do. We were supposed to use our compass courses but this was a problem as I always seemed to get lost!) At Cranfield I saw the letter 'X' on the tower roof, which was the letter I had to bring back to prove I got there and this was often changed during the day. Then I set course for Aston Down again, stuck right to my maps and hit it perfect. When I was near Little Rissington, I was flying in the bottom of a heavy cloud layer and I happened to look up through a little break in the solid dirty grey mass, and there through the break went three bombers in a straggling 'V' formation. I could swear they were Heinkel 111s, they then disappeared into the clouds. It shook me. I landed at Aston Down at 1.50 p.m.

Later today I was ordered out on another cross-country, only longer, up into Wales. I figured out my course and headed off in my Spitfire again. It was lousy weather, visibility was 2 miles with rain squalls everywhere, ceiling 1,000ft. I got on course and flew instruments most of the time. Some of the rain squalls were pretty thick, water came dripping in on me. I got lost in the mountains, some of them were over 1,000ft and the ceiling was under that. I finally got to Shrewsbury and then right on course to Brize Norton where I had a little dogfight with another Spitfire and then stayed on course to Aston Down. Total flying time was 2.05 which was a long flight for a Spitfire. *[Ross writing in retrospect:]* The problem for me on cross-country flights was that I was used to flying by the seat of my pants, looking at the ground as I didn't have much confidence in the compass of other instruments and England's landscape was just too jumbled for me.

We waited around for a late flight but didn't make it. I have about 23 hours in Spitfires now. I think I go on air firing next week. The latest gen is that the kid that crashed the other day was shot down, they found bullet holes in his ship, so I guess I have to keep my eyes open around here.

14 AUGUST

Ross's Diary: I spent the whole day at the Flight today, starting at around 8 a.m. Flew No. 4 in a formation, a tough position to hold. After lunch I went up and did glide landings – almost landed with my gear up once as I was concentrating on a guy who was cutting me out. Later after tea I went up again to do some low flying. We really had a time. It was raining from about 1,500ft and there was a fog layer coming in around 900ft. I ran into four other Spitfires and we had a big fight. I formed up with one of them on his wing and he dived low over a town, then he banked sharply at me. I swerved to keep him from hitting me and came awfully close to the ground doing around 300mph. Oh! I was cold inside after that. Later I flew under that railroad bridge again and after picking two or three more dogfights, I came in low for fuel. I had been running the engine hard and had been up 1.30 hours. I felt tired tonight but tired the good way after a good day of flying. I put in almost 4.30 hours today, that's what I like. I left the Flight at 7 p.m. after 11 hours on the job, except for eating. I am enjoying it here now, but have not had any letters in over a week now.

15 AUGUST

Ross's Diary: It stormed and rained today and all flying was cancelled. I went into Stroud this morning and took my laundry and battle dress and got my other uniform and got my pictures from the shop. I went back to Stroud this afternoon and saw *Santa Fe Trail* with Plt Off Yi, my Burmese friend. I also bought a shaving kit and a book of Longfellow's works.

16 AUGUST

Ross's Diary: I didn't get to fly this morning, I was authorised for some dogfighting with Plt Off King but my Spit wouldn't start. This afternoon I went over to the decompression chamber. Five other guys and I were put in and given oxygen masks and earphones so we could talk and hear. The thing was closed and bolted and we started up. We went to 23,000ft, adjusting our oxygen flow every 5,000ft. At 23,000ft No. 1, an Englishman, was told to take his mask off and turn off his oxygen and then take a pencil and pad and start writing his name. He wrote his name for 3 minutes, then slumped over and started convulsing. He was ordered over the R/T to reach up and turn his oxygen on but he couldn't control his hands, he tried to loosen his tie, but his hands just shook near his throat. His face got red and he passed out convulsing. I hooked up his oxygen, turned it on and he came round pretty well. We then went up to 27,000ft and they asked for someone to volunteer to take his mask off. Everything went quiet so I volunteered. I took my mask off and got the pad and pencil in my hands and started writing my name. I began getting hot, my hands got out of control, all in a space of about 8 minutes. I barely remember being hunched over on my right knee, time seemed to end until I heard someone on the R/T saying 'go on write your name'. I began writing and things straightened out, I could feel the flow of oxygen coming up in my mask. I had gone out and they had turned my oxygen on for me. I guess I was a pitiful sight. I could see the initial writing, very legible, then an area of scribbling, then nothing, then my signature coming back again after they turned the oxygen back on again. I did not realise that I had lost consciousness. An Englishman volunteered next; he lasted 6 minutes. When he went out he just shook a bit and went to sleep. We were in the chamber 1.30 hours. It was an effective way to teach us what our individual symptoms were when being deprived of oxygen and also to warn us about what would happen if we should try to fly at high altitude without oxygen – we believed them!

I went up later and did some dogfighting with Plt Off King. We were up 1.35 hours, my ship was running pretty rough but we had a good flight, also practising stern bomber attacks and breakaways. Jack Ludlow just came in from a flight in the same ship I was in earlier; the engine went out, a connecting rod came out through the lock and he force-landed at another drome. He was almost blinded by black smoke so he was lucky to get down. That guy is living on borrowed time around here! (It was also indicative of the quality of our aircraft maintenance, obviously there was a reason the aircraft would not start for me earlier in the morning and for the roughness in the flight.)

17 AUGUST

Ross's Diary: I went to the Link Trainer this morning right after breakfast, spent 1.30 hours doing dead reckoning interceptions. I didn't fly until after lunch. Walt and I went up in Spits with Sqn Ldr Cooper and Sqn Ldr Ironsides – a four-ship flight. I was Black 3 and Walt was Black 4. We practised section attacks (two ships) on a Master. We really had a great time peeling over and attacking the Master, then doing those mean quick breakaways to keep the rear gunner from getting a shot at us. We did diving rolls coming out in the opposite direction which blacked you out every time. We also did some low flying.

Later Walt and I went up in the Master together as a target aircraft. I was supposed to be the rear gunner and some other guys practised shooting us up. I was to check on their breakaways to see if they showed their vulnerable bellies or tops as they broke off. It was great fun. I took a lot of pictures of WO Bill Mart in formation with us.

18 AUGUST

Ross's Diary: Today is the fifth week of me being at Aston Down. I have put in over 30 hours on Spitfires and 10 hours on the Master. I flew the Link today. Beam approaches. I didn't get up in a Spit today but did get around 2.15 hours in a Master. Took the squadron leader over to South Cerney, left him and went up and stooged around as a target ship for three Spitfires as they made section attacks on me. Then I dived down from 12,000ft and went back to South Cerney to pick up the squadron leader. He took one of his friends up for a ride, then we returned. While I was on the ground there I saw Vassar again, he was duty pilot [in the] tower [for] aerodrome control. I also met another guy from a class behind us at Aero Centre – Class 33, and we talked about old times for a bit. I took a few pictures in the air today. Got a letter from dad – sure was glad as it was the first for around two weeks. I have an appointment with the Station Commander tomorrow morning regarding the commission.

19 AUGUST

Ross's Diary: The British Army put out a report this morning that they had raided France [on the German-occupied port of Dieppe] and that operations were still in progress. This may mean the invasion of the Continent, maybe the big show has begun. I'm waiting for more bulletins. Apparently this is not an ordinary commando raid so now I see what all those Channel sweeps and bombings were for. The interview with the group captain lasted almost 2 hours. I was trying to sell myself and pointed out to him why I should have a commission. I think it worked, he gave me four forms to fill out and I think he is going to put through a recommendation for all four of us. I never talked and explained so much.

20 AUGUST

Log Book: 1. Master Local. 2. Spitfire section formation.

Ross's Diary: Well they stayed in France 9 hours yesterday and then came back from Dieppe. It was supposed to be a probe to test German defences. Mostly Canadian soldiers, very high casualties. I wondered at the time about all those Canadians that sailed over with us on the *Banfora*. Ninety-seven RAF fighters and eighty Germans were apparently shot down in the terrific air fighting over the operations. It was a hard blow to both sides. I think twenty-one RAF pilots out of those shot down were saved.

I flew three times today. The first was in a Master as target ship with Hirstich, a New Zealander, as a passenger. Then I flew in a flight of four Spits on a climb to 31,000ft. We really had a wild time. On the way up my engine almost quit. When we got to 31,000ft we were making beautiful vapour trails. We dived down to 21,000ft and did some section attacks. Then I got on the squadron leader's tail and we dived down to about 3,000ft at around 420mph. It was so cold coming down so quick, that all the instruments were covered in ice and frost. I was wearing my heavy flying suit for the first time, I also wore two pairs of gloves, one silk and a heavier pair over them, and also heavy boots. I was supposed to dogfight with Ludlow but I never saw him. I had all sorts of dogfights with every Spit I met. I attacked an Anson bomber, though he must have got excited because he fired the colours of the day as I came in on him. He must have thought I hadn't recognised him as friendly and was going to shoot him down.

I went into Stroud yesterday afternoon and left my watch to be fixed. After eating and seeing a movie, *Jungle Book*, I joined Roach and Mart at the Imperial Bar for a half-hour, then returned to camp. Later Jack Ludlow and I stopped in at the dance at the Sergeants' Mess then hit the hay.

21 AUGUST

Log Book: Spitfire height climb.

Ross's Diary: I was on the first flight this morning: a formation trip. We went up to 8,000ft above some fog-like clouds and did some wild line astern tail chasing. Later we did some section attacks. First I was the stooge, then White. I blacked out pretty bad once after I had attacked. I broke off just as I was about to hit the ship and did a roll straight down and started pulling out. I was conscious but paralysed. I could hear the roaring but could not shake free. I went dashing off a couple of miles from the others before I got control. We then did some low flying and came in. It is raining again and flying was called off after lunch. I went into Stroud and saw *Blood and Sand*. Got part of my laundry from the shop and will have to get the rest tomorrow. I hitched a ride back to camp in a RAF truck. We were paid this morning. Jack owes me a pound and Joe, two pounds. Jack paid me ten shillings.

22 AUGUST

Log Book: 1. Master with Sqn Ldr Sunderland. 2. Spitfire, section formation.

ORB: Miles Master AZ282 with Sgt R.P. Fenton struck a concrete picketing block while taxying and damaged the tail and tail wheel.

Ross's Diary: I went to X Squadron today – the gunnery squadron at Aston Down. I twice flew camera gun excercises. I flew a Mk II Spitfire, 1,150hp for the first time. I went up and practised shooting at another Spitfire using the camera gun. One time today I almost landed on the wrong runway. The CFI warned me not to do it again. I went to Stroud again and saw *Jungle Book* again. I met a pilot officer friend from Arizona and had a beer and something to eat before returning tonight.

24 AUGUST

Log Book: Spitfire, section formation.

Ross's Diary: I didn't get to fly yesterday at all. Shot forty rounds at clay pigeons and hit sixteen. Later I went into Stroud and saw *Scarlet Pimpernel* then went to the Lamb pub.

I met a girl there I had met at a little place about three weeks before. Another pilot and I walked her and her girlfriend home. The girlfriend's mother offered to let us spend the night there, so we did.

25 AUGUST

Log Book: Spitfire cloud flying and section formation.

ORB: B Squadron moved to Chedworth this afternoon. Instructors, pupils and servicing personnel of the squadron are now attached to that station. No. 19 Course was posted to squadrons today. Because of the extension to twelve weeks the course was able to attain the excellent average of 72 Spitfire hours per pupil. Thirty-six pilots were posted and three were retained as staff pilots. The course was keen throughout its training, particularly in intelligence and armament instruction. A considerable number of interception exercises were carried out, some of them controlled by Colerne over VHF which is now installed in the final phase training machines.

Ross's Diary: I went down to X Squadron this morning and saw the pictures I took yesterday while firing on the drogue. The camera gun runs during firing. It is raining hard and flying is off. I am going to town tonight.

29 AUGUST

Log Book: Spitfire, section formation.

ORB: Minchinhampton police today reported that two parachutists had been seen in the neighbourhood of Brimscombe. A patrol by the RAF Regiment and another by the 30th Gloucestershires were sent out from the station, but as a result of enquiries it was established that the parachutists were meteorological ones and one of them was recovered and handed over to the Intelligence Officers.

The station has been much concerned in farming operations during August. The weather has been unfavourable for harvesting and every moment of sunshine has had to be carefully used. Station personnel have been working overtime at Aston Farm and it seems that PSI will make considerable profits for their enterprise in undertaking the running of such a large farm.

30 AUGUST

Log Book: Spitfire, section formation.

Ross's Diary: Haven't had much time for writing lately and have been going out almost every night. Last night I went with a group of friends from Thrupp on a farewell to a lady's son who is joining the RAF. I was with a nice girl. I am happy when I am with them, almost like home. I have another date tomorrow night. I have been at X Squadron all last week and have done air firing about six times in Spitfires, three times I used cannons but got no cannon hits. Cannons are good only in line astern attacks and you can't shoot from directly behind or you'll hit the towing ship. On one of my firing passes I became so intent that I ended up almost directly behind the drogue, and my bullets were coming close to the Fairey Battle tow plane and they fired red flares for me to break away. I am well above average in my scores.

This morning I flew the Link Trainer again 1.15 hours practice beam flying. This afternoon I flew the Spitfire with cannons again, shooting at targets floating in the Bristol Channel. It was a lot of fun. I hit the target with my cannons perfectly. My four machine guns really cut up the water. Also had fun low flying and 'shot up' my girlfriend's house. I got fined a shilling for doing a climbing turn off the deck against the traffic pattern in my Spit – it was still fun.

3 SEPTEMBER

Log Book: Spitfire, section formation.

ORB: Today the national day of prayer; the BBC service at 1100 hours was relayed over the station tannoy and all sections stopped work during the broadcast.

4 SEPTEMBER

Log Book: Master Chedworth and return.

Ross's Diary: I finished at X Squadron with two good scores and am now back with my old C Squadron. I flew 1.30 hours with Walt this afternoon. We flew out across the Bristol Channel near Wales. I flew formation on Walt. We had a lot of fun. I have about 47 hours in a Spitfire now. I feel right at home in them. It won't be long before I am in the scrap now. My views have certainly changed since I joined this outfit. It won't be long before I am 19.

5 SEPTEMBER

ORB: Sgt Pilot Freel, an American pupil pilot on No. 20 Course, had a spot of trouble while flying a Spitfire at Chedworth today. In order to make his plight known, Sgt Freel took off his Mae West, wrote on it 'wheels don't work, wireless don't work – love Steve' and flew low over dispersal to drop it off. He flew so low that he struck a stationary Miles Master which was cut in two and written off as a consequence. Sgt Freel is reporting to Brighton tomorrow for a three-week course as our first representative there. We feel that they may improve his discipline and perhaps his grammar, but the directness of his recorded prose writings leaves nothing to be desired!

6 SEPTEMBER

ORB: An enemy aircraft, believed to be a Ju86A, flew over the station today at some 30,000ft.

Ross's Diary: Yesterday I flew down the Bristol Channel across a section of south-east England and came out on the south Channel coast. I flew up over rough coast lines, once through a break in the clouds I saw a web of vapour trails out over the Channel towards France. I was a little scared as I didn't have any guns and there are Fw190s around there. I came up on the coast at Bournemouth and warped it a couple of times, then checked out a couple of Whitleys who were out hunting submarines. I then came back down the coast and looked over an Albacore [Fleet Air Arm aircraft]. Then I went up through the clouds, which were getting low, and set a course of 360 degrees and in a few minutes I let down through the stuff and came out right over the Bristol Channel. The ceiling was down to 300ft so I hedge-hopped up the River Severn, past Bristol and got back to Aston Down with 20 gallons left. I had been gone 1.30 hours.

7 SEPTEMBER

Log Book: Spitfire, section formation.

ORB: Flt Lt Aldridge, who has been a most capable and conscientious OC Maintenance Squadron, was today posted to India.

Ross's Diary: Flying was called off yesterday afternoon so John and I went into Stroud and saw a movie. I flew two formation trips today. The first as Black 3 in a flight of four and later as 2 in a four-ship flight. We had a good formation, had a little fun when we broke up, dived down from 7,000ft to 3,000ft, pulled her up at about 380mph and did a couple of rolls straight up to 6,000ft. Then after a dogfight I landed. Am going to hit it early tonight. Hupe and his friend are here looking at my picture album.

8 SEPTEMBER

Log Book: Spitfire, section formation

Ross's Diary: Yesterday I flew twice, one Miles Master flight and one in a Spit. I went up dual on an aerobatic check with the CO. We did loops, Immelmans and rolls. Later I went up in a Spit on a short formation hop as No. 4. Last night I went into Stroud and spent the night there. I hitched a ride to camp in a truck after breakfast and got to the squadron just in time. It is almost noon and I don't fly until about 4 p.m. I have about 55 hours in Spitfires and this course only goes up to 58 or 60 hours and I may be moved to a different field to finish up. I saw another guy from 121 Squadron; a flight lieutenant. He said he would speak to them about me. I hope I get into the squadron before it transfers to the US Army Air Corps.

9 SEPTEMBER

Log Book: Spitfire – weather test and formation.

ORB: We learn today that Plt Off V. Cukr has been appointed acting flight lieutenant. Cukr came to the unit when it was first formed as a sergeant pilot and is the first instance of an NCO being commissioned at this unit and reaching flight commander rank while still serving with the unit.

---

10 SEPTEMBER

Log Book: Spitfire formation.

ORB: Flt Lt Wheeler was today posted to a squadron. He has been with us as an instructor for more than a year and for his work here gained the award of an AFC.

Ross's Diary: Didn't fly yesterday, met my date in town last night. We saw a movie and I let her have my picture book for a couple of nights. I came back on the 9.45 p.m. camp bus with my laundry.

I flew two formation flights today, both 1.20 hours. Fenton, a friend of mine who lives in the same hut here, was killed today. He was doing formation flying at the same time as I was; he was in a three-ship vick, he was No. 3. He went down under the leader and then pulled up. The leader's wing cut his tail off. They were at 1,000ft and Fenton went right in, too low to bail out. Hayes, the No. 2 man, circled the wreckage. He saw a wing in one field and other pieces scattered around. Fenton was still alive when they reached him but he died soon after. He must have been torn up. I just can't believe it, but it is so I guess. I ate breakfast with him at 8 a.m. this morning. You never know when you are looking at a friend's face for the last time.

Went into Stroud on a bender.

---

11 SEPTEMBER

ORB: While flying a Spitfire P7676 over the River Severn today, Sgt Pilot Grant, a Canadian of No. 20 Course, struck the water and was killed.

Ross's Diary: Grant, a Canadian friend of mine, was killed today. He was up dogfighting around 8,000ft. He suddenly dived down to a very low altitude over the River Severn and he banked too low over the water and his wing went in. They got his body out. He was a swell looking guy, in No. 20 Course, just ahead of us, and he only had five days left at the OTU. I guess he figured he could do anything with a Spitfire – that seems to be the way most guys get it, over-confidence. They start going west at the end of their courses so I'll have to watch myself. I may be getting too reckless, every day I seem to be doing crazier things, every day I seem to miss getting it a little closer, taking too many chances, going between narrower gaps in trees and wires.

---

12 SEPTEMBER

Log Book: Spitfire weather test.

ORB: Sgt Pilot Kureen of 22 Course was killed while flying Spitfire P3284 near Hungerford. Bystanders report that a wing of the aircraft came off in mid-air.

Ross's Diary: I flew 40 minutes more at X Squadron yesterday to finish up. I went for a jumping exercise (a mission on which we were attacked by instructors who acted as enemy aircraft and tried to jump us by surprise). Once when I was jumped, I did my first accidental spin in a Spitfire. I stalled out in a turn; was watching the attacking Spitfire and hauled it in too tight. Around and around I went, spinning. I had enough altitude and got out of the spin okay and carried on.

Life on the airfield continued with training, and the daily routine was normal apart from the odd exception, such as an air raid or one of the trainee pilots being killed or injured in an accident.

23 SEPTEMBER

ORB: The station was subjected to a spray attack from the air today. The liquid used was a substitute mustard gas and more than half the hangar area was heavily contaminated. 111 Station personnel took part in the exercise, reconnoitring, decontaminating and cleansing squads fully manned.

Representatives of the Air Ministry, MAP and most of the Command Gas Officers were present including Air Commodore Robertson CB, DFC, to observe the effects of the spray and our methods of dealing with it.

29 SEPTEMBER

Log Book: Master with Sgt Woxon, cross-country and aerobatics and Spitfire air test.

ORB: An Air Ministry Film Unit showed the film *The First of the Few* to a large and very appreciative audience in the theatre hangar this evening.

Gp Capt Ironmonger, Officer Commanding RAF Station Quedgeley, visited the station.

The principal event of the month has been the opening of the Chedworth satellite and the consequent changes in the training programme. In future each course is to spend the last three weeks of its time at Chedworth and is to form there a squadron – No. 552 – which is to be semi-operational. The idea is that it should be used for occasional convoy patrols by a sector operational station. The station is rather too far from the coast for this but an attempt is being made to use a station nearer the coast for this purpose whenever necessary. It is a present disadvantage that only one dispersal at Chedworth is ready for use and that therefore only half the course can be accommodated there.

Farming operations have again claimed a large amount of time and attention, but the harvest has been gathered as well as weather conditions have permitted and a start has been made at digging and clamping the potatoes under the direction of the Padre, Sqn Ldr F.J.E. Britnell.

14 OCTOBER

Log Book: Spitfire, section formation.

ORB: Sergeant Pilot Morton, a pupil on No. 22 Course, was killed while flying Spitfire I, AR227 near Babdown today.

15 OCTOBER

ORB: Today has been quite the worst for fatal accidents in the history of the unit. Plt Off Beange, a New Zealand pilot of No. 24 Course, was killed when flying a Spitfire II, P7966. He was doing a height climb and the aircraft dived into one of the sheds at Quedgeley Maintenance Unit killing a civilian woman worker and injuring others. The shed was set alight and considerable damage was caused.

A Miles Master II, AZ364, in which Flg Off Lawton, an instructor, was giving dual instruction to Plt Off Holt, an English pupil pilot on No. 24 Course, collided on the aerodrome circuit with a Spitfire I, X4059, flown by Sgt Williamson, an Australian pupil pilot on No. 24 Course. Both machines crashed and all three pilots were killed. This was felt as a very real loss, both to the unit and to the RAF as Flg Off Lawton had been an instructor at the unit for nearly six months and had worked hard and conscientiously. Plt Off Holt had been in the A&SD Branch for some two years and had been acting flight lieutenant, but had transferred to the GD Branch and sacrificed seniority in order to train for flying duties.

17 OCTOBER

Log Book: Spitfire formation and low flying.

ORB: Sgt Winther, a Norwegian pupil on No. 23 Course, was killed while flying a Spitfire II, P7543, today. Sgt Winther had been on a dogfighting exercise, the weather deteriorated and he was recalled. Encountering low cloud on the way back he climbed into it and crashed at Babdown, presumably when trying to get down under the cloud.

22 OCTOBER

ORB: Lt Kreutzer, a Norwegian naval chaplain, and Lt Lund, an officer of the RNAF HQ, attended the funeral of Sgt Winther at Cirencester today. Lt Kreutzer conducted the ceremony at the graveside.

October had clearly been remarkable for the unfortunate series of fatal accidents. Apart from these there was only one other accident reportable.

2 NOVEMBER

ORB: A farewell cocktail party was held in the Officers' Mess this evening for Wg Cdr M.H. Rhys. He has been in command of the Training Wing of the unit for the past eleven months during which he has put in a lot of hard work. The best wishes of all at the unit will go with him to his new posting as Inspector General of the Iraq Air Force and we look forward to seeing photos of him in his new uniform complete with fez! Sqn Ldr J.H.

Lapsley DFC is posted to us as OC Training Wing in place of Wg Cdr Rhys. Lapsley had been acting as the Satellite Commander at No. 58 OTU.

17 NOVEMBER

ORB: No. 22 Course was posted to squadrons today. The nine American pupils on the course all transferred direct to the USAAC.

November at Aston Down has seen us getting into our stride with our night-flying programme. In future all pupils should have 5 hours dusk and dark flying at this unit and the old D Squadron dispersal has been turned over to a newly organised night-flying flight with aircraft to be used only for that purpose.There has been a good deal of experimenting with flare paths and lighting but the Flight is now running smoothly.

Three instructors have been summoned to Buckingham Palace during the month for Investitures. Plt Off Paul Brennan received his DFC and DFM at the same time. Flg Off Graves received the DFC and Flt Sgt Schade the DFM. During the month F Squadron moved to Chedworth so that the senior course is now all at the satellite and has been formed into No. 552 Squadron, and they are to undertake convoy patrols under the control of an operational station and are to form a semi-operational squadron.

Barney continued to instruct during the month, accumulating his flying hours.

3 DECEMBER

Log Book: Spitfire, section formation, escort Huns!

ORB: An exhibition of German aircraft equipment arrived at the station today and is staying here until 5 December. Organised tours of the exhibition are being held for station personnel.

8 DECEMBER

Log Book: Spitfire – weather test and formation.

ORB: No. 23 Course completed training today and was posted with an average of exactly 58 Spitfire hours per pupil. The course was a satisfactory one but the weather during the final phase of training was poor and 552 Squadron at Chedworth was not able to get in as many cine-gun practices and affiliation exercises as was hoped. The seven Norwegian pupils on the course were outstanding and all received above average assessments.

26 DECEMBER

ORB: Our training has been interrupted by the proposal to establish a Fighter Leader Course at Chedworth. For this purpose the satellite is being taken over for the next three months and our courses will be confined to Aston Down. Since the new course is also taking over our aircraft at Chedworth, the pupil strength will have to be cut down and the proposal is that we are to have only two instead of three courses on the unit at a time. For this reason no new course was posted in today and No. 25 Course is remaining here instead of going to Chedworth.

31 DECEMBER

Log Book: Leopard Moth, W/C Cunningham and self return to base.

ORB: A demonstration rifle flight of the RAF Regiment gave an interesting display during the afternoon.

Christmas at Aston Down was a thoroughly enjoyable and satisfactory occasion for all concerned and the thanks of the whole unit must go to the station administrative officer, the catering officer, and the entertainment officer who have all worked so hard and well to ensure our comfort and entertainment. The Christmas programme included a pantomime *Babes in the Wood* or *Two of our Erks are Missing* which were performed by the station personnel in the theatre on Christmas Day and on the following Tuesday and Saturday. It also visited Chedworth. This show reached heights to which we have never before aspired and was voted thoroughly satisfactory by all who saw it. Some forty personnel took part in the show, the chorus was well-drilled and their costumes colourful, and the many topical allusions delighted the audiences and the whole show added greatly to the Christmas entertainment. The airmen's dinner was served in the dining hall by officers and sergeants, and the menu was most attractive and filling. Airmen and airwomen dined together and thoroughly enjoyed both the food and the entertainment provided by the station band. The main dish was roast pork produced on the station farm.

John Cunningham had become the leading RAF night-fighter pilot of the Second World War after chalking up nearly twenty kills. He had numerous decorations and had been rested in the summer of 1942 and was now Wing Commander of 81 Group, and the OTU at Aston Down formed an element of this group. It was only right that he was at the end-of-year celebrations. To Barney, he seemed a modest man and he recalled that he was fêted like a film star. Nicknamed 'Cat's Eyes', a description he never liked, he had exceptional skill at night flying after British scientists had developed a sophisticated radar system which allowed pilots to home in on enemy aircraft. Barney's wife Dorothy was also at the end-of-year celebrations and remembered Cunningham as well, but for different reasons. Barney was at the bar for most of the evening and the charming Cunningham asked her for a dance. He was an excellent dancer but Barney was not impressed.

'Why did you dance with him?' he asked.

'Because he asked me to,' was the quite natural answer. It was left at that!

1 JANUARY, 1943

ORB: The opening of the New Year finds us faced with many problems in connection with the organisation of the Fighter Leaders' School at Chedworth. While the organisation of the school is to be in the hands of Wg Cdr Woodhouse and a staff of instructors posted in by Fighter Command, the aircraft and their servicing and maintenance has to be found from No. 52 OTU. As a result we are restricted to two courses of twenty pupils each and all our flying is to be done from Aston Down. Thirty-six Spitfire VB aircraft for use at the Fighter Leaders' School are to be held against our strength, thus reducing the number available for our normal training programme. We are all very sorry today to say goodbye to Flt Lt V. Cukr and Plt Off J. Kaucky who have been with us as instructors since the formation of the unit. They have both done good work at this unit, particularly in the training of the Czech and French pupils, and Flt Lt Cukr has been Officer Commanding B Squadron for the last six months.

Vaclav Cukr had come to England and joined 310 (Czech) Squadron based at Duxford in August 1940 and had transferred to 6 OTU at Sutton Bridge later the same month. Posted then to 43 Squadron, he was shot down in September and suffered wounds. He was sent to 253 Squadron based at Kenley before he was rested from operations in March 1941. Following that he was posted as an instructor to 52 OTU, being based at Debden before it transferred to Aston Down.

Jan Kaucky had also joined 310 (Czech) Squadron at Duxford in July 1940 and flew with them through the Battle of Britain, before he too was posted to 52 OTU as an instructor in March 1941.

ORB: They are both transferring to No. 20 Maintenance Unit, also at Aston Down, on Test Pilot duties. Flt Lt R.S. Hartree is also being posted today so we are losing another of our old hands. He was at Aston Down when the unit moved here and, as accountant officer, his caustic wit has enlivened many Officers' Mess meetings during the discussion of Mess finances. Wg Cdr Macbrien is also leaving us today. He has been here as a pupil, having commanded a training station in Canada, and is going to command a Canadian fighter station in England. He has made many friends during his short stay here and proved a pleasant surprise to flight commanders who were a bit doubtful how to treat a wing commander pupil.

2 JANUARY

Log Book: Spitfire, formation and doggers, 1.10 hours.

ORB: Sgt Pilot Britto was killed while flying Spitfire I, AR220. His engine stalled during flight and he tried to make the airfield but the aircraft spun in and hit the ground near the watch office building. Britto was from Jamaica and was one of the most popular pilots on No. 25 Course.

9 JANUARY

Log Book: Spitfire, formation 1 hour.

ORB: The first of our monthly gas exercises was held at the station this morning. [Sgt] A. Griffiths, who had been attached from 81 Group as full-time gas officer, organised the exercise, which assumed that from 0900–1200 hours we were living under gas warfare conditions. As the first of these exercises it was considered successful, though minor points which needed attention were observed.

16 JANUARY

Log Book: Spitfire, formation attacks, 1.15 hours.

ORB: Routine orders today announced a Mention in Despatches for Wg Cdr R.W. Jackson and Sqn Ldr J.E.M. Stebbings of the unit. There can be no doubt that these are well earned. As Chief Technical Officer, Wg Cdr Jackson has had a large share in the satisfactory training the unit has been able to give its pupils. Because of his keenness and efficiency the largest wing on the station runs smoothly and satisfactorily and the record of flying hours compares favourably with that of any other OTU. As PMC of the Officers' Mess since last October he has provided amenities and comforts which have made a tremendous difference to officers living in the Mess. Sqn Ldr Stebbings was station Admin Officer from November 1941 to September 1942 and was notably hard working. Many of the farming headaches fell to his lot and the satisfactory running of the farm last year owed much to his care and attention.

17 JANUARY

ORB: Plt Off V.P. Brennan DFC, DFM was posted today, we understand, back to Australia. A successful pilot from Malta and a keen and interesting personality, Paul Brennan quickly made his mark at this station and has done a good job here particularly as the Officer Commanding Night Flying Flight.

18 JANUARY

ORB: The station cinema started tonight its new service of presenting films on six nights weekly with a change of programme twice weekly. This enterprising step should add greatly to station amenities. A twin projector has been installed and the film and sound are reproduced in a faultless manner. The first film, Walt Disney's *Dumbo*, was shown to a large and appreciative audience. Average attendance of 300 per night proves that this provision is necessary.

19 JANUARY

ORB: No. 25 Course output, due today, has been postponed for a fortnight because flying times are so low, but following a new command policy a new course has been posted in. We will thus have two courses to cope with at one flight. This means that the new course will not get much Spitfire flying until the old one leaves, but arrangements are being made for the night-flying unit to give them some Master flying and the CGI is to get the lecture programme as far advanced as possible before full flying can be started. The new course is only twenty-strong and the majority are not pupils in the normal course of training, but they have been doing stooge jobs as target towers or instructors at glider-towing schools and so on. A course of this kind is normally more difficult to run than a normal one so A Squadron may have some problem children to deal with.

26 JANUARY

Log book: Spitfire, formation and Rhubarb, 1 hour.

ORB: Sgt Caldwell, a Canadian pupil on No. 26 Course, was killed today when his Spitfire II, P2808, which he was flying was seen to plunge into the River Severn after colliding with a Spitfire flown by Sgt Clark. Sgt Caldwell was a member of the detail waiting to attack the towed drogue on the air firing range, but joined in the attack while an earlier detail was operating. As a result of the collision Sgt Clark landed his machine on the shore near the river but Sgt Caldwell's machine was lost in the Severn. Attempts to recover his body failed so that Caldwell is officially posted as missing, though eye-witness accounts make it certain that he was in fact killed.

30 JANUARY

Log book: Spitfire, weather test, 0.30 hours.

ORB: Two more of our instructors were posted today. Flt Lt De Naeyer to 602 Squadron and Flg Off Wigley DFC to 19 Squadron, both at Perranporth. Both have got their flights and Wigley put up the extra ring before leaving us. We are sorry to have them go but both were keen to get back on ops after a tour of duty here, during which both had worked hard and well. Wigley's promotion is particularly pleasing to us all, as he is an ex-pupil of the OTU. No. 27 Group Cirencester extended an invitation to certain officers of the station to attend a film show including *Flying Officer X*, which was given at their headquarters, and at which Her Majesty Queen Mary had expressed her intention of attending. The Station Commander, Wg Cdr Lapsley, Sqn Ldr Whittle and Flg Off Hagerty from the station attended and had the honour of being presented to Her Majesty.

January had been a month of uncertainty as far as the training programme was concerned. There had been uncertainty both in terms of the size of course to be sent to them and the dates on which they should have arrived. The training programme had to be adapted to meet the new situation. With smaller courses, it had been found better to send the whole course to flights in flying weather and confine the ground training to non-flying days. This had enabled them to get in a satisfactory number of flying hours and to do justice to the pupils, despite their troubles. The formation of the Fighter Leaders' School had thrown extra work on the Maintenance Wing who had to take charge of thirty-six Spitfire VBs, to see that they were inspected and put into service quickly, and to prepare for the dispatch of the thirty-six Spitfire I and IIs which were allocated away from the unit. In spite of the extra work, their own training had to be carried on and serviceability had to be well maintained at the flights. The 81 Group scheme of flying planning had been brought into operation during the month and had been very useful in setting out, for the benefit of all concerned, the work that had to be got through in the three-week period. The flying charts showed daily and three-weekly targets and had proved valuable to use; they justified the time and trouble taken in their preparation.

1 FEBRUARY

ORB: The AOC-in-C of Fighter Command, Air Marshal Sir Trafford Leigh Mallory KCB, DSO, visited and inspected the station. It is understood no major criticisms were made.

2 FEBRUARY

ORB: The remainder of No. 25 Course were today posted to squadrons; thirteen pupils of the course have been placed on overseas draft and seven left today to join squadrons. The course was an average one but established a record for the unit in only suffering one reportable accident. The average number of Spitfire hours for the course was 51 and they averaged 14 hours formation flying.

6 FEBRUARY

ORB: The funerals of two sergeant pilots were held at the station today. They were members of the crew of a Wellington from Moreton-in-Marsh which crashed at Stroud while night flying.

Sgt Pilot Burden, a Canadian pupil on No. 27 Course, baled out about 3 miles east of the aerodrome today. Spitfire I, P9446, sprang a glycol leak and the cockpit filled with fumes. Burden baled out and was not injured; the plane crashed near Sapperton and was a write-off.

7 FEBRUARY

ORB: Sqn Ldr P.M. Down, who was Chief Flying Instructor at Chedworth until the formation of the Fighter Leaders' School, was posted as CFI at Rhoose, the Llandow satellite.

9 FEBRUARY

Log Book: Spitfire; 1. Formation 1.10 hours; 2. From Chedworth 0.30 hours; 3. To Charmy Down 0.40 hours.

ORB: Routine orders announced a standardisation and tightening up of leave policy, and particularly of the time at which personnel may leave the station when starting leave. This is a needed step as the time of starting leave has varied considerably from section to section. No. 26 Course was posted today. Of the twenty-one pupils, three were posted overseas and the remainder to squadrons in England, six of them to 11 Group. The course averaged 50½ hours of Spitfire flying and the wing commander reported it as being a 'good average'. The course was unable to carry out sector affiliations because they lost their VHF when they lost Chedworth, but the other advanced training reached a good standard. Some good squadron formations were laid on during final training.

No. 28 Course arrived today; it numbers twenty-one and includes nine officers, several of whom have been in Training Command.

12 FEBRUARY

ORB: Flg Off W.H. Winter was posted with effect from today to flying control duties at 51 OTU. He has been with the unit since August 1941 and has reigned over the watch office during that time. Popular with everyone in the Mess, his going will leave a void in the billiards room.

13 FEBRUARY

Log Book: Spitfire, formation 0.40 hours.

ORB: The Under-Secretary of State for Air Lord Sherwood, accompanied by Lord Winterton, visited the station today.

22 FEBRUARY

Log Book: Spitfire, section attacks 0.45 hours.

ORB: Flt Lt Griffiths, who was adjutant of the wing that went to Murmansk in 1941, visited the station and gave an interesting lecture on Russia to all personnel.

27 FEBRUARY

Log book: Spitfire, formation and doggers, 1.05 hours.

ORB: The Station Commander kicked off a charity football match at Stonehouse.

28 FEBRUARY

Log Book: Spitfire, formation, 1.10 hours.

ORB: [In summary for the month] February had been notable for fine weather and good flying times. The unit flew 2,441 hours of which 2,169 were in Spitfires. The total included 600 Spitfire hours by the Fighter Leaders' School, but the number at the unit provided evidence of the good work done by the Maintenance and Training Wings. To get in so many hours with so few machines available meant that the servicing teams were kept on their toes all the time and accidents and minor prangs were kept to a minimum. In fact the accident record for the month was much better than that of any other OTU, the average hours per preventable accident was 1,220 against an average for the Group as a whole of 355. There were only five accidents reportable, and only two classed as avoidable. No pilots were injured. The average number of aircraft on charge daily was 126. Spitfire numbers serviceable were 68, and unserviceable 28. Masters serviceable 15, unserviceable 7 and other aircraft serviceable 6, unserviceable 2.

The training programme had again been subject to improvisation since it was not practical to follow the training syllabus exactly when courses were as small. The machinery for disposing of unsuitable pupils seemed to have again jammed and the unit found itself with too many pupil pilots unfit for flying and up for transfer, but who were left with the unit for months on end with nothing to do. The position was most unsatisfactory, both for the unit and for the pupil pilots and they made representations to the Group on the subject.

2 MARCH

ORB: Two members of the Soviet Military Mission, Major Rooday and Captain Diky, visited the unit today for the purpose of studying the administration and organisation of a fighter OTU. They were accompanied by Flg Off Hills of the Air Ministry. They were greatly interested in the work of the unit and as each of the Russian officers appeared to speak and understand our language there were many interesting discussions and exchanges of views on matters in general and air forces in particular.

7 MARCH

ORB: Sgt J.W. Callinan, one of the Canadian pupils on No. 27 Course, was unfortunately killed at Slimbridge today when his Spitfire collided with high-tension cables in the low-flying area.

9 MARCH

Log book: Spitfire; 1. Affiliation 1.15 hours; 2. Formation 0.45 hours.

ORB: Flg Off Mike Graves DFC, was posted from us to 57 OTU to a Flight Command. Mike had also served in Malta and had come to us and done good work at Chedworth, later returning to Aston Down where he spent most of his time on the staff of the Air Firing Squadron.

10 MARCH

Log Book: Spitfire, Doggers 0.45 hours.

ORB: Sqn Ldr P.W. Lefevre DFC, who has been Officer Commanding Air Firing Squadron since March 1942, was posted to 129 Squadron. A very popular flight commander who got results, he had an inimitable sense of humour and was always on top form. The funeral of Sgt Callinan took place today at Cirencester.

12 MARCH

Log Book: Spitfire, Doggers 1.00 hour.

ORB: Plt Off Phillip Charron posted to us as an instructor. Charron had been one of the NCO pilots on No. 16 Course and had been posted back to Aston Down from Malta.

21 MARCH

ORB: Gp Capt F.E. Rosier DSO assumed command of the station.

23 MARCH

ORB: No. 27 Course was posted out today. An average course in all respects, average flying times per pupil was 54.20 hours. No. 29 Course arrived with an intake of thirty-three pupils, the largest since No. 23 course arrived back in September 1942.

28 MARCH

Log Book: Spitfire, weather test, 0.15 hours.

ORB: In celebration of the 25th anniversary of the formation of the RAF, a well-attended church parade was held at Minchinhampton parish church.

The average number of aircraft on charge daily [this month] was 104. Spifires serviceable 59, unserviceable 21. Masters serviceable 10, unserviceable 6, and total flying hours for the month was 2,344. It was with regret that we said farewell to our old CO and we think he was not anxious to leave us. We have been happy under his command and wish him all the best at Church Lawford. We will do our best for the new CO in his quest to maintain the station at its present good standing.

During the month the unit's training wing adjutant, Flt Lt R.F. Lane, transferred from the RAF to the USAAF. His loss is greatly regretted as he took quite an interest in the preparation of the records of the unit.

1 APRIL

ORB: In celebration of the 25th anniversary of the RAF a ceremonial parade and march passed, with the Station Commander taking the salute in front of the watch office. Later in the day the CO addressed the personnel of the station over the tannoy reminding us of our inheritance and exhorting us to greater efforts. The celebration ended in great style at an all-ranks dance being held in the NAAFI in the evening.

2 APRIL

ORB: Another goodbye, this time to our Wing Commander Training, Wg Cdr J. Lapsley DFC, one of the best. He has been with us for five months but now returns to operations.

He and his good wife have been very popular and his good work has been apparent. He is succeeded by Wg Cdr P.M. Brothers DFC, who is already well known to many at the unit.

CLOSING ENTRY: 3–7 APRIL

ORB: An epidemic of postings to our junior instructors with Flg Off N.G. Jones, Flg Off R.R. Barnfather and Plt Off 'Junior' Tayleur, all of whom have been with the unit for more than six months, leaving us for further spells overseas. Tayleur was commissioned with us and has been a popular member of both the Sergeants' and Officers' Messes. Flg Off Webster who had rendered good service for three months also departed for 234 Squadron.

CHAPTER 6

Operation Torch – The Final Throes

72 Squadron in North Africa May 1943

Following the initial deliveries of Spitfires to Malta, the next theatre earmarked to receive them was North Africa. As early as April 1942 the personnel of two Spitfire Squadrons, 92 and 145, had arrived in Egypt. Malta still had first call on the tropically modified Spitfires and as Malta's need was greater than expected, it was met by diverting the fighters from the two units sent to Egypt.

The delivery route of short-range aircraft to Egypt was even more difficult than that to Malta, with crated aircraft being shipped to the port of Takoradi on the Gold Coast (now Ghana) where they were assembled and test flown. They then flew through Nigeria, French Equatorial Africa and the Sudan to Egypt in preparation of meeting the large German and Italian offensive in North Africa. They made rapid progress eastwards. The Axis advance was famously halted at El Alamein, within 60 miles of Alexandria on 25 June. During the ferocious air battles surrounding El Alamein which accompanied the ground battles, the Spitfires' main task was to provide top cover so that other RAF units could perform their ground attack and support functions without being attacked from above.

On 8 November 1942, just as the Axis defensive line in Egypt was in the process of collapsing, Allied forces opened a new front in North Africa with the intention of trapping the Axis forces between simultaneous advances from the east and west. Codenamed Operation Torch, troops landed at widely separated points in Morocco, on the north and south coasts near Casablanca, and in Algeria at Oran and Algiers. The landings at Oran were with 18,500 American troops, the landings at Algiers were with 18,000 American and British forces and Major-General Patton led the Moroccan landings with a further 24,500 American troops.

As soon as airfields had been secured ashore, RAF and USAAF units flew into them and began operations. The intention was that the RAF would organise much of the air defence of the supply ports, forward cover for the troops and tactical cooperation with the army, with strategic bombing left to the USAAF. It was planned initially to send out eleven RAF squadrons with the convoys, seven with Spitfire Vs, three with Hurricane fighter-bombers and one with photo-reconnaissance Spitfires. These would then be joined by four squadrons of Bristol Blenheim Vs and two of Bristol Beaufighter night fighters, and would fly direct. The units would be grouped into three wings:

322 Wing – commanded by Gp Capt C. Appleton and led by
Wg Cdr P.H 'Dutch' Hugo
   81 Squadron – Spitfire V (Sqn Ldr Ronald 'Razz' Berry)
  154 Squadron – Spitfire V (Sqn Ldr D.C. Carleton)
  242 Squadron – Spitfire V (Sqn Ldr D. Secretan)

323 Wing – commanded by Gp Capt Edward-Jones and led by
Wg Cdr M.G.F. Pedley
  43 Squadron – Hurricane II (Sqn Ldr M. Rook)
 253 Squadron – Hurricane II (Sqn Ldr L.H.T. Bartlett)

324 Wing – commanded by Gp Capt Ronnie Lees and led by
Wg Cdr D.A.P. McMullen
  72 Squadron – Spitfire V (Sqn Ldr Bobbie Oxspring)
  93 Squadron – Spitfire V (Sqn Ldr G.H. Nelson-Edwards)
 111 Squadron – Spitfire V (Sqn Ldr Tony Bartley)
 152 Squadron – Spitfire V (Sqn Ldr J.E.J. Sing)
 225 Squadron – Hurricane II

324 Wing had originally been formed in September 1942, then also under the command of Gp Capt Ronnie Lees DFC. After an intensive training period that included such items as battle and general hardening and toughening-up courses, the wing had embarked for North Africa in October 1942 arriving at Maison Blanche airfield near Algiers early in November. It was the first fighter wing to land in North Africa.

Lloyd Snell, a Canadian radar expert with 43 Squadron, the 'Fighting Cocks' (later to join 72 Squadron as part of 324 Wing), recalled:

I had been posted to 43 Squadron to maintain the IFF (Identification Friend or Foe) that all Allied aircraft carried to show them as friendly when picked up on radar. This was the most secret place of the radar and it carried a detonator to destroy the circuitry before it fell into enemy hands. 43 had been preparing to go overseas and on 1 November we had left the United Kingdom with our destination unknown. On 8 November we were told the landings had been made at Casablanca, Oran and Algiers and we would be on the next convoy to land at Algiers. That night we went through the Straits of Gibraltar. There were lights on the Spanish coast; Gibraltar was in darkness but silhouetted against the sky. On 12 November we pulled into Algiers. All the white buildings looked very clean from a distance and the next morning we were offloaded with full kit, sten guns, eight magazines with twenty-five

rounds in each magazine, and headed towards Maison Blanche airfield which
was about 16 miles away.

The landings in Algeria and Morocco developed into a race, with Allied troops
struggling to build up their strength ashore and advance into Tunisia while
German units moved rapidly into that country to establish defensive positions.
When they met there were some fierce initial clashes but, as the winter set in, the
situation developed into a stalemate. The poor state of the roads in Algeria meant
that Allied forces in the east of the country and in Tunisia were often short of
supplies. Moreover, there were few airfields in the area equipped for all-weather
operations which meant that aircraft often became bogged down in quagmires of
mud following periods of heavy rain. These factors imposed severe restrictions on
their sortie rates. The Germans by contrast were better placed in the early part of
the campaign. Numerically they were the weaker force but their airfields in central
Tunisia were better equipped and the arrival of Jagdgeschwader 2 (JG2) and Focke-
Wulf Fw190 fighters gave the Germans a measure of technical superiority. As a
result there were occasions when the Germans were able to establish air superiority
over the battle area, yet for much of the winter poor weather prevented effective air
operations being performed by either side.
    The airfields remained targets for the Germans. Lloyd Snell again recalled:

> There were frequent raids and the spent ack-ack landing on the tin roof was
> very noisy. One evening Eric Boutell, Jim Hillis and I walked down a road
> to a bar that they had seen at Maison Carée. We drank wine with some old
> timers who were at the bar. When we got back to the gate of the airfield an
> air raid was just beginning so we went across the road into a field of grapes,
> near a Bofors gun emplacement, a little off target. First a number of parachute
> flares were dropped that lit up the whole area until the raid was over. Besides
> bombs they had dropped canisters of spikes made up of sheet metal with
> four points so one point would always puncture aircraft tyres. The canisters
> would always open on the way down so the spikes were scattered over a wide
> area. Anti-personnel bombs were also dropped in canisters. When a bomb
> stopped whistling on the way down we knew it was a canister of one or the
> other and they were dropped in sticks of four. This night the bombs were
> heading straight for us: one, two, three each getting closer, the fourth landed
> past us and bounced off the ground. We had been taught to keep our heads
> off the ground to avoid concussion (on our elbows with our hands behind
> our necks) so the three of us were fine. When the raid was over we picked our
> way back to the airfield by the light of one of the flares still working. A scary
> moment but I learnt that you could survive a close one.

Early in the New Year the weather improved and the situation swung rapidly in
favour of the Allies. Following a vigorous airfield improvement programme their air
forces were able to bring greater strength to bear and from then on until the end of
the campaign there would be a high rate of air activity with both sides experiencing

losses. At the end of January the first Spitfire IXs became operational and these were able to provide top cover for other forces. Meanwhile, the tightening air and sea stranglehold on the Axis supply routes from Italy made it increasingly difficult for them to move supplies and equipment to Tunisia. Under Operation Flax the Allied air forces launched a major campaign to defeat the Axis airlift of supplies, and scores of transport aircraft were shot down, drastically reducing the German carrying capacity. From the beginning of April it became clear that the battle for control of Tunisia was entering the final phase.

In the south, at the Mareth Line, General Montgomery and his 8th Army had tried during the final week of March to pierce the German line without success. The Mareth Line was actually a fortification system built before the war by the French to prevent the Italians from spilling over from Libya into Tunisia. It extended westward from the Mediterranean Sea, straight inland for about 22 miles to the Matmâta hills, flanked by impassable salt lakes. FM Rommel had occupied the line, reinforcing the gun emplacements, pillboxes and strongholds with German arms and ammunition and had effectively blocked the Allies' entry into Tunisia from the south. Frontal attacks by the British had failed which prompted Montgomery to order his New Zealand troops to march inland far enough to encircle the line and launch an attack on Rommel's rear. Once the New Zealand troops were in position, Montgomery also launched a simultaneous attack at the front again, forcing the Germans to withdraw, albeit slowly. During the next few weeks' delay, the American and British armies prepared for the final push through extremely difficult mountainous terrain against the well-prepared German defence.

In preparation for the final onslaught several significant changes had been made at the top of the Allied chain of command. While General Eisenhower remained the supreme commander-in-chief of all Allied forces in North Africa, the British general, Alexander, became his deputy, bringing with him his great experience and intelligence. On the German side, FM Rommel was recalled to Germany, partly due to ill-health, and relinquished his command to General von Arnim with Kesselring retaining his position as supreme commander of Italy, Sicily and North Africa. Of more concern to the RAF was the appointment of ACM Tedder to command all air forces, with Air Vice-Marshal Harry Broadhurst directing the operations of the Western Desert Air Force that had been operating with the 8th Army.

15 APRIL, 1943

Barney's odyssey to North Africa began on 15 April when he joined the transport ship SS *Franconia* at Liverpool docks bound for Algeria. The ship arrived safely on 23 April after successfully eluding the prowling German U-boats and slipping through the Straits of Gibraltar.

Log Book: Perfect trip thanks to the Navy. Three days in Algiers and then to 324 Training Wing at Kalsa Jderda. Five days doing nothing and then at last to 72 Squadron in the famous Souk Valley.

At the time, 72 Squadron together with 93, 111 and 243 Squadrons made up 324 Wing, which was part of 242 Group in the North African Tactical Air Force under the overall command of the Australian, Air Marshal Arthur 'Maori' Coningham. Following the departure of Sqn Ldr Oxspring, Flt Lt Stephen 'Danny' Daniel had been appointed to take over command of 72 Squadron. Daniel was a Scotsman from Dumfries and had joined 72 Squadron early in 1942, flying sorties over France before being posted to the Mediterranean arena in November 1942 for the landings in Algeria and Morocco. He would end the war with sixteen confirmed kills.

There were a number of airfields constructed in the Souk-El-Khemis valley which were all given names of London railway stations: Paddington, Victoria, Waterloo and Euston. They were quite good airfields, being built on sand with Sommerfield Track runways, consisting of canvas covered by steel netting. Although this stabilised the ground, it did not remove the dust. This proved to be quite a problem with a lot of the starter motors. As a result, the Spitfire Vs were fitted with the Vokes tropical air filter for the carburettor intake that had a distinctive big filter housing beneath the nose of the aircraft.

There were no buildings whatsoever on the airfields and practically no trees for cover, and being only 20–30 miles from the front line they were vulnerable to enemy attacks.

The Allies were now firmly on the offensive and close to gaining air superiority. No. 324 Wing had been engaged in offensive patrols over the battlefront and providing escort to Allied medium bombers as the ground forces prepared for the last big push in Africa. Montgomery's 8th Army had won the battle of the Mareth Line and the German and Italian armies were being forced into a smaller and smaller area around the Tunisian peninsula. The April weather was brilliant; the Germans were still over most days which was difficult to understand as most of their airfields had been destroyed. On Palm Sunday two squadrons of the wing shot down thirty-six Jerry transports loaded with petrol and supplies for the Afrika Korps.

Barney's North African campaign was to be conducted in circumstances quite different from those with which he had become accustomed to in England. In North Africa everyone was in tents and they carried their own bedrolls. The aircraft were dispersed, they were not covered and only sometimes camouflaged.

---

5 MAY

ORB: Briefed with the Commanding Officer addressing the pilots in the Officers' Mess. The final big assault will begin at dawn tomorrow, the programme has been amended, the bombers with their fighter escorts are to blast a way for the army.

Gen von Arnim was issuing printed orders of the day to his men: 'Behind you lies the sea, before you lies the enemy. You must go forward, you must fight to the last man and the last round.' But the German position was not desperate. The minefields, mortars and machine guns still stretched like a web around Tunis and Cape Bon. There were still over 250,000 Axis troops on the field of battle and they had petrol, food, guns, tanks and ammunition. It was only the Luftwaffe that seemed to have packed up as most of it had already disappeared back to Sicily.

---

6 MAY

Log Book: Spitfire IX sweep Tunis area x 3.

ORB: Flying commenced again on 6 May, the day of the final push to defeat the combined German and Italian armies in North Africa.

It was the air force that started the battle, and at dawn the next day the squadron was at readiness and watched the sun rise – a beautiful morning. The squadron's task was to escort the medium bomber Bostons all day. It was a tribute to the number of sorties flown (Barney flew three) and the Allied air superiority that no aircraft were lost; over 1,000 sorties were flown. Pilots were returning with stories that they had nothing to bomb, the remaining aircraft had either gone or been hidden, because there were certainly none in the sky. There were no vehicles on the roads and there was no sign of German activity near the front. There was practically nothing to hit or to strafe. The Germans had gone to ground, heavily camouflaged and dug-in, and from the air the ground looked dead and deserted. By 10 a.m. that morning the advancing armies were ahead of schedule. Every objective had been taken and the advance units had to slow down to allow the flanks to catch up.

In the afternoon, twelve Spits from 72 Squadron swept over the battle area at 1400 hours flying at 14,000ft. Bad weather over Tunis prevented much from being seen there, but north of Bizerte sixteen Me109s were encountered. Wg Cdr Gilroy led a section down on them from 10,000ft but they fled. The rest of the squadron climbed rapidly and followed them, getting in among them and a terrific battle ensued during which Flt Lt Hagger claimed one and one damaged. Plt Off Keith claimed two and a probable and Flt Lt Prytherch and Plt Off Shaw claimed one each. Two more were damaged.

Later on, at 1745 hours, a further twelve Spits from 72 Squadron took off to patrol the Gulf of Tunis at 10,000ft. Four Me109s and two Fw190s dived out of the clouds west of Tunis and engaged them and Flt Lt Hagger damaged one of the Fw190s. Heavy flak was seen during the mission and a Boston was lost at around 1800 hours.

---

7 MAY

Log Book: Sweep Tunis area. No joy – last reported bogies, some flak.

ORB: Tunis orbited up to 17,000ft with twelve aircraft including Wg Cdr Gilroy and Sqn Ldr Boddington. Took off at 0905 hours but no aircraft encountered. There were between a dozen to twenty motor transports on the Protville–Tunis road. All aircraft landed safely at 1025 hours.

Log Book: Sweep La Goulette area. Pranged corvette, MTB and tug in Gulf of Tunis. Wizard.

ORB: 8/10 cloud at 10,000ft when Sqn Ldr Daniel and eleven other pilots took off at 1805 hours. Tunis patrolled at 8,000ft and there was much small shipping to the north of Tunis. Our aircraft went down and attacked off the mouth of the River Medjerda. Four barges left smoking and a destroyer, and three smaller craft also attacked. Destroyer left on fire and two of the smaller craft sank. Light flak encountered. Plt Off D.N. Keith was hit and crash-landed at Medjez el Bab but was unhurt.

The speed of the advance had taken the Germans by surprise and news filtered through that Tunis had fallen.

In the late afternoon Bizerte fell and the noose around the German forces was drawing tighter. Most of the remaining German fighters were ordered to fly out of Tunisia.

8 MAY

Log Book: 1. Sweep south of Tunis, pranged transport on road but cannons jammed; 2. Sweep Cape Bon area, no joy. Light flak again.

ORB: Squadron flew at 10,000ft in the Cape Bon area, weather and visibility good. Motor transport seen moving between Hammet-Kelibia and Kerda al Medzel and were attacked. Came across twenty Me109s and one He111 left on the ground. Flt Lt Hagger destroyed two, Sgt Clarkson damaged two and Flg Off Hughes damaged a third. Squadron later flew again around Cape Bon area and though no enemy aircraft reported, fifty plus motor transport seen at and observed north-east of Soliman. Heavy flak encountered at Soliman.

9 MAY

Log Book: 1. Sweep Cape Bon area. Boost control still unserviceable; 2. Sweep Cape Bon again – still some ground fighting but nothing for us.

ORB: Flying at 12,000ft in fine weather, both coasts could be seen, but no enemy aircraft reported or seen. Heavy flak encountered. Shipping seen at Korbous and Cap de Forbas.

The Germans were doomed and they were forced into the confines of the Cap Bon peninsula, while in the La Sebala area they hung on for another few days only to be wiped out eventually, with just a few escaping. There were some remnants in the Enfidaville area who, despite being totally surrounded, continued to fight on valiantly.

Realising the hopelessness of the situation they surrendered in vast numbers and it was here that Gen von Armin was taken prisoner.

10 MAY

Log Book: Sweep Cape Bon.

Losses, however, were very low and they continued to harass the evacuating troops right up to the next day when it was considered that the North African campaign had ended. Freelance patrols continued and for a few days the odd fighter was encountered, but after this their only concern was flak which was still heavy and accurate. They were flying over Tunisia at 10,000ft now, whereas a week before it had only been safe to fly at 25,000ft – a mark of the quickly changing position. They continued to strafe shipping, parked aircraft, transports and troops, but this was stopped because the Allied troops were advancing so rapidly that it was difficult to identify targets accurately. To their knowledge they never made the mistake of attacking their own forces, but this was as much down to good luck as to good management.

11 MAY

On the ground, troops were advancing on Tunis. The roads were packed with tanks and troops following the advance and there were constant traffic jams. An advance party was sent through and reported back that the smell and the flies were awful and bodies remained everywhere.

13 MAY

Log Book: To La Sebala ex-Hun drome.

No. 72 Squadron followed their ground crew and moved from Souk-el-Khemis to La Sebala, an airfield about 8 miles north-west of Tunis where the squadron next established itself. La Sebala was still under construction. It was here that only five days beforehand Me109s had taken off and taken on the Spitfires from 81 Squadron. La Sebala was an excellent aerodrome, wide and flat, completely grass-covered with no litter or useless material left lying around; but it was not the same on all captured airfields. Many others were littered with shells, grenades, dead men and animals. On the aerodrome itself there were ten burned-out Ju52 transport planes which lay broken and crippled at the edge of the airfield, but several Me109s stood intact and untouched in their bays, hidden in the orange groves at the southern edge of the airfield. They dared not touch anything since there was the chance that they had been rigged with explosives, which would have been set to go off with the slightest touch by an unwary trophy hunter or a scrounger. Often the most innocent-appearing object would be wired so they had to be extremely careful. The journey by the advance party had solved one problem, and that was how the Germans had kept flying after most of their airfields had been bombed: they had used long straight stretches of roads with parking bays built by the roadside. These had camouflage nets to hide the aircraft. The Germans had also left a parting gift at the airfield other than the booby traps and mines, as most of the squadron went down with dysentery. While the water bowsers had filled the wells, on examination they contained dead animals.

Despite this, and to observe the victory, a number of pilots were dispatched with 4-gallon tanks and orders to fill them with local wine. Several hours later they reassembled to drink and revel. Barney recalled that they drank and drank for ages without anything happening. Eventually, somewhat disgusted, they retired still seemingly sober. By morning, however, they were all drunk – the slow-acting date wine finally revealed its potency and they were drunk for most of the day. Nothing else ever compared to that potent Tunisian wine. 'Lunatics' Broth' it was called, and they had access to gallons of the stuff, so they made full use of it.

14 MAY

Log Book: Patrol Bizerte.

ORB: Four aircraft patrolled harbour and town at 5–10,000ft. No incidents to report. Dusk landings made.

17 MAY

Log Book: Scramble 23,000ft.

ORB: Flg Off Barnfather and Plt Off H.S. Lewis scrambled at 1005 hours to attempt to intercept a bandit over the sea. Plots faded and no contact was made so the pair recalled.

20 MAY

Log Book: Bizerte–Cape Bon to cover V parade in Tunis.

ORB: Flg Off O.L. Hardy led the squadron of twelve Spitfires on a patrol at 18–20,000ft in the Gulf of Tunis to intercept any enemy aircraft that might attempt to attack Tunis during the Victory Parade. None seen or reported and all landed safely.

21 MAY

Log Book: Scramble. Sex [WO 'Sexton' Gear] got Me210 today.

ORB: Two aircraft, Sgt L.A. Frampton and Flg Off R.R. Barnfather, scrambled to intercept enemy aircraft 25 miles north-west of Bizerte but no contact made.

Four aircraft led by WO A.H. Gear scrambled at 1715 hours to intercept enemy aircraft 10 miles north-east of Bizerte going west at 23,000ft. Section climbed to 26,000ft and a visual was obtained but soon lost. This was regained and enemy aircraft identified as a Me210. WO Gear fired two bursts from above and the port engine caught fire and it spun and crashed into the sea off Tabarka leaving only a patch of oil. All aircraft returned safely.

22–31 MAY

ORB: No operational flying but squadron moved from La Sebala to Mateur.

On 31 May there was a liberty run into Tunis for most of the squadron. According to the Operations Record Book, cars and motorcycles in various states of repair began to appear around the campsite. Trophies of the campaign were eagerly sought after by many and German helmets, rifles and badges became popular souvenirs. A few managed to get hold of cars and motorcycles, and with wheels they were able to explore further afield far more quickly. Approaches to any of the towns were littered with the carcasses of horses and bodies of soldiers which were surrounded by hordes of flies in the intense heat. The stench of decaying flesh was overwhelming.

Tunis, however, was marvellous and a popular retreat with wide streets and lined boulevards, and the pilots were able to shop in the stores. The army had managed to drink the two breweries dry in the week following its capture before Gen Montgomery had instructed the Redcaps to move in to restore some sort of order. The pilots and ground crew drank wine and champagne around the bars and clubs near the docks and harbour, over which they had flown only weeks beforehand when the medium bombers had attacked the very same targets. It was also clear that the medium bombers had succeeded in destroying a large amount of shipping, readily evident from the masts, funnels, debris and keels protruding above the waterline. Even though the harbour was in close proximity to the city itself, very few bombs had gone astray and the city lay virtually untouched.

The pilots were able to relax in the warm water and on the beaches and they quite quickly became tanned. The ancient city of Carthage, with the temple of Apollo, became a regular haunt. The sunshine, mountains and brilliant blue of the sea and sky and the areas of historical interest enabled the pilots to almost forget that there was a war. Happy days.

The success of both 322 and 324 Wings in the months of March, April and May was even more spectacular when one considers the opposition they were up against, and the conditions under which they had to operate. Their opponents had principally been JG51 and JG53 flying the latest Me109s, and JG2 flying Fw190s. These units had been based on the permanent all-weather aerodromes around Tunis and Bizerte and their pilots were among the most experienced in the Luftwaffe. The Allied squadrons had operated under much worse ground conditions than the Germans and were frequently unable to fly because their airfields were under water. This made living conditions intolerable and it was also evident that the German communication and warning systems were much better than those of the Allies. In addition, the Germans could use the main highways for emergency landing grounds whereas the Allies frequently had to deal with quagmires of mud. The Allied squadrons had no hangars and there was always a shortage of spares for the aircraft when they were damaged or unserviceable. Ground crew had to be ingenious and resilient and along with pilots had to endure bombing raids and ground strafing attacks in the open. The ground crews, unlike the pilots, had little opportunity to rest or take a holiday but their commitment and efficiency was undoubted and without them the pilots would have been helpless.

Despite this, there is no question that Allied air superiority meant the campaign ended swiftly and without further unnecessary loss of life. The Germans later admitted that they could not fight against the tremendous concentrations of aircraft that the Allies were able to bring to bear exactly where and when they were needed, and this accounted for the sudden collapse of the enemy in the Cap Bon peninsula. Under such superior air cover it was clear that the Germans were not prepared to try and evacuate their trapped troops. In short, some of the Germans' best and most experienced troops were sacrificed. Had they been saved, they could have been used effectively later on. Along with the troops (some 290,000 in all) were twenty-six generals and hordes of equipment, machinery and supplies, food and ammunition. The amount captured was staggering and must have had some effect on the Germans' ability to fight and later counter-attack when the Allies landed in Sicily and Italy. Most of the German prisoners were detained in open sites around Carthage.

Relaxation came to an end as the pilots became bored with almost too much spare time. Reading, writing, swimming and seeing the sights were a far cry from trying to operate aircraft from muddy quagmires and difficult, almost impossible, conditions. Disease was becoming rife as the diet was so limited and they were constantly warned about taking precautions to avoid contamination. Sanitation was very basic: a spade for digging a hole in the ground. At one stage they had large lidded galvanised buckets with a tented screen, but the Arabs stole the lot so they had to return to the spade. They also used petrol cans cut in half with holes bored in the bottom and filled with sand. Jerry cans had not been invented then and the cans they used were thinner and leaked all over the place but when empty were extremely useful. The Arabs treasured the cans as well, called them 'bedays' and used them for a whole host of reasons, even to build shacks. They became valuable because they could be traded for eggs and fruit or used as a stove (bottom filled with water, top filled with sand and petrol) that could be used for cooking and laundry.

The squadron was being prepared to move again at short notice. They did not know where and little was Barney to know that he was shortly to end up back in Malta.

CHAPTER 7

The Return to Malta

1 JUNE, 1943

ORB: After spending a few days rest at either Tabarka or Tunis all the pilots returned to Mateur today. Included in the party were four new pilots posted to the squadron, Flg Off J.F. King, Sgt C.R. Piper (NZ), Sgt L.C.R. Morris (Australian), and Sgt K.C. Weller.

Ground personnel working at full pressure today in preparation for the squadron movement. All aircraft are being recamouflaged from the desert colours to a dark-green colour similar to that employed at home. The difficulty is that no proper spray paint is obtainable and at the moment it is a matter of trial and error. All the squadron's motor transport is being prepared and marked with the squadron's numbers and letters. A definitive scale of kit to be taken has been laid down by 242 Group, which only allows one kit bag per man.

Signal received at 0830 hours advising 'as many members of the squadron as possible to proceed to Carthage to be addressed by an important personage between 1100 and 1200 hours'. As time was short and there was such pressure of work only a few airman attended. It was guessed that the important personage would be the Prime Minister and this proved to be correct. At about 1310 the familiar figure of Winston Churchill appeared from the cabin door of an Avro York at El Aouma. His aircraft had been escorted in by six P-38s. As he stepped from the aircraft he was given a rousing welcome and seemed in great spirits.

Churchill left later for Carthage where in the famous amphitheatre overlooking the Mediterranean he made a further speech to the 1st Army. He said that he had come on behalf of the king and the nation to thank the members of the 1st Army for their glorious victory in Tunisia. Many more victories would fall to the lot of the 1st Army but none would be so glorious and significant as that accomplished in Tunisia.

Work continued on very hot days with conditions at Mateur not ideal. All ground personnel were living in tents on a very dusty plain, beside the landing ground and miles from the sea. Pilots remained in Tunis where similarly no adequate arrangements had been made, for example they had to cook and eat their own food in the passages of the hotel where they stayed. General opinion was that all personnel could have camped by the sea and arrangements been made for the guarding of the aircraft. Lack of organisation led to considerable unrest. It was perhaps fortunate that the squadron was resting and off operations. The ground crew continued to have to work hard with maintenance needed on the grounded kites and the overhaul of equipment and motor transport. Little work was done in the heat of the afternoon, so after a light lunch many would jump in whatever transport was available and drive to Ferryville, where, beside the blue lake, they would sunbathe and swim all afternoon. There they had the use of spring boards, high boards and a water polo pitch and most of the squadrons mingled with each other. They would normally return to the aerodrome in time for tea, and then if necessary the ground crews would work gently in the cool of the evening.

Options for entertainment in the evening included the 'flea-pit' cinema in Mateur, dancing or watching a film held on the side of a hill with a screen set at the bottom. It was invariably watched by thousands, including the troops who would sit or stand around on the grass, or try and get a better view by gaining a vantage point on one of the lorry transports. The temperature made for warm and peaceful nights.

Now that the Axis forces had surrendered in Tunisia, the next stage of the Allied plan could be put into action: the aerial assault against, and the ultimate capture of, the island of Pantelleria.

4 JUNE

The first elements of 322 Wing began arriving in Malta from Tunisia. No. 81 Squadron landed at Takali led by Wg Cdr Colin Gray, the new wing leader, while 322 Wing's former leader, Gp Capt Piet Hugo, was appointed OC Wing. No. 81 Squadron was joined by four other squadrons: 152 Squadron led by Sqn Ldr F. Lister, 154 Squadron led by Sqn Ldr A. Wiseman, 232 Squadron led by Sqn Ldr C. Arthur (known as 'Duke') and 242 Squadron led by Flt Lt G. Sylvester.

Advance elements of another Spitfire wing, 244 Wing, also began to arrive led by Wg Cdr Peter Olver DFC, with 145 Squadron led by Sqn Ldr L. Wade and 601 Squadron led by Sqn Ldr J. Taylor. They went into Luqa from where they were to operate for the forthcoming invasion. The arrival of the other squadrons was also imminent with 92 (RAF), 417 (RCAF) and 1 (SAAF) Squadrons on their way. With so many Spitfires at Takali and Luqa, the squadrons already resident there moved to a new strip at Safi and became the Safi Wing commanded by Wg Cdr Duncan Smith.

Most of the squadrons on Malta were being re-equipped with brand new Spitfire IXs. For the last couple of years the defence of the island had been in the hands of the older Spitfire Vs, but the Germans had introduced the Me109G and the Fw190 into the Mediterranean theatre which were superior in performance to the older Mk Vs. The Spit IX was slightly heavier, due to the larger engine, but it had the same airframe, lovely loose ailerons, an additional 250hp, a four-bladed propeller and a supercharger that came in with a tremendous kick at about 21,000ft. Its introduction would give the Allied air forces the advantage over the German aircraft.

5 JUNE

ORB: At 0700 hours 324 Wing units, including 43, 72, 93, 111, and 242 Squadron [from 322 Wing], began to move off to Sfax. 140 vehicles were involved and very good time was made. Convoy camped for the night en route.

6 JUNE

ORB: Arrived in Sfax.

7 JUNE

ORB: Vehicles of wing and squadron embarked on transport. Axis fighters beginning to put in an appearance against the American bombers relentlessly targeting Pantelleria.

8 JUNE

ORB: Embarked. All possible motor transport was loaded onto [tank landing ship] LST 403 and this was to be their home for the voyage. These mass-produced craft have a very shallow draft and a retractable bow to enable transport to be loaded and unloaded on beaches where no proper docking facilities exist. The convoy of LSTs with a corvette escort, HMS *Roxina*, sailed at noon. Conditions at sea were ideal, with very little swell or wind. After a quiet night, land came into view at 0630 hours – the destination: Malta.

With the island of Malta in the background Wg Cdr Brooke, Senior Padre of 324 Wing, conducted a short religious service on the upper deck. The ship's captain, Lt Cdr J.D. Row RNR, was asked to say a few words at the end and he expressed his satisfaction with the conduct of all troops on board and expressed the opinion that the stay on Malta would be short, for they had a major part to play in the forthcoming offensive. By 1300 hours all personnel had disembarked and reached Hal Far camp.

For the first time in seven months the squadron would not be required to live and sleep under canvas, as the billets were empty houses in a small but picturesque village. By evening most of the airmen were installed and they spent their free time bathing in the sea.

The build-up of aircraft, and how Malta managed to handle and sustain so many extra units preceding the invasion of Sicily, was an astonishing story of efficiency in supply and organisation. The island had been turned into a gigantic aircraft carrier supporting twenty-three Spitfire squadrons, five night-fighter squadrons and a large number of bomber, strike and reconnaissance squadrons. The two Spitfire wings had now left Cross's 242 Group and transferred to the Western Desert Air Force under Air Vice-Marshal Harry Broadhurst, who besides being experienced in tactical operations, had led the Western Desert Air Force in support of the 8th Army through the Libyan and Tunisian campaigns.

Many of the pilots and ground crew appreciated the newly acquired comforts of Malta. Conditions had only recently improved following the ending of the siege of the island at the beginning of 1943. Before then conditions had been as primitive, if not worse, than North Africa, and food was in such short supply that the island's occupants were slowly being starved. After the insufferable conditions of Tunisia – the extreme heat, dust, flies and lack of a suitable diet – Malta, with its cool buildings, fresh water, and a reasonable diet, now that the supply lines had been kept open, was positively idyllic by comparison. It was a pleasure to sit down in a Mess and be served dinner by the Maltese staff, without being hounded by the flies.

With the build-up of Allied aircraft in Malta, the German air raids that had been almost a daily feature of island life for the previous two years became less frequent. The battle scars remained, however: the harbours at Sliema Creek and Valetta were filled with masts of sunken ships. While food remained in relatively short supply and rationing still in place, beer and wine were plentiful again as it was made on the island. The girls were lovely and they too were plentiful, and friendly. Many were half-English, with soldier fathers. They were bilingual and all of them wanted an English husband to be able to get off the island. Dances were held in Valetta most nights, and at weekends at the other RAF stations such as Hal Far, Luqa and Kalafrana. Valetta also had a notorious street called the Straight, known to servicemen as 'The Gut'. Every building was a pub, café, doss house or brothel. No officers were allowed, but for a small fee hats could be exchanged so that they too could enjoy the fruits and delights of Malta's nightlife.

Flying from Malta would also bring about a change in tactics, not only because they would be flying over enemy territory, but also because the large expanse of water between Sicily and Malta was a difficult enough barrier to overcome when aircraft were fully serviceable, let alone if anything happened to them. Sir Keith Park lost no time briefing his pilots on arrival at Malta – in approaching Sicily they might be at 25–30,000ft in the hope of catching the enemy fighters either coming up towards them, or be in a position to see them below. He also stressed the importance to all ground staff that maintenance was vital for this new over-water role.

10 JUNE

Log Book: Sweep Sicily. Conducted tour of prospective battlefield and later air test.

ORB: For everyone a very busy day, at noon the aircraft had arrived from Mateur and the rest of the day was spent in servicing the aircraft and completing checks and unpacking stores. Pantelleria taken after a huge aerial assault.

11–14 JUNE

ORB: No operational flying. Sqn Ldr H.S.L. Dundas DFC posted from HQ NATAF for Wing Commander flying post. Aircraft of 43 and 243 Squadrons also arrived.

15 JUNE

ORB: 324 Wing, including twelve aircraft from 72 Squadron, carried out a sweep over Sicily flying at 26,000ft. Some flak over Comiso but nothing else to report. New Wingco, Wg Cdr H.S.L. Dundas, of 324 Wing succeeding Wg Cdr Gilroy, who has been promoted to group captain, flew with the squadron this morning but had to return early due to engine trouble.

16 JUNE

ORB: Further sweep over Sicily, again flak over Comiso. Total of thirty-five Spits up from 324 Wing over Ragusa, Comiso and Gela in late morning.

Fortunately, or unfortunately for Barney, depending on how you viewed it, he was again confined to hospital at Imtarfa. It was at Imtarfa where he had recovered from his collision about a year before, but this time he was being treated for impetigo. Later, Barney's Log Book was to say: 'Once again at the 90th General Hospital at Imtarfa with impetigo. Meawhile the squadron swept Sicily. Waited with mixed feelings for the do to commence which it did on 10 July and 72 Squadron got cracking. I joined them again on the 13th and learnt they had already shot down twenty-three!'

17 JUNE

ORB: It appears that the enemy is using the same tactics as he used in Tunisia; he refuses to react to purely fighter sorties and will only use his fighters when bombers are operating. Only six Me109s seen by the whole of 324 Wing (thirty-seven Spits from 72, 93 and 111 Squadrons and led by Wg Cdr Dundas) and they all avoided combat. Sweep was a prelude to the bombing of Comiso and Biscari by US Liberators, the bombing force themselves covered by a force of about seventy Spits drawn from 322 Wing and the Krendi and Safi Wings.

18 JUNE

ORB: Not a happy day for the squadron. Despite the fact that the squadron opened the wing score when Plt Off Keith destroyed his fourth Me109 with the squadron over Sicily in the morning, the squadron lost Flt Lt Dalton Prytherch, who baled out because of engine failure off the Sicilian coast. The engine failure was not due to enemy action. He was seen to bale out successfully but then appeared to be dragged along by his parachute in the water. WO Gear flew at 50ft just after the parachute was seen in the water but no trace of the pilot was seen. Search carried out with no results. Flg Off George Keith RCAF, a Canadian from Alberta with three victories already in Tunisia, was separated from the rest of the squadron, and as he was crossing the coast on his return, spotted the two Spitfires of Clarkson and Gear circling looking for Prytherch, but with an Me109 poised to attack them both. He attacked the Me109 from above, closed to within 300yd, fired a short burst, observed strikes on the wing root and glycol pouring from its radiator. He fired another burst and saw the cockpit hood and other pieces fall off and the pilot then baled out.

Flt Lt Prytherch was an experienced pilot and a valuable leader and his loss was a heavy blow to the squadron.

19 JUNE

ORB: Offensive sweeps over the south-eastern corner of Sicily continued but no enemy aircraft encountered, even when escorting nine US Liberators which bombed Reggio de Calabria and San Giovanni.

20 JUNE

Today for the first time the people of Malta saw their king, George VI. He arrived on HMS *Auron*, escorted by four destroyers, at Valetta early in the morning and spent the day inspecting the island. The squadrons at Hal Far only caught a fleeting glimpse of him as he drove along the perimeter track towards Kalafrina. He was dressed in the uniform of an Admiral of the Fleet and was accompanied by Lord Gort.

ORB: It has been the turn of the squadron to be at readiness from dawn until dusk. Five scrambles were ordered but only one produced any results. At 1830 hours Wingco and three other pilots, Flg Off Gordon Sharp, WO Alan 'Sex' Gear and Sgt Keith Clarkson were scrambled to investigate hostile plots over the Malta channel. They climbed to 26,000ft and flew towards the Sicilian coast and found two enemy aircraft flying south-west towards Gela. The formation split up, two aircraft going in pursuit while the remaining two provided top cover for them. The enemy aircraft crossed the coast and then saw our aircraft between them and the coast. They turned away and were about 600yd in front. The enemy leader then did a slight left-hand turn and with a wide deflection shot, hit the aircraft flown by Flg Off Sharp, who had in turn been warned by WO Gear to take evasive action. The Spitfire turned on its back and dived into the ground near Biscari. WO Gear at once turned onto the enemy leader and with a 3-second burst blew the cockpit hood off and the enemy aircraft also turned on its back and dived into the ground at Biscari. The operation therefore ended on equal terms.

It became known today that the squadron was to lose its Spitfire IXs and be partially equipped with Spitfire Vs. This move brought both 322 and 324 Wings into line with the fighter wings of the Western Desert Air Force formerly operating with the 8th Army. The idea was to allow the most experienced pilots in the squadron to benefit from the superior performance of the newer Merlin engine.

21 JUNE

ORB: Wg Cdr Dundas leading, the squadron carried out a further uneventful sweep over Sicily. The transfer of ten Spitfire IXs to other squadrons in the wing took place this evening and at the same time ten Spitfire Vs were received as replacements. Four Spitfire IXs took part in a fighter sweep over Comiso and again no enemy reaction was seen. This serves as confirmation to the fact that the enemy is employing the same tactics as in Tunisia by conserving his aircraft to deal with bomber raids and to ignore the fighter operations.

23 JUNE

ORB: Four Spitfire IXs acted as top cover to Spit bombers who intended to attack the aerodrome at Comiso but target was obscured by cloud so an alternative target was attacked. Two Me109s seen and Flg Off Hughes attacked one without results.

24 JUNE

ORB: Readiness dawn to dusk. Two small missions carried out without incident. Visits by the 'top brass' were not over and airmen of 243 and 72 Squadron assembled near the windsock on Hal Far to hear an address by Sir Archibald Sinclair, the Secretary of State for Air, who on behalf of His Majesty's Government, thanked the squadrons for their services in North Africa.

25 JUNE

For the first time since the squadron had arrived on Malta it was released from duty for the day. A rare day of pleasure was spent visiting Valetta. A large quantity of mail arrived. The effect of the mail was noticeable; spirits rose, conversation became animated and a general feeling of satisfaction was apparent as soon as the mail was distributed. There was no doubt it had a tremendous effect on morale and any news from home lifted spirits even more. The more they got the better, as far as the pilots were concerned.

A large formation of B-17s from North Africa had raided Messina in the morning and inflicted much damage.

27 JUNE

ORB: Since arriving on Malta there have been seventeen cases of malaria reported so the use of Alabrine will be resumed. It is thought that the use of the drug will keep the disease under control. Offensive sweep by ten Spits of 72 Squadron in morning but brought no reaction again from Axis fighters.

28 JUNE

ORB: ASR Wellington sent out to search for missing Wellington bomber which had crashed into the sea off the Sicilian coast during the night. Escort provided by twenty-four Spits from 324 Wing. Dead body in flying clothes, empty dinghy and debris found over a wide area but no survivors.

29 JUNE

ORB: Further large amount of mail arrived. News arrived of Plt Off F. Malan (missing since 26/4/43) regarding his fate. It appears that his aircraft disintegrated in mid-air and he died a few minutes after being rescued by the 15th Light Field Ambulance.

30 JUNE

ORB: Further day of release for the squadron again spent in Valetta. This ends the month of flaming June. On the whole it has been a trying month for the squadron and its difficulties have been increased by the loss of Flt Lt Prytherch. Despite this however, the squadron at once has taken its place as the top-scoring squadron in the wing.

CHAPTER 8

The Capture of Sicily

Operation Husky, the intended Allied invasion of Sicily, had been the subject of intensive planning by the American, Gen Dwight Eisenhower, and the British commanders in the Mediterranean theatre, ACM Tedder, Gen Alexander and Adm Cunningham.

The Allies had some success in subduing the small island of Pantelleria, midway between Malta and Sicily, solely by naval and aerial bombardment. The Allied leaders had hoped to knock out the Luftwaffe and Regia Aeronautica on their Sicilian airfields and achieve air superiority before the beach landings. Attacks on the Sicilian airfields had begun on 15 June and continued on an almost daily basis with raids by heavy bombers. The build-up to the planned invasion was to see intensive action erupting in the skies above and around Sicily for the whole of July, entirely in contrast to the relative quiet of June.

There were to be three main phases in the air plan. The first had begun as soon as Tunisia had fallen and comprised the systematic bombing of Italian industry and Axis airfields, with care taken to distribute the attacks so as to give no hint of where the amphibious landings would take place. RAF bombers from England would attack Italy and Germany, while more bombers from the Middle East would attack the Dodecanese and Aegean Islands. Until 3 July, a week before D-Day, strategic bombing attacks were to be made against the principal enemy airfields of Sardinia, Sicily and southern Italy. The second phase for a whole week before D-Day was aimed at destroying enemy fighters and communications in Sicily and Sardinia, but in order to maintain surprise, no beach defences were attacked. The third phase was to be the all-out attack on local airfields coordinated with the attacks made by the land forces.

It was considered that the day after D-Day would be the most hazardous for ships approaching or lying off the beaches, since by then the main Allied concentration points would have been revealed. The fighters would then be transferred from their offensive roles to the task of protecting the shipping from enemy bombers. This would be needed day and night from the Spitfire squadrons within range on Malta.

Now assembled on Malta, and on the neighbouring island of Gozo, in readiness for the impending invasion of Sicily, were no fewer than twenty-three Spitfire squadrons, one photo-reconnaissance squadron, and one tactical recce squadron comprising about 400 Spitfires.

1 JULY

ORB: Sweep over Sicily to escort eight Spit bombers of 1435 Squadron bombing Biscari aerodrome. Squadron engaged twelve Me109s and although they quickly dived away, Sqn Ldr Daniel damaged one Me109 after firing a 3-second burst. Squadron suffered no losses. Judging from reports from the strategic bomber force and the reports of the Malta pilots, it would seem that the tempo of the battle over Sicily is now being stepped up quickly and a tremendous amount of damage is being inflicted both night and day.

2 JULY

ORB: Flg Off R.R. Barnfather and WO A.H. Gear admitted to SSQ today, but no operational flying.

4 JULY

ORB: Wing cooperated on American Independence Day with American elements of the strategic air force by acting as top cover to B-17s attacking Catania in Sicily. Long-range tanks were used. Fleeting contact with Me109s and MC202s but no claims were made. Three B-17s attempted to land Malta on their return, two landed at Hal Far but one crashed into the sea, the crew having baled out. A member of the crew was sadly mortally wounded. One B-17 which landed claimed they had destroyed a Me109 and had seen at least fifty enemy aircraft.

For the first time the medium bombers of the Tactical Air Force, which had played such an important part in the Tunisian campaign and the capture of Pantelleria, were in action over Sicily.

5 JULY

ORB: Squadron transferred to Middle East Command. US bombers again pounded the airfields. Escort to B-17s heading for Gerbini were met near Ragusa by more than 100 Me109s. Flg Off Tom Hughes claimed one Me109 as damaged.

6 JULY

ORB: Acted as cover for three squadrons of P-40s of the Tactical Air Force, the target being Biscari. No enemy reaction apparent. No doubt that the full Allied bomber strength being used to batter Sicily with the Malta wings, including 72 Squadron, provided fighter cover for the bombers.

7 JULY

ORB: Squadron escort to Mitchells bombing Biscari, again no opposition. The weight of the attacks now appear to be having an effect.

8 JULY

ORB: Tremendous pounding being meted out to Sicily and it is clear that air superiority is now clearly in our hands. The softening process seems well under way and the ground offensive cannot long be delayed. The squadron was successful when acting as withdrawal cover to B-17s over Comiso aerodrome.

Plt Off Roy Hussey at 14,000ft saw enemy fighters circling to land which he at once attacked and destroyed an Me109 with white tips. Sqn Ldr Daniel also destroyed a Me109 and a third crashed without being attacked. Flt Sgt Hermiston and Sgt Scott also damaged two Me109s. The airfield at Comiso was then attacked and a Ju52, Fw190 and Hs129 were damaged together with admin buildings and wireless operations.

9 JULY

ORB: Large numbers of invasion barges arrived in Malta and the plan was today unfolded. Two conferences, one of squadron commanders and one of intelligence officers, were held where the broad strategic and technical plans were outlined. The broad plan is as follows: Intention is to attack Sicily and capture it by use of air and seaborne troops, the assault to be divided between British and American forces. The British troops will force the south-east coast and the American troops will attack from the south-west. Parachute and airborne troops will be landed at strategic positions in advance of the sea landings. Enemy dispositions show that the assault is expected in the west and the only German units in Sicily are located in this area. Airborne troops are to land soon after 2200 hours and the seaborne troops will land tomorrow morning. For the rest of today the vast armada of landing craft will proceed to their objectives and we will provide them with continuous air cover from Malta. The long-awaited day is about to dawn.

In a few hours from now, British and American troops will be fighting for a foothold on Hitler's Europe. The fight will be hard and there may be heavy losses, but the RAF have little doubt that the Royal Navy and the Army will be successful, protected by a complete air umbrella and spurred on by the success of the Tunisian campaign.

For the Axis forces, the first warning that Sicily was about to be invaded came after reconnaissance aircraft, on a routine patrol in the Mediterranean, had spotted five convoys in the sea south of Malta heading towards Sicily, each with about 150–180 landing craft. Later, additional convoys, with two battleships, two aircraft carriers (HMS *Formidable* and HMS *Indomitable*), four cruisers, and considerable Allied air power, came into play. All Axis garrisons on Sicily were put on full alert. At nightfall on 9 July the water off Sicily had seemed deserted, yet despite the windy weather and rough sea, the Axis forces on the island were aware of the presence of a huge fleet of ships and vessels somewhere in the darkness moving towards the island. The Axis forces could do little except wait for the resumption of the Allied air bombardment that would signal the start of the invasion.

In fact, the start of the invasion was heralded by British gliderborne troops of the 1st Airborne Division who had been tasked to attack and hold strategic positions south of Syracuse, though the operation was to go horribly and tragically wrong.

The majority of the gliders were towed by C-47s of the US 51st Troop Carrier Wing and the remainder by RAF Albemarles and Halifaxes. Winds of up to 35mph buffeted and blew the gliders and heavy flak forced many of the pilots of the towing aircraft to take evasive action, which dispersed the formation and caused some pilots to release their gliders early. Confusion reigned and some planes even opened fire on each other. Others turned around and headed back towards Tunisia. Of the 136 gliders that had set off, about half ditched in the sea, many paratroopers were drowned and the remainder were spread over a 25-mile area between Cape Passero and Cape Murro di Porco.

At the same time as the ill-fated 1st Airborne Division assault on the area around Syracuse, the Americans planned a similar airborne assault to the east of Gela. About 200 C-47s were to transport 3,500 men of the US 82nd Airborne Division from airfields in Tunisia. Again, the high winds and inexperienced pilots meant that the paratroopers were dropped along 50 miles of coast. Both airborne operations were disastrous failures. The few airborne troops and partaroopers who landed in the right place at the right time contributed to the success of the landings. The harsh lesson from the British perspective was not to rely on American transport aircraft with inexperienced pilots because the troops were too valuable to be wasted.

---

10 JULY

ORB: Sicily invaded. Operations appear to be proceeding to plan and penetrations made inland after an intense naval barrage. Comiso already in our hands. Squadron stood by from dawn but were not called upon until late afternoon when they provided bomber escort, completed without incident.

Despite the battering that Sicilian airfields had taken in the build-up to the invasion, and the toll of aircraft destroyed in the air and on the ground, the Axis forces still posed a major threat to the invasion forces. Montgomery later reflected, however, that: 'Allied air forces had definitely won the air battle and this was quite apparent from the first moment the troops landed on the shores of Sicily because the enemy air force was swept from the skies and were not allowed to inconvenience them.'

The Western Naval Task Force carried the US 7th Army and made landings at three designated areas, codenamed 'Cent' near Marpina, 'Dime' near Gela and 'Joss' near Licata, with the first troops landing at 0245 hours. Some resistance was seen; small formations of Fw190s, Me109s and Ju88s and Italian fighter-bombers began dropping flares and attacked the troops, as well as the USS *Philadelphia* and USS *Jefferson*. Spitfires based on Malta covered the landings all day and in turn. The first over the landings were flown by 242 Squadron between 0500 hours and 0530 but were met by indiscriminate fire from American gunners who were later to riddle Wg Cdr Warburton's PR Spitfire. Warburton had been briefed to photograph the landings but his plane was severely damaged and he only just managed to get back to Malta.

The British landings were further east. The Eastern Naval Task Force beached on the Sicilian coast at around 0500 hours on five designated areas, codenamed

'Acid North' near Cape Murro di Porco, 'Acid South' near Avola, 'Bark East' near Marzameni, 'Bark Middle' near Cape Passero and 'Bark West' from Pozzallo to Pachino. The British 8th Army overcame a few elements of an Italian division which did not put up much resistance. Some troops remembered seeing that they had fighter cover from first light, and the Spitfires from 324 Wing led by the OC 324 Wing, Gp Capt 'Sheep' Gilroy, were over the landings at about 0530 hours and came across a Ju88 south of Syracuse. The next patrol was led by Wg Cdr Dundas and its job was to maintain air cover over the Syracuse area throughout the day, in squadron strength, with each squadron due to spend about 35 minutes on patrol over the beaches. This timing was critical for fuel conservation and depended on formation leaders to head back for Malta once their time was up, and provided they had been relieved by the next squadron and were not engaged by the enemy. From the first patrol led by 'Sheep' Gilroy the Spitfires were delayed before returning to Malta, so much so that Flg Off Leslie Connors had to ditch his aircraft about a quarter of a mile from Hal Far. Although he was seen swimming for the shore, by the time a launch arrived he had disappeared, presumed drowned. Three other Spitfires landed short of fuel at Safi rather than at Hal Far, which must have been critical because Safi was less than 2 miles from Hal Far.

Patrols were maintained throughout the day, and twelve Spitfires from 92 Squadron encountered Me109s near Cape Murro di Porco. On duty that day with 92 Squadron was Flg Off Milton Jowsey, RCAF, who had been with Barney and 234 Squadron back at Ibsley in Hampshire in 1941–2. After encountering the Me109s, where no claims were made, they came across six Ju88s attacking shipping. One was shot down by Flt Lt Tom Savage, who was then believed to have been hit by gunfire from the warships and, unable to bale out, was lost with his aircraft. Milton Jowsey recalled:

> Over the landing craft we found six Ju88s, numerous MC202s, Me109s and Ju87s. We came in too fast and overshot the Ju87s. I saw Flt Lt Savage shoot down one Ju88 and while in pursuit of another, at about 10,000ft, he was shot down by Royal Navy flak. We were very loathe to pursue enemy aircraft near RN ships as they only seemed to get close to us.

Another Ju88 was claimed by Johnny Gasson but a second Spitfire was also shot down with Flt Lt Dicks-Sherwood, who had been with Barney in 603 Squadron in Malta, having to bale out into the sea. He was picked up and taken back to Malta.

The problem with friendly fire continued when the Spitfires of 93 Squadron, led by Wg Cdr Duncan Smith, were back over the beachhead in the afternoon. They sighted six Ju88s bombing shipping with some Macchi C.202s as escort which they chased away without any claims being made. As the Spitfires swept down over the beach the AA gunners put up a heavy and accuarate barrage, which hit two of them. Wg Cdr Duncan Smith managed to nurse his damaged aircraft back to Malta but Flt Lt Raoul Daddo-Langlois crash-landed on the beach and suffered a severe fractured skull. He was carefully removed and placed aboard a small lighter to take him aboard a hospital ship but another bombing raid came in and the lighter was sunk. Daddo-Langlois – or 'Daddy Longlegs' as he was affectionately known – a veteran of the air battles in Malta a year beforehand, was lost.

Further sweeps and more claims and successes followed, though 72 Squadron were not required until the late afternoon and did not encounter any Axis aircraft. US bombers and fighter-bombers from North Africa continued to pound the Axis airfields and defences and with the onset of darkness further raids were carried out against Trapani, Milo and Gerbini. Allied forces had by the end of the day captured Syracuse, Pachino, Gela and Licata.

---

11 JULY

ORB: First operation of the day was fourteen Spits led by Gp Capt Gilroy and Sqn Ldr Daniel who, together with twelve Spits from 43 Squadron, patrolled the beaches south of Syracuse but failed to locate any aircraft. Second operation of the day was more successful when Sqn Ldr Daniel led the squadron and in the course of the mission encountered some twenty Macchi C.200s, which were being very roughly handled. The CO shared a Macchi C.200 destroyed with Flt Lt Christopherson, and two others were claimed as damaged by Flt Sgt Hermiston and Plt Off Roy 'Jack' Hussey. With the squadron fairly short of fuel, south of Syracuse, Flg Off Keith became detached and did not return with the other pilots. It was thought that he had crash-landed short of petrol. Later he returned, complete with serviceable Spitfire, and explained that before he had made a forced landing at Pachino in Sicily he had also destroyed a Macchi C.200 and a Ju88.

The landings appear to continue to go well and with the exception of Gela and Comiso, enemy opposition appears to be steadily reducing. Further squadron sweep over the Noto beaches in the evening but again uneventful.

During the night the main attacks on Sicily were delivered against air and supply bases in the west of the island. Mitchells bombed Bo Rizzo airfield and Wellingtons did likewise against Trapani, Marsala and Mazzaro de Vallo. More Wellingtons bombed Porto Corvino Ravella airfield near Salerno on the Italian mainland where German bombers were stationed. Liberators and Halifaxes from Cyrenaica attacked Reggio di Calabria airfield and pressure on the Axis defending forces continued.

Allied land forces were also on the move. US 7th Army troops occupied the important airfield at Comiso where repairs started immediately. In addition, the US 82nd Airborne Division dropped its second paratroop wave in front of the Allied landings at Gela. Again it proved disastrous and out of the 144 C-47s involved, twenty-three failed to return and thirty-seven were severely damaged. It turned out that many had been hit by friendly fire from Allied shipping offshore that had not received instructions that the air armada carrying the paratroops was friendly. The ships' gunners had been instructed to fire on any aircraft flying at low level over their vessels. It seemed incredible that the RAF would lay on such a hazardous low-level flight over the assault area, and over Allied shipping that was committed in combat and which had been subjected to enemy raids for the previous two days without any warning.

1. Barney Barnfather in a Spitfire cockpit, RAF Ibsley, April 1942. *(K. Gamble)*

2. Barney Barnfather with his wife, Dorothy, on the day he was awarded his wings and became a sergeant pilot, 13 September 1941. *(Author's collection)*

3. Barney and Dorothy at Keynsham, 1942. *(Author's collection)*

4. Flt Lt Dave Glaser, Sgt Barney Barnfather, Sgt Keith Gamble and Sgt Wiggy Webster, RAF Ibsley, April 1942. *(K. Gamble)*

5. Barnfather (far left) and Keith Gamble (centre), others unknown, RAF Ibsley, April 1942. *(K. Gamble)*

6. USS *Wasp*, from which the Spitfires of 601 and 603 Squadrons took off for Malta on 20 April 1942. Malta was a strategically important British base that needed protection from the Luftwaffe. (*Imperial War Museum/A9232*)

7. Spitfires being warmed up and tested on the flight deck of USS *Wasp* with HMS *Eagle* in the background, May 1942. HMS *Eagle* had delivered the first batch of Spitfires to Malta on 7 March 1942. (*US National Archive*)

8. The pilots of Operation Bowery on the deck of USS *Wasp*, May 1942. Barney is seated in the second row from front, third from the left. Operation Bowery was the codename for the second delivery of Spitfires to Malta; the first delivery had suffered an intensive attack by the Luftwaffe within 90 minutes of their arrival. (*US National Archive*)

603 SQUADRON MALTA G.C.

Year 1942		Aircraft		Pilot, or 1st Pilot	2nd Pilot, Pupil or Passenger	DUTY (INCLUDING RESULTS AND REMARKS)
Month	Date	Type	No.			
		—	—	—	—	TOTALS BROUGHT FORWARD
MAY	9	SPITFIRE Vc	Z	SELF		ALGIERS — MALTA
"	12	"	W	"		SCRAMBLE - 'S 109 destroyed
		SUMMARY FOR MAY 1942	TYPES			
		UNIT 603 SQUADRON	SPITFIRE			
		DATE 1·6·42				
		SIGNATURE ...	FLT. O.C. "A" FLIGHT.			
					s/LD. O.C. 603 SQUADRON	
JUNE	2	"	N	SELF		PRACTISE FLYING.
"	4	"	Z	"		SCRAMBLE
"	6	"	W			Practise
"	15	"	W			"
"	20	"	N			"
"	21	"	T			"

Details of flight remarks (right-hand page):

From U.S.S. "Wasp" Good trip but lost.
a ftre en route
Collided with F/Lt. Douglas. Both strolled down O.K. Shared 109 with Douglas & Hurst.

Jack Slade & I trounced by 109's. Spun off turn and lost Jack, the others, and bags of height.

GRAND TOTAL [Cols. (1) to (10)]
TOTALS CARRIED FORWARD

9. Pages from Barnfather's Log Book: Barney describes the flight from USS *Wasp* to Malta, May/June 1942. *(Author's collection)*

10. Grumman Martletts and Spitfires lined up on the deck of USS *Wasp*, May 1942. (*US National Archive*)

11. Spitfire taking off from USS *Wasp* bound for Malta as part of Operation Bowery, May 1942. (*US National Archive*)

12. Anti-aircraft guns, Valetta, Malta, 1942. (*Imperial War Museum/GM946*)

13. Spitfire service: a Maltese civilian lends a hand with a horse and cart, Malta, 1942. (*Imperial War Museum/CM3226*)

14. Spitfires at readiness, Malta, 1942. (*Imperial War Museum/CM3270*)

15. Naval personnel and RAF ground crews re-arming a Spitfire, Malta, 1942. (*Imperial War Museum/CM3232*)

16. The Investiture Ceremony led by Lord Gort in front of the Castille, June 1942. This ceremony marked the apparent victory over the German and Italian forces that had been constantly attacking Malta. (*Imperial War Museum/GM1361*)

17. A Spitfire in North Africa, May 1943. (*Imperial War Museum/CNA121*)

18. Comiso, Sicily, July 1943. Following an Allied invasion from Malta, Sicily was captured and Barnfather's 72 Squadron was moved over to Comiso on 15 July. (*Imperial War Museum/CNA1056*)

19. Flt Sgt Keith Clarkson and Flg Off Barney Barnfather give their combat reports to the Intelligence Officer after both shooting down two Fw190s and a Me109 in Italy, October 1943. (*Imperial War Museum/CNA1890*)

20. 72 Squadron Spitfires at Comiso
in Sicily, 1943. (*Imperial War Museum /
CNA1130*)

21. Plt Off Roy Hussey, Sicily, 1943.
Roy and Barney were very good
friends and lived about 15 miles apart
in the West Country. Roy is buried in
the churchyard at Coxley, near Wells.
(*Imperial War Museum / CNA1050*)

22. Sqn Ldr S.W.F. 'Danny' Daniel, CO 72 Squadron in Italy, October 1943. At the time, the Allied forces were continuing to push back the retreating Germans. (*Imperial War Museum/CNA1889*)

23. Barnfather at Lago in Italy, covering the Anzio landings, January 1944. (*Author's collection*)

24. 72 Squadron pilots, including 'Spy' Brill, Squadron Intelligence Officer, at Lago in Italy, January 1944. *(Author's collection)*

25. 72 Squadron pilots at Lago in Italy, January 1944. *(Author's collection)*

26. Barney's Spitfire, Lago, Italy, January 1944. *(Author's collection)*

27. *Below left:* Sqn Ldr Russ Foskett, CO 94 Squadron, October 1944. *(Author's collection)*
28. *Below right:* Barnfather in Sedes near Salonica with 94 Squadron, March 1945. The uncertainty at this stage of the war meant very little operational flying. *(Author's collection)*

29. 72 Squadron Spitfires, Klagenfurt, Austria, 1945. On arrival at Klagenfurt airfield, Barnfather's squadron witnessed row upon row of abandoned Luftwaffe transports – a sad reflection of the once powerful German air force. (*Imperial War Museum/CNA3630*)

30. Barnfather as a member of the Royal Air Force Volunteer Reserve, 1950. (*Author's collection*)

31. Barnfather after his retirement, in Keynsham, 1980. He is happy despite having suffered a stroke which left him paralysed down one side. *(Author's collection)*

32. Pages from Barney's Log Book: 'News of Sarah's birth arrived today . . .' Sarah being the author's mother, December 1943. *(Author's collection)*

12 JULY

ORB: A record day for the squadron. In three sorties to the Syracuse-Augusta area in Sicily, the squadron destroyed thirteen enemy aircraft (eight MC200s, four Me109s and one Ju52), probably destroyed three Me109s and damaged a further ten (four MC200s and six Me109s). The squadron losses were two aircraft missing [Sgts King and Morris] and two slightly damaged. Sgt Morris later reported to have been picked up from the sea by the Royal Navy.

Move of the wing [324 Wing] from Malta to Sicily began today with the departure of the Wing HQ party.

Squadron attitude at the end of 'a hell of a day' was 'let them all come'. 72 Squadron's big show had already caught the eye of the 'high-ups' hence receipt of the following signal from the AOC Malta: 'Well done 72. Congratulations on your magnificent combat this morning when you destroyed eight enemy aircraft without loss to yourselves.'

The main effort for the day was still the provision of fighter cover for the landing beaches and Allied shipping in the occupied harbours. Near the end of the first patrol, south of Syracuse, a number of pilots saw two aircraft go down in flames: victims of 72 Squadron that had encountered about six Me109s and a few MC202s near Augusta. Flt Lt Arthur Jupp claimed one Me109 probably destroyed and Sgt Keith Clarkson claimed a second, which dived into the sea. Flg Off Keith then shot down a MC202 but Sgt J. Morris was forced to land his Spitfire near Malta. It was badly damaged and he was given a lift back to Malta on a LST and arrived back two days later.

On the second patrol of the day, just before midday, the squadron led by Sqn Ldr Daniel came across a large force of thirty Me109s, six MC202s and more fighter-bombers escorting a single Ju52 in the Augusta area. The Ju52 was quickly shot down by Plt Off B. Ingalls, RCAF, who also damaged a Me109. Sqn Ldr Daniel also claimed a Me109 shot down and a further that was damaged by Flg Off Cameron. In addition, five fighter-bombers were shot down by Flg Off Tom Hughes, Flg Off John King, Sgt A. Griffiths (two) and Flg Off Rodney Scrase who also claimed a damaged. One probable was claimed by Flt Lt M. Johnston and Sgt Scott. All this for no losses.

On the third patrol of the day at about 1700 hours, twelve Spitfires led by Flt Lt Arthur Jupp engaged a large number of Me109s and MC202s north-east of Carlentini between 9,000 and 12,000ft. They had been attacking Allied tanks and motor transport advancing over the Catania plain. The squadron tore into the enemy fighters and two Me109s were claimed by Plt Off Roy 'Jack' Hussey and Sgt Scott, while Plt Off Eric Shaw, RNZAF, claimed a MC202. Flt Lt Jupp and Flg Off George Keith each claimed a Me109 and three more were claimed as damaged by Sgt Keith Clarkson, Sgt Pearson and Flg Off J. King. Another Spitfire flown by Sgt King failed to return and he later became a POW. Sgt Griffths returned to Malta with his aircraft badly damaged and Plt Off Hussey landed despite damage to his tail.

For its successes during the day, AOC Malta sent a letter of congratulations to Sqn Ldr Daniel and the pilots of 72 Squadron.

13 JULY

Log Book: Sweep Syracuse. Nothing. Two air tests.

ORB: Squadron flew four sorties/sweeps over Sicily. During the second, Plt Off Hussey destroyed a MC200 and shared a Me109 with Sgt Griffiths. News of the squadron move to Sicily arrived in the evening and arrangements for the move were started with an advance party to leave Hal Far early tomorrow morning.

Last day on which the enemy put up any effective aerial resistance over Sicily. Coastal radar installations had been lost to the invasion forces and other key installations, including airfields at Catania, Milo and Trapani, were attacked by B-17s and Marauders. No. 72 Squadron relieved 111 Squadron on the patrol line over the beaches between Augusta and Noto at around 10 a.m., and came across a group of Axis fighters that included Me109s and MC202s. 'Jack' Hussey shot down a Macchi before he joined Sgt Bert Griffiths and between them they shot down another Me109 which crashed into the Syracuse–Catania area.

Reduced aerial activity in the afternoon with only small groups of Axis fighters making an appearance. Patrol by 72 Squadron led by Wg Cdr John Louden but nothing was seen. It seemed that the Axis forces knew that air superiority had been gained by the Allies.

Overwhelmed and exhausted, the surviving German and Italian pilots were withdrawn to the mainland leaving behind many unserviceable aircraft. During the night more British paratroops were dropped over the plain at Catania to secure the key bridge over the River Gornachunga at Primosole, but as had happened before, the operation proved to be costly with several C-47s, Albacores and Halifax towing aircraft lost. The remaining paratroops did however succeed in capturing the bridge and removing the demolition charges.

14 JULY

Log Book: Sweep Syracuse. We were bounced. Keith and his boys got three. Later sweep Catania. Nothing.

ORB: Sgt Morris reported missing on the 12th and then picked up by the Navy; rejoined the squadron today. The Hal Far Wing's Spitfires, including 72, flew three further sweeps with three Me109s claimed as destroyed, one by Plt Off Keith.

By morning the British 8th Army had encountered enemy rearguard at Monterosso while the German counter-attack on the seaplane base at Augusta was beaten back. US troops captured further airfields at Biscari, Mazzarino and Canicatta, so the ground fighting was now going the Allies' way.

First patrol of the day from 72 Squadron was at about 0745 hours when eleven Spitfires saw several Me109s in the Augusta area and attacked them from above. Three were promptly shot down and claimed by Flg Off George Keith and Flg Off Ken Smith, and George Keith and 'Jack' Hussey claimed a further one shared between them. US B-17s, Mitchells and Marauders from the NWAAF, and Liberators from the US 9th Air Force, continued to pound Messina.

15 JULY

Log Book: Sweep Catania. Flak!! Hal Far–Comiso, Sicily!!

ORB: Squadron as an operational unit left Hal Far for Sicily ready to conduct further operations from Comiso. One uneventful patrol flew over Catania from Hal Far and then in the afternoon the following pilots flew their Spits to Comiso: Sqn Ldr Daniel, Flt Lt Jupp, Flt Lt Johnston, Plt Offs Hughes, Shaw, King, Flg Offs Smith, Hussey and Barnfather; and Sgts Clarkson, Connolly, Scott and Griffiths.

After the capture of the important bridge at Primosole, the British 8th Army began to fan out over the plain at Catania. Despite numerous patrols, it proved to be relatively quiet in the air. More squadrons moved across from Malta to Sicily and 72 Squadron at Comiso was joined by 43, 93 and 111 Squadrons. The general state of the airfield and buildings paid tribute to the accuracy of the Allied bombing effort. Hangars and buildings had been completely wrecked and the airfield was littered with damaged Axis aircraft. It was also remembered because of the thick clouds of red dust thrown into the air as the Spitfires took off, and the flies and mosquitoes that were everywhere, infesting cuts and scratches. Comiso was also only about 30 miles from Gerbini, and the Axis-held airfields close to it were not captured until 21 July so this made life interesting for a while.

US fighter-bombers continued their attacks on retreating German motor transport and positions around central Sicily. USAAF Mitchells continued to bomb Palermo and the railway yards at Termini to hinder troop movements further.

16 JULY

Log Book: Sweep Catania. Bit of a shambles. Con got 109.

ORB: Bulk of the squadron had a great day at Hal Far and bathed. Flg Offs Keith and Cameron flew further Spits to Comiso where operationally the squadron swept the Catania area.

The British 8th Army continued to advance across the plain at Catania towards Gornalunga and the landing grounds at Gerbini, and the Canadians took the Caltagirone further east. In the morning nine Spitfires from 72 Squadron, led by Flt Lt Arthur Jupp, patrolled north of Augusta and across the Catania plain at around 10,000ft and engaged about fifteen Me109s 3 miles west of Augusta. Sgt Bert Griffiths was seen to shoot down one Me109 but his aircraft appeared to be hit by the fragments and it fell out of control and crashed. One parachute was seen to open but it was unclear whether the parachute was German or that of Bert Griffiths. Later, however, Bert's body was recovered from the wreckage of his Spitfire.

In the evening warships that were laying off Syracuse, including HMS *Rodney* and HMS *Nelson*, bombarded Catania.

17 JULY

The British 8th Army continued its push and advance across the Gornalunga; the Canadians captured Ramella and its airfield; and the Americans took Pietraperza. More Spitfire squadrons made the move across to Sicily from Malta.

18 JULY

Log Book: Sweep Catania. Chased 110s. Roy and Pip shared one.

ORB: Early morning patrol over the Catania plain and came across four Me110s with an escort of Me109s bombing Catania harbour. One Me110 was claimed shot down and shared by Sgt Cliff Piper (RNZAF) and Roy 'Jack' Hussey after their first bursts had hit the rear gunner and stopped him shooting. The plane was seen to crash north of Mount Etna.

19 JULY

ORB: Patrol by squadron failed to find any enemy in morning patrol in the Catania area but a large convoy was seen and attacked. Two lorries were destroyed by Flt Lt Arthur Jupp and Flg Off John King, then the Kittyhawk fighter-bombers were called up and destroyed half a dozen more.

On the ground the British 8th Army had run into stiff opposition against the crack German Hermann Göring Division, which had been reinforced by the 15th Panzer Grenadier Division. The Canadians had also run into stiffer opposition as the Germans fought hard to keep open the road that ran eastwards to help with troop movements.

20 JULY

Log Book: Sweep Catania. F.A. squirted at transport on road.

ORB: Rest of squadron personnel arrived from Malta. Convoy from marshalling yards completed the tortuous route through Pachino, Ispica, Modica, Regusa and then to Comiso. Camp-site at Comiso attractive, with plenty of shade.

21 JULY

Log Book: Sweep N. Sicily. Saw Kittis bomb.

ORB: Camp-site converted into home. Pilots who had flown the Spitfires in on the 15th and had sleeping quarters in the wing were moved into the camp-site. Aerodrome was a mess, but offered ample evidence of the thoroughness of the air attacks before our occupation. Two further patrols over Catania.

22 JULY

ORB: Squadron dug in and a lone raider dropped bombs and shot up the aerodrome. Squadron provided escort to Baltimores bombing Adrano.

23 JULY

Log Book: Escort Kittyhawks. Flak. Jetty at Catania.

ORB: Comparatively quiet.

Squadron provided cover for Kittyhawks bombing Catania and Baltimores over Misterbianco.

24 JULY

ORB: First mail arrived, with a considerable number of airmail letters and bags of parcels and newspapers.

News that in the operation in Sicily itself, Palermo had fallen and the Allied forces held the whole island with the exception of a line north of Palermo–Catania.

25 JULY

Log Book: Escort Baltimores.

ORB: Air-raid alarm. Lone bomber dropped several bombs in the aerodrome area but no more than a nuisance value. Squadron provided escort again to Baltimores over Adrano, Bronte and Gerbini.

26 JULY

Log Book: Shipping recco. Musso resigned. Badaglio now PM. King Emmanuel now C-in-C Armed Forces.

ORB: News that Mussolini had resigned reached the squadron. Squadron function changed to shipping reconnaissance and four sorties were flown, each with several aircraft.

Flg Off Cameron was posted missing from the first of the day, last seen a few miles north of Messina.

27 JULY

ORB: Reconnaissance from the previous day on shipping had meant the bombers of the American 57 Group were able to successfully attack them NW of Reggio.

Squadron operations included bomber escort again to attack the shipping off the coast of Sicily.

---
28 JULY

Log Book: Escort Kittibombers. Messina. Bags of flak. Whew!!

ORB: Squadron [took part in] four missions escorting Kittyhawk bombers: twice to Milazzo, once to Randazzo and one ASR trip to an upturned sighting of a dinghy.

---
29 JULY

Log Book: Escort Kittibombers. North coast of Sicily. Duff weather.

ORB: Less operations but news that another move for the squadron planned, indicated by the order that the 'A' party consisting of approximately sixty personnel were to be prepared to move out at short notice. Nobody particularly happy about this move as it is doubtful whether flying or general facilities will be as good as those at Comiso. Kittyhawk bombers were twice escorted today and the Spitfire pilots saw the railway station at Schettino destroyed by a direct hit from the bombers.

---
30 JULY

ORB: Move to Pachino commenced. 'A' Party moved off shortly after midday and later that evening the squadron aircraft flew to Pachino, six landing after an armed recce during which nothing was seen. Other operations included escorts to Kittyhawks whose targets were Milazzo, Risposto, and Ciardini. Sqn Ldr Daniel flew the captured Me109 regarded as a trophy.

Pachino was about 30 miles south-west of Comiso, on the southernmost tip of Sicily. It would not be the first time the squadron had operated from a dust strip, as it was similar to those in Tunisia, but this one was only about 800yd long and had been ploughed up and then prepared by the Royal Engineers, assisted by members of No. 3201 RAF Servicing Commando who had come ashore immediately behind the assault troops. There was some concern over the length of time needed for the squadron to take off and form up, because if they waited for the thick clouds of dust to clear after each pair took off (and the strip was only wide enough for pairs of aircraft to take off), valuable fuel would be wasted in forming up. The only solution was to set the gyro and take off blind into the dust! Flies and mosquitos continued to be the scourge of squadron personnel, but this was compensated for by the luxury of a plentiful supply of grapes and melons around the dispersed aircraft.

---
31 JULY

Log Book: Escort Mitchells. Randazzo. Wizard bombing. Moved to Pachino.

ORB: Move to Pachino completed, apart from small party remaining at Comiso on unserviceable aircraft. No. 72 Squadron made three bomber escort trips, two with

Kittyhawks to Giardini and Randazzo and the third escorting B-25 Mitchell bombers to Randazzo. Remarkably accurate bombing by the Mitchells.

---

1 AUGUST

ORB: A little more achieved towards completing the move from Comiso to Pachino. Especially happy day for 'Sexton' Gear to whom Gp Capt Gilroy, OC 324 Wing, brought news about the award of his DFC. CO Danny Daniel also had a Bar to his DFC, Roy Hussey the DFM and Sgts Connolly, Morris and Scottie all continued to put up the squadron score. Tom Hughes' second stripe had also come through and he became a flight lieutenant.

Squadron provided bomber escort to Adrano and Randazzo. Weather on second trip closed in and bombs had to be dropped away from target.

Some of the pilots and ground crew evidently did not appreciate the move. Was Comiso too good for us? It had a 2,000ft runway, a camp and was in pleasant surroundings. In true air force fashion, the move was made to a strip where taxiing threw up dust and taking off was blind! Comiso lay in a flat valley at the foot of a ridge of hills. Fruit was available everywhere, bunches of grapes, lemons or peaches. Over the ridge was a town called Ragusa which was untouched by the war and beautiful and 'Sicilian'. It was built around the junction of two gorges and consisted of a new town and an old town. The new town had straight streets criss-crossing, a cathedral and a square where the male population met in the evenings. There appeared to be shops that were well-stocked, though none had windows.

---

2 AUGUST

Log Book: 1. Escort Bostons Adrano. Good bombing; 2. Escort Mitchells Adrano.

ORB: Two further sweeps as bomber escort to Adrano but a third rendezvous was not kept by the bombers so Spitfires from 72 carried out an armed recce instead which proved to be uneventful. Echelon moved into Pachino South from Comiso and several aircraft which had been left at Comiso undergoing repairs were flown over. With the sea being in close proximity to the camp-site, daily bathing parades were organised.

---

3 AUGUST

ORB: Fairly quiet day, squadron provided escort to bombers again over Adrano and an armed recce west of Etna. Few enemy aircraft were being encountered, the main problem continued to be friendly fire either from other Allied aircraft or from Allied troops or ships.

---

4 AUGUST

Log Book: Escort Bostons Biancaville. Strafed road north of Catania. George in drink (died same night).

ORB: Today the squadron lost one of its outstanding pilots, Flg Off George Keith. While he was attacking ground targets in the Catania area, his aircraft was hit by flak and he had to bale out into the sea. He was soon picked up by the Air Sea Rescue Walrus but he had hit his leg on the tailplane when he baled out and his left leg had been smashed. An operation was carried out at No. 25 Military Field Hospital but he died the same day.

He was buried at Casabile the following morning. His loss had occurred during the second of the day's three missions which were primarily bomber escorts to Adrano. George was killed before news of his DFC and Bar had come through.

---

5 AUGUST

The fall of Catania to the Allied forces made good news. No. 72 Squadron again provided cover to bombers over Adrano. Catania had shown signs of being difficult to take until the Hermann Göring Division defending it pulled out, so when British forces entered on the morning of the 5th there was little opposition. It was clear that the Germans were making preparations for their withdrawal to the mainland across the Straits of Messina, and they started to pull out immediately. For their part, the Allies needed to be in a position to press home their advantage by using the full weight of their naval and air superiority.

Air Vice-Marshal Harry Broadhurst, AOC Western Desert Air Force, was also clear when he wrote to the AOC Tactical Air Force, AM Coningham, 'that a combined naval and air plan was required but that the flak on both sides of the Straits of Messina would need the use of US Fortresses to prevent the evacuation'. The Germans could probably muster about 100 fighter and fighter-bombers to cover the evacuation, plus about 100 long-range bombers. The plan was to use the Wellingtons of the Strategic Air Force to bomb Messina at night while B-17s would do the same in daylight as well as bomb the landing grounds in Crotone and Scalea.

---

6 AUGUST

Log Book: Escort Bostons Bronte. One Boston down but crew baled out OK.

The CO, Sqn Ldr 'Danny' Daniel and Flt Lt Arthur Jupp returned from a motor trip with a good yarn to tell and various trophies. It was an unofficial tour to see the army at work. They visited Catania where, under mortar fire for an hour south of Catania, they watched enemy positions around Adrano being bombed and shelled. The squadron again provided escort to bombers over Adrano and Bronte.

---

7 AUGUST

Log Book: Escort Baltimores Randazzo. Spits tried to bounce us!

ORB: Allied bombing attacks increased today on Randazzo, numerous trips during the day, with Spitfires providing the escort. Troina fell to the Americans. Further landings at Sant Agata by the Americans to try and outflank the Germans.

8 AUGUST

ORB: No. 72 Squadron provided three further bomber escort trips to Randazzo.

9 AUGUST

ORB: Squadron stood down at midday.

A Me109 had been made serviceable from one of several Me109s left lying around Comiso in various states of disrepair, and had been brought across to Pachino when the squadron had moved. The one chosen had just had a prop change so with the help of Tom Hughes, a German dictionary and various experiments, it flew!

'Sexton' Gear took the Me109 up and got mixed up in a barrage of ack-ack fire over Pachino because he had not told the gunners that the Me109 would be flying, nor did he have a Spitfire 'escort'.

Most of the squadron lay on the ground anticipating that 'Sex' and the Me109 would be shot out of the sky, but Tom Hughes ran out to a parked Spitfire, climbed in, started it up and took off into the flak and machine-gun fire. By circling the Me109 and weaving gently, waggling his wings he was able to persuade the gunners the Me109 was friendly so 'Sex' was able to land, very shaken but otherwise unhurt, though he bent the Me109 when landing on one wheel.

Lloyd Snell, a Canadian radar expert with 43 Squadron which was based on the same airfield as 72, recalled:

> We were lined up for our evening meal in a clearing about a quarter of a mile from the landing strip. We were on a rise where we could look down at the airstrip. In the background was the sea in a wide arc. Suddenly a Me109 passed over, just above the tree tops and everyone scattered. Then the ack-ack opened up and we saw a Spit take off, and as it got close to the 109 I thought I was going to see a close-up kill but it waggled its wings and I realised it must be from Comiso. We watched the Me109 land on one wheel and the Spit follow it in.

10 AUGUST

Log Book: Escort Baltimores Randazzo.

ORB: Three further escort trips to bombers over Randazzo again. Sgts Leach and Gridley posted to the squadron.

11 AUGUST

ORB: Three further escort trips to bombers over Randazzo. Had news of a large raid by the Germans on Lentini where some twenty-six Spitfires and Kittyhawks were hit and unserviceable and twenty-seven were killed, mostly from 244 Wing.

12 AUGUST

Log Book: Escort Mitchells Navarro. Bandits reported!!

ORB: Three trips, this time to Falconi and Olivari, Navarro and Massoli, and a patrol covering shipping in the Catania area.

13 AUGUST

Log Book: Escort Bostons north of Catania.

ORB: Two bomber escorts to Piedmont and Falconi and a high-cover patrol north-east of Etna.

14 AUGUST

Log Book: Escort Bostons Messina.

ORB: Patrol to the north-east of Sicily and bomber escort to Messina.

15 AUGUST

ORB: Flg Off Tom Hughes had to bale out of another captured Me109 he was flying which had developed a glycol leak.

He landed in a vineyard not far from Pachino and returned unscathed and apparently all the happier for his experience.

16 AUGUST

ORB: No operational flying, the end of the Sicilian campaign is evidently near.

Although No. 72 was not required, other Allied squadrons continued the relentless assault on the retreating Axis forces across the Straits of Messina. Despite this, the vast majority were able to evacuate safely to the mainland. Of the 122,000 Axis troops taken prisoner, about 119,000 were Italian. There would be recriminations on the Allied side when the success of the German evacuation was realised; the Germans for their part could not believe their luck and could not comprehend why they had been allowed to get away. Gen Montgomery was livid, and noted:

There has been heavy traffic all day across the straits of Messina and the enemy is without doubt getting his stuff away. I have tried to find out what the combined navy–air plan is to stop him but I have been unable to find out and I fear the truth is there is no plan. The trouble is there is no high-up grip on this campaign – Eisenhower the Supreme Commander is in Algiers, Cunningham the Naval C-in-C is in Malta, Tedder the Air C-in-C is in Tunis, and Alexander, in command of land forces, is in Syracuse. So it beats me how you think you can run a campaign with the commanders of the three main services about 600 miles from each other. The enemy should never be allowed to get all his equipment out of Sicily and we should round up the bulk of his fighting troops.

Following the withdrawal, an inspection of the airfields in Sicily revealed over 600 aircraft abandoned and in various states of repair.

17 AUGUST

Log Book: 1. To Lentini West; 2. Patrol nautics – what a bind!!! Monitor shelling; 3. More nautical patrol! 4. From Lentini. Organised resistance in Sicily now ended.

ORB: Allied troops in Messina. No. 72 Squadron sent four aircraft to Lentini where they flew five patrols escorting naval vessels and Kittyhawk bombers to Palmi.

18 AUGUST

ORB: All organised resistance in Sicily now over. No operational flying.

19 AUGUST

Log Book: Tank test.

ORB: Plt Off Shaw, WO Caldwell and Sgt Pearson all left the squadron as tour-expired.

20 AUGUST

Log Book: Aircraft flown – Caproni Vizzola with 'Spanner' and various erks. Line shoot mostly for 2 hours.

ORB: Twelve aircraft went to Lentini and provided escort to bombers across southern Italy.

'Spanner' was the nickname for Greggs Farish, an engineer officer who had been with the squadron since November 1942 in North Africa. The Italian-made Caproni Moth had also been rendered serviceable enough to fly just as the Me109 had been. The Caproni was a dual-control biplane made of wood and fabric with a six-cylinder air-cooled Alfa Romeo engine that was pretty new. The ground crew called it the 'Maggie' but the pilots called it the 'Pisser'. It was a joy to fly, faster than a Tiger Moth and safer than a Maggie. They had to modify the tailwheel forks to take a Spitfire tyre because no spares were available. It was pranged one day when Roy Hussey and Scottie took it across to Lentini to try and find Griff's grave (he had been lost when debris from a Me109 hit his Spitfire on 16 July). During the trip they got shot at by ack–ack and were beaten up by two Me109s. When they returned Scottie, who had not flown it before and who was evidently in the front cockpit, asked Roy to land the plane because the crosswind was a bit awkward. Roy duly landed but touched down too fast and they found themselves heading towards a bomb crater and a pile of rubble. Roy hit the brakes and they both ended up in the front cockpit, the plane with a broken undercarriage. It took about a month to mend it.

21–25 AUGUST

Log Book [for 25th]: Practice shambles!

ORB: No operational flying, though Plt Off A.H. Gear left for hospital, tour-expired.

26 AUGUST

Log Book: 1. To Agnone; 2. Sweep south-eastern tip Italy; 3. Patrol Catania; 4. Back to base.

ORB: Fifteen aircraft moved to Agnone for the day and from that landing ground carried out a bomber escort to Bianco in southern Italy. Two further patrols over Augusta and Catania.

News of the DFC to the late Flg Off Keith was received. Flt Sgt Hermiston left the squadron tour-expired.

27 AUGUST

Log Book: To Pane Bianco.

ORB: Remainder of Wing HQ and squadron left Pachino and proceeded to Pane Bianco and squadron aircraft followed. Just after their arrival a thunderstorm broke and the ground quickly became a quagmire that made the erection of tents impossible.

No further operational flying in the month but 'big events in the air'. Conference at Wing Headquarters for a proposed move north and further preparation on operations.

30 AUGUST

ORB: Landing area still bogged down after the deluge and the airfield remained unserviceable, not fit for landing. Instructions received to proceed to Milazzo area tomorrow, pending embarkation.

CHAPTER 9

Italy Invaded

It had been agreed by the Allied Chief of Staff as early as 20 July that Italy was to be invaded as soon as Sicily had been captured. Amphibious operations, however, were to stretch the limits of the fighter cover based in Sicily and the key to the invasion would again be air superiority. The early capture of airfields was therefore considered to be a priority.

The plan was that the Allies were to put three divisions ashore around Salerno, a small port on the west of Italy about 50 miles south of Naples, under the codename Operation Avalanche, and further divisions would be landed at Taranto, again a port, right on the 'heel' of the foot of Italy under the codename Slapstick. Once established ashore, fighter squadrons would fly into Monte Corvino airfield near Salerno to provide air cover. The landings at Salerno would be under the command of General Mark Clark and his US 5th Army, and the landings at Tarranto and Messina would be under the command of Gen Montgomery and his British 8th Army. The plan was for the two armies to link up following the 8th Army drive north from their landings at Messina and Tarranto. It was also hoped that Rome could be seized by a *coup de main*, dropping a US airborne division to reinforce the Italian troops when they suddenly switched sides.

From 18 August to 2 September, the Allied air forces mounted a concerted attack on lines of communication in southern Italy, dropping over 6,500 tons of bombs.

---
1 SEPTEMBER

ORB: Initial movement for squadron in Operation Avalanche for which 324 Wing squadrons, including 72 Squadron, were to operate under the American 12th Army Air Support Command. Flt Lt Pearson moved off with the wing advance party. Having just settled at Pane Bianco the squadron was once more on the move and headed for Casala, which is less likely than Pane Bianco to be unserviceable in the event of further rain. The CO and 'Spanner' [Greggs Farish], the Chief Engineer Officer, flew across in the 'Pisser' to make preliminary arrangements. Unfortunately when they were about to return, Flg Off Farish was seriously injured when trying to start the engine by swinging the propeller.

Danny Daniel and Spanner had gone across to Casala near Gerbini to have a look around as preparation for the squadron to move in. They had chosen the dispersal when Danny had apparently climbed into the front cockpit of the 'Pisser' as Spanner was preparing to swing the propeller to start the engine, which was the only way of doing so. Apparently, Danny waited for him to climb aboard with the engine then running but he did not appear, so he put the brakes on to stop the 'Pisser' rolling forward, jumped out to find Spanner underneath, unconscious and covered in blood. He apparently managed to shove Spanner in the rear cockpit and flew him back to base, still unconscious, where he was rushed to No. 21 Field Hospital nearby with severe wounds to his head and hand. He remained critical for several days but regained consciousness and made a full recovery.

---

2 SEPTEMBER

Log Book: To Casala then scrambled.

ORB: Squadron moved to Casala from Pane Bianco. WO Price arrived on attachment as replacement for Flg Off Farish.

---

3 SEPTEMBER

Log Book: 1. Patrol Augusta, Italy invaded across Messina Straits; 2. Patrol Augusta. Twenty plus Me109s reported, no joy.

ORB: Italy invaded in the south by the 8th Army at 0430 hours today. There was still no rest for the squadron. Warning notice that the 'A' party, comprising roughly half the ground crew strength and a few pilots, are to be ready to travel tomorrow with half the squadron motor transport and ground equipment to Falcone on the north coast of Sicily. Packing soon in full swing. Squadron patrolled three times today over Allied shipping north-east of Augusta. No observations made. Sgt Pilots Johnstone, Pullen and Street reported for duties.

At 0430 hours on 3 September, under the cover of a massive artillery barrage and the fire-power of fifteen Royal Navy warships, XIII Corps of 8th Army began the crossing from Sicily to Italy in 300 landing craft under Operation Baytown. The 5th Division landed to the north, while 1st Canadian Division led the attack on the southern flank. The Italian coastal units surrendered almost immediately, leaving a single German regiment to defend 17 miles of coastline. That evening, British Commando forces were landed in the rear of the Germans, at Bagnara, securing the success of the immediate landings. However, the difficult terrain in Italy – the dominant factor in the fighting for the next two years – coupled with skilful German demolition operations, slowed the advance. The roads in Bagnara itself had been so badly damaged that only troops on foot could enter the town. The 16th Panzer Grenadier Division covered the German withdrawal north as 8th Army slowly advanced through Calabria. In reality the crossings had gone by the book because the Germans never had any intention of fighting for the strategically useless 'heel and toe' of Italy, they merely wanted to delay matters as much as practically possible to allow the Axis ground forces to withdraw in good order and re-establish themselves to contest the landings at Salerno. Most enemy airfields in the 'toe' of Italy were abandoned.

4 SEPTEMBER

Log Book: 1. Patrol Messina; 2. Patrol Messina – 109s above and engaged. No luck; 3. Patrol Messina. Showed the flag!!

ORB: Flt Lt Hughes left squadron to become a flight commander in 43 Squadron. 'A' Party left for Falcone in the early afternoon. Squadron escorted Kittyhawk bombers to the 'toe of Italy' and landing beaches. Operated between 5–10,000ft patrolling Messina Straits. Flak was reported but no enemy aircraft encountered.

Later patrol at 1245 hours again over Messina Straits, contacted five Me109s and these were chased north-east to Capistrano, but had to give up the chase because our boys were short of fuel.

5 SEPTEMBER

Log Book: 1. Patrol Messina; 2. Patrol Messina.

ORB: 'A' Party already at Falcone, 'B' Party at readiness for same move. Squadron was to be based here to provide high cover for the landings at Salerno. The latter party were unlucky as their ration wagon went astray and they were more than a little hungry by the time it followed them into Falcone. Two patrols over the landing beaches and Allied shipping east of Augusta with a Ju88 reported but not seen.

The problem with any sorties was that they could only be made with the aid of 90-gallon drop tanks. This was to test the Spitfire capabilities, especially as they would be flying across 180 miles of sea.

6 SEPTEMBER

Log Book: From Casala to Falcone.

ORB: All squadrons released. Everything a bustle at Casala. 'B' Party started for Falcone and the aircraft flew to the new location shortly after the motor transport departed. The route taken by the M/T was interesting with magnificent scenery, though tortuous and hilly. Travelling as the 'A' Party had done before, via Catania, Misterbianco, Palermo, Adrano, Bronte and Randazzo, they saw something of the havoc and destruction wrought by the Allied bombing during the fighting.

The party camped at 4,000ft up a hillside overlooking Vittoria and allthough chilly, everyone was in good humour, despite the rain which meant that numerous temporary shelters were rigged.

When the squadron aircraft arrived at Falcone, Flg Off Scrase crashed on landing, but only received minor injuries.

His log book recorded candidly: 'Spitfire 9 to Falcone – hit tree at end of runway, aircraft Cat. 3 damage.'

7 SEPTEMBER

ORB: 'B' Party continued journey to Falcone which they reached at about 1800 hours, through Floresta, Naso and Cape D'Orlando. All pilots attended a briefing by Gp Capt Ronnie Lees, its former CO, where they were briefed on the proposed landings at Salerno and Operation Avalanche.

8 SEPTEMBER

Log Book: Tank and acceptance check. Nice kite.

ORB: The struggling vehicles on the Casala–Falcone journey, due to mechanical troubles, finally arrived. Squadron learnt that their role in Operation Avalanche will be to support and then make landings on the Italian mainland south of Naples. More preparations for the sea party move.

9 SEPTEMBER

Log Book: 1. Cannon test. Heinie man resisting. Landings by Anglo-Americans. Italy unconditionally surrendered; 2. Cover invasion beaches. South of Naples. We cover with 90-gallon tanks. Whew! No air opposition today. Area full of P-38s, A-36s and Spits.

Although General Castellano had signed the Italian surrender in Sicily on 3 September, it was not declared until 8 September, as the convoys carrying the Allies neared their target at Salerno. The plans to seize Rome had to be abandoned, after a covert Allied reconnaissance visit decided there was no possibility of successfully reinforcing the Italian garrison sufficiently. The German 2nd Parachute and 3rd Panzer Grenadier Divisions quickly overran the Italian troops in the capital. However, at Taranto, six Allied cruisers safely put ashore the 1st British Airborne Division to help the Italians secure the important naval base.

Meanwhile at Salerno, in the early hours of 9 September, Operation Avalanche saw the British 46th and 56th Divisions of X Corps land on the northern flank, with the US 36th and 45th Divisions coming ashore to the south. Three German armoured divisions – the Hermann Göring and the 15th and 16th Panzer Grenadiers – were in the area and launched a series of counter-attacks. By the end of the day Italy had unconditionally surrendered, as the culmination of arrangements made (according to broadcasts) on 3 September. The squadron's first operation under Operation Avalanche was patrolling the beaches south-east of Naples and although fitted with 90-gallon drop tanks, they could only maintain standing patrols over the beaches of about 25 minutes. The 90-gallon drop tanks extended the range of the Spitfire's flying time by about an hour or so and although they increased drag, did not affect the handling of the aircraft to any great extent. Initially they were jettisoned once empty, but after several trips, when it was realised there was little enemy air opposition, they were retained. In this way the aircraft could be airborne for up to 2 hours 40 minutes.

ORB: Beaches patrolled were Peaches beach in the Salerno area, with the Mark VCs at 16,000ft and the IXs [including Barney] at 20,000ft. Landing craft and M/T reported but no enemy aircraft in the air.

10 SEPTEMBER

Log Book: Cover invasion beaches. 2.45 hours. Found SM79 and brought it home!

ORB: 'A' Party moved to marshalling yards at Milazzo for waterproofing the vehicles prior to embarkation to Italy, where they are to support the 5th Army in the Salerno area. Flt Lt Johnston badly shaken when his aircraft overturned on take-off. Two uneventful patrols over Peaches beach again near Salerno. Plt Off Kennedy from 111 Squadron destroyed a Fw190 in the morning over Peaches beach.

Gp Capt Gilroy had also flown with 111 Squadron during the day. He liked to keep his hand in and often flew with one of the squadrons whenever he could. He also had a reputation for being able to spot enemy aircraft before anyone else had spotted them. Peaches beach by this time appeared to be a complete shambles. Men and equipment, tanks and landing craft, smoke and flashes of guns and shell bursts made flying hazardous. Allied ships continued to fire on targets inland. The rest of the wing were at Monte Corvino and were told that the American 31st Fighter Group were to occupy the aerodrome, so they had to move to Tusciano landing ground. Very little sleep was had by anyone on the aerodrome and camp-site as they were located in front of three artillery batteries. The noise of the shelling together with the anti-aircraft fire made sleep impossible.

11 SEPTEMBER

Log Book: Delouse invasion area. 2.35 hours. No lice! 93 had Yank flak trouble. Pretty bloody.

ORB: During the first two patrols of Peaches beach, Flt Sgt Leech landed at Paestem in Italy due to engine trouble but returned to Falcone later in the day. Sqn Ldr Mackie from 243 Squadron destroyed a Dornier 217 over the beaches in the morning. Plt Off Newman reported as Engineer Officer in place of Flg Off Farish, posted from the unit, non-effective to RHQ DIAF in view of his injuries. News was also received that Plt Off Shaw, formerly of the squadron, now tour-expired, was awarded the DFC.

Reference to '93 Yank flak' trouble rather glibly, but sadly, recorded the death of a former 243 Squadron flight commander, now Sqn Ldr Macdonald of 93 Squadron, who was shot down and killed by American ack-ack gunners near Battipaglia. 'Friendly fire' casualties were becoming a real concern, with aircraft regularly being lost and aircraft recognition at a premium. The solution was the painted black and white 'invasion' stripes which would aid aircraft recognition and would be available to the Allied air forces for their landings in Normandy the following year.

12 SEPTEMBER

Log Book: Cover usual area. 2.30 hours. Twenty plus Me109s. The Mark Vs chased but no catchee. Con one destroyed, one damaged. Smithy one damaged and Bruce one destroyed, one damaged all in Mark IXs.

ORB: While 'A' Party was being embarked at Milazzo, the LSTs sailed at about 1900 hours, the pilots operating from Falcone continued to push up the squadron score. During the first of the two days' patrols over Salerno, seven Me109s were encountered and two were destroyed by Plt Off Ingalls and Sgt Connolly and two were damaged by Flg Off Smith and Sgt Connolly. Flg Off Smith's aircraft was hit by flak and Plt Off Ingalls, short of fuel, had to crash-land on his return to Milazzo West.

The initial successes on the ground for the Allied ground forces were reversed when FM Kesselring's Panzers counter-attacked with some force and recaptured Battipaglia from the British, just three days after the first beach assault.

13 SEPTEMBER

Log Book: 1. To Tusciano. Italy!! 4 miles from front line. 25-pounders behind us!!! 2. Escort Dakotas u/s.

ORB: Aircraft of 72 Squadron and 243 Squadron arrived at Tusciano so squadron was able to begin operations from the Italian mainland. Flt Sgt Clarkson overshot on landing and damaged his aircraft but was unhurt. First job was to patrol Dakotas to Stromboli and then patrol Peaches beach again, both without incident. 'A' Party disembarked while the navy were shelling enemy land positions. Some enemy air activity reported and a few bombs were dropped in the vicinity of the camp during darkness. One enemy aircraft bought down north of the camp. With guns all around pounding away there is not much sleep to be had. The recent death of Sqn Ldr Macdonald had served to highlight the dangers of aircraft operations and recognition in close proximity to the battle area, so in moving to Tusciano they would be the first RAF unit to operate in front of their own artillery, not that the pilots were told before they arrived!

The British 25-pounders were situated in olive groves on the seaward side of the landing ground and appeared to fire continuously over the landing strip, even when Spitfires were in the circuit. Barney recalled later that the landing at Tusciano was probably the most nerve-racking experience he had faced since his landing on Malta some 18 months earlier from the USS *Wasp*. Coming into land, they had to turn over the enemy positions at a greatly reduced speed with wheels and flaps down. The concussion of the gunfire caused the Spitfires to rock and buck with the very real danger that they would lose flying speed and control at such a low altitude, making a fatal crash inevitable. They were told later that the gunners did not, at least in theory, fire when aircraft passed in front of them. The Wingco, 'Cocky' Dundas was told 'in any event, whoever heard of a 25-pounder shooting down a Spitfire!'

What few tents the squadron had were pitched that night on the southern end of the runway and the personnel and pilots lost no time in digging in their slit trenches. Sleep was impossible because of the noise of the 25-pounders, so most of them stayed awake and watched the vivid flashes of the guns, followed by the screams of the shells. The tents shuddered under the gunfire. There was a small enemy raid when the aerodrome was dive-bombed and a small fire was started at the end of the drome.

On the ground the Germans re-took Altavilla and Perano from the Americans. Plans for other squadrons to move to landing strips on the beachhead had to be delayed because there was a real danger that the beachhead would be lost. The Luftwaffe was largely kept at bay from interfering with Allied troops and supplies because of their air superiority, but it was undoubtedly accurate and destructive naval fire power that helped turn the Germans back.

---

14 SEPTEMBER

Log Book: Cover battle area. Bombed and shelled during night. Whacko!

ORB: 'B' Party moved from Falcone to the marshalling yards near Milazzo, the beginning of a long and later tedious wait there until the shipping was available on the 21/9. At Tusciano, the remainder of the squadron saw evidence of the increased Allied air attacks on enemy positions and the bombers passing overhead were almost endless. During the night, again disturbed by gunfire.

Gp Capt Gilroy flew with squadron on the first of the day's two missions, comprising bomber escort to Avellino and a further patrol of the beach area. Aircraft of 43 Squadron arrived at Tusciano. Wg Cdr Dundas flew.

Sgt Connolly reported the enemy gun positions and the army was informed. Pilots were instructed to sleep with pistols at hand in case of enemy paratroops or intruders, as the potential was there for enemy attacks at will.

Sleep remained impossible because of the noise of the barrage, ack-ack fire and shells. The mosquitoes also proved to be everywhere; the large fierce variety that proved resistant to all repellents. Such arduous living and operating conditions sapped the strength of the men. Within a few weeks many would be suffering from malaria. Examining the aircraft each morning also became a chore to assess any damage caused during the night. Shellfire damage was an obvious risk, but several aircraft were damaged by great white oxon. The beasts roamed the field at night and scratched their hides on the wings which damaged the all-important pitot head extensions, the externally mounted tubes that measured air speed. The field guards had the thankless task of trying to keep the huge creatures away from the aircraft, occasionally firing their own guns at them to deter them, but it was quickly realised that any bullets just bounced off their tough hides. They were not to know it, but 14 September appeared to be the turning point in the battle. About 700 sorties were flown that day by Allied fighters and fighter-bombers, largely against German transport near Eboli.

15 SEPTEMBER

Log Book: 1. Cover battle area; 2. Cover battle area – chased nine plus 109s. Clueless me! CO got one destroyed, Johnny one damaged and Smithy one probable.

ORB: Bombers again lively over Salerno, encountered intense flak. Enemy aircraft encountered during the second of two Peaches beach patrols. Sqn Ldr Daniel destroyed a Me109 and later in the Naples area Flg Off Smith probably destroyed a Fw190 and Flt Lt Johnston damaged another Fw190.

16 SEPTEMBER

Log Book: Cover battle area. Found four 109s at 22,000ft. Chased them home and squirted. I got one Me109 damaged. Pip force-landed behind enemy lines and got one Me109 destroyed.

ORB: Three patrols of Peaches beach with more squadron successes and the start of a great adventure for Sgt Piper who, after shooting down a Me109 during the second patrol, crash-landed because of engine trouble near Lacino, within the enemy lines, and was reported missing. On the same patrol Flg Off Barnfather damaged a Me109 and during the last operation of the day Flt Lt Pearson and Flg Off Leach destroyed a Fw190. The enemy aircraft destroyed by Sgt Piper was the 200th destroyed by the squadron.

Barney's Combat Report for the day was as follows:

Spitfire Vc, Coded RN-J
Up 1345 hours and down 1505 hours from Tusciano
Nil Cloud, visibility good and general weather good
Peaches Beaches Patrol

I was flying Yellow 111 on the Peaches patrol, controller came through at 1355 hours and told the leader to fly to 25,000ft. We reached patrol height and patrolled the Peaches beach for 10 minutes and were flying due south from Salerno and saw a gaggle of aircraft 2,000yd clear of us at same height (25,000ft). We closed with them and identified them as Lightnings in this manoeuvre. We lost height to 22,000ft and we saw four aircraft flying 1,000/1,500ft above us flying due north which were identified as Me109s. We turned to port, the enemy aircraft doing likewise, we and they doing a complete orbit. (The enemy aircraft did an orbit and a quarter finishing up flying north-west.) We continued our turn and straightened out behind and still below the enemy aircraft. Enemy aircraft then put their noses down and dived away on north-west coast. We dived after them and they were then over the shipping off Salerno and made a starboard turn approx 45° and we slowly closed the range and I eventually chose the enemy aircraft on the starboard outside and managed to close the range to approx 400yd at 4,000ft at Lago-di-Laceno (N9346). Enemy aircraft began to draw away (the tit having been pressed as he gave off black smoke) so I pulled the nose up and gave five short bursts. No observed results until the very last burst at 1410 hours when a white flash was seen on the starboard side of the pilot's cockpit. Enemy aircraft did a tight turn to port. I followed round in a three-quarter turn but had to break away because the remainder of the enemy section were in a favourable position to attack.

Claim: One Me109 damaged

Some of Montgomery's 8th Army moving up from Calabria in the south joined with the Americans at Salerno beach. It appeared the crisis and threat of being stuck on the beachhead, or even turned back into the sea, was averted. The beachhead had been secured.

17 SEPTEMBER

Log Book: Squadron reached 200 destroyed yesterday/last night. Smithy: one destroyed; Leech: one damaged and Jack: one destroyed.

ORB: Artillery fire in the Tusciano locality abated, the guns evidently having moved forward in the wake of the enemy retreat. Between the two squadron patrols over the beaches, Sqn Ldr Daniel and Flt Lt Jupp were to have shared in the protection of P-38 Lightnings on a ground strafing expedition, but the P-38s did not keep the rendezvous. The two therefore did their own ground strafing and damaged enemy aircraft on the ground. Enemy aircraft reported over the beaches and, despite an intense barrage, one ship in the bay was bombed.

18 SEPTEMBER

ORB: Comparatively quiet day with only one operational mission, another patrol over Peaches beach in the Salerno area. News of the 8th Army advance towards the 5th Army was encouraging. The landing of more British and American troops on the beachhead ensured the Germans began their withdrawal towards Salerno.

19 SEPTEMBER

Log Book: Cover battle area.

ORB: Two beach patrols and over Naples. Two unknown pilots baled out in camp vicinity.

20 SEPTEMBER

Log Book: 1. Escort Mitchells – good bombing Avellino; 2. Air Test – OK. Roy got two Dornier 217s.

ORB: Twice today Fw190s made low-level bombing and machine-gun attacks on the aerodrome and camp-site. Casualties in other units but none to 72 Squadron. Squadron escorted bombers to Avellino and subsequently patrolled the beaches. On the patrol

Plt Off Hussey destroyed two Do217s. Six Me109s were engaged by 243 Squadron but they had to break off thinking 72 Squadron was also enemy aircraft. The same Me109s were attacked and Flt Lt Pearson got one damaged and Plt Off Ingalls got one probable.

An interesting story comes from one of the other squadrons. They were on patrol at 23,000ft when they saw a group of Fw190s at very low altitude that just appeared to be stooging around. The squadron came down in a steep curving dive and just as they came up the back of the still unsuspecting Fw190s, about 400yd away and ready to fire, the front armoured windscreens clouded over completely and they could see nothing. It was evidently the result of leaving a very cold altitude at 23,000ft for much warmer air in a very short time. This strange and disquieting occurrence would happen several times in Italy.

21 SEPTEMBER

Log Book: Cover battle area. Pip came home. Four exhausting but interesting days. Good show.

ORB: 'B' Party having languished in the marshalling area for a week were embarked at Milazzo and sailed for the Italian beaches at 1900 hours. Two beach patrols were flown.
   Sgt Piper returned to the squadron with a grand story to tell, the truth was at least as thrilling as the fiction! At first befriended by an Italian soldier in the hills with other Allied troops who were seeking to escape from enemy lines. The Germans persistently patrolled the scene of Pip's crash and searched houses and buildings. When Pip eventually reached Capagnia, there were evidently doubts to whether it was still occupied by Allied troops or Axis troops. While Pip was being brought back by road by the Yanks to the Tusciano area, some Piper aircraft were noticed in a field and the offer of one of the pilots to fly Pip back was readily accepted, so that on arrival at his home landing strip, Sgt Pip Piper was bought back by a Piper!

22 SEPTEMBER

Log Book: Cover battle area.

ORB: A 'hit and run' bomber dropped bombs near the runway at Tusciano. Two freelance patrols between Salerno and Capua and on the beaches. 'B' Party disembarked on the beach a short distance from Tusciano while the bay was under heavy shellfire so they were not able to reach camp until darkness.

23 SEPTEMBER

Log Book: Cover 'push'.

ORB: Squadron ground personnel working normally. Three patrols of Peaches beach, Battipaglio and Salerno. Aircraft of 93 and 111 Squadron's arrived Monte Corvino.

Montgomery and his 8th Army linked up with Clark's 5th Army and started to push the Germans back.

---

24 SEPTEMBER

Log Book: To Falcone.

ORB: Our aircraft covered the reconnaissance Spitfires over Naples and later in the day patrolled the Salerno area led by Wg Cdr Dundas (Wingco Flying) who shared with Flt Sgt Larlee, a Canadian, the destruction of a Ju88.

Also escorted transport near the Volturno river. Heavy flak over Capri though Tusciano area now quiet.

---

25 SEPTEMBER

Log Book: Cover battle area. Gp Capt led a flag showing effort.

ORB: Enemy motor transport and railway transport seen during a sweep north of Naples and reported to the ALO with a view to bombing them. Squadron afterwards patrolled Salerno again.

---

26 SEPTEMBER

Log Book: Cover battle area.

ORB: Following a morning patrol north of Naples, the position of enemy flak batteries was also reported to the ALO. Later the squadron patrolled over Salerno again.

---

27 SEPTEMBER

ORB: No activity. Airfield unserviceable following heavy rain in the early morning. First sign of the weather, that it, along with the Germans would be difficult during the coming winter. 243 Squadron had to divert to Paestum because Tusciano was unserviceable, but there two collided on the runway on take-off and a third lost power and crashed into a tree.

---

28 SEPTEMBER

Log Book: Cover battle area. Duff weather.

ORB: Squadron's first offensive sweep between Benevento and Gaeta was curtailed because of cloud. The second patrol of the Salerno area reported that our own motor transport appeared to be under fire from our own guns.

Torrential rain and a thunderstorm in the night wrought havoc in the tented accommodation.

29 SEPTEMBER

ORB: Aerodrome unserviceable due to rain. Fortunately a fine day that helped with the drying out.

30 SEPTEMBER

ORB: Aerodrome still unserviceable. During the afternoon flak batteries fired at enemy aircraft high above the camp but no bombs were dropped.

1 OCTOBER

ORB: Six aircraft Peaches beach patrol. Good news for the CO, Sqn Ldr Daniel, who was awarded [Second] Bar to his DFC. Also news that DFCs had been awarded to acting Sqn Ldr Evan Mackie and Flt Lt Bam Bamberger of 243 Squadron, so celebrated in the Mess that evening with Gp Capt Gilroy as guest of honour. More general good news in that Naples had fallen to the Allied forces.

2 OCTOBER

Log Book: Patrol Naples.

ORB: Ten aircraft Peaches patrol. More torrential rain shortly before noon made the aerodrome unserviceable for the rest of the day. US Tomahawks had prepared the ground for a further 8th Army landing at Termoli on the Adriatic by bombing and strafing troops and transport on the roads north and west of the town.

3–4 OCTOBER

ORB: Aerodrome unserviceable. No flying. Some of the pilots took the opportunity to head towards Naples as this would be their next home. It was a journey of some 60 miles through Battipaglia, which had been totally destroyed, from Salerno, which remained heavily damaged, and numerous hill towns. Battipaglia had been obliterated by carpet bombing by the US, there was practically nothing left standing. Civilians had not been spared in the bombing, many had perished and were still left under the ruins judging by the stench and the steady stream of flies gorging themselves on the rotting flesh.

Massed supply columns crowded the roads and slowed their progress but the countryside was also battered. There were refugees of all ages and descriptions lining the road and heading in both directions which hampered movement. Some were probably trying to get home, some were trying still to escape the destruction and seek safety. Some carried a few belongings while others pushed wobbly carts laden with salvaged possessions. The mud and rain covered everyone and everything in a grey filth but it appeared that they all ignored the discomfort. There seemed to be huge masses of people on the move but it was their helplessness and pitiful condition that remained etched on the minds of many pilots and personnel that . . . witnessed the scenes.

The 8th Army landings at Termoli were assisted by fighter-bombers and B-25 bombers that hampered German transport movements despite the appalling weather, and then helped the army hold the bridgehead against determined German efforts and counter-attacks.

---
5 OCTOBER

ORB: Six aircraft 72 Squadron patrol Naples area.

On the Adriatic, Kittyhawks and US Warhawks (the P-40 was known as the Kittyhawk in RAF service, and as the Warhawk by the Americans) helped break up the main enemy concentrations by hitting their transport hard on the roads from Termoli, Isernia and Chieta.

Following the landings at Termoli, Allied troops now occupied a line running from the Adriatic at Termoli itself, through Ielsi, Circello, north-west of Benevento and along the rivers Calore and Volturno. The airfields around Foggia and Naples had been captured and provided bases for operations to continue. Following the capture of the Foggia airfields the 8th Army was given the task of advancing towards the Rome Line, the name given to the lateral road running from Pescara, through Avezzano to Rome. There were two further water barriers to overcome, the rivers Trigno and Sangro. The Germans would choose the latter as the basis for the long hard winter defence because on the south side there was an escarpment and on the north side a steep ridge framing the long shallow plain. With the winter rain the Sangro would also flood making it impassable.

---
6 OCTOBER

ORB: Six aircraft 72 Squadron patrol Naples area.

7–10 OCTOBER

ORB: Aerodrome unserviceable. No flying. Change of administrative control as the squadron moved from Middle East Command to NWAAF, announced in Western Desert Air Force Routine Order 347 dated 3/10/43.

In the evening [the] Wing [Commander] intimated that tomorrow an advance party from the squadron was to make preparations for the squadron move, with the rest of the wing, to the main airfields around Naples. During its stay on Tusciano, the squadron (and the other squadrons that formed the wing) had remained under canvas, but this was becoming increasingly uncomfortable as winter began to set in. Aircraft had to be serviced outside and rations were poor. Bread and meat were at a premium, compo rations were the order of the day, except notably when some of the 243 boys took a three-tonner and 'discovered' a lost cattle beast, shot it and brought it back so that everyone had fresh meat. Occasionally they would try and barter with the Americans on adjacent landing strips. A precious bottle of whisky could be exchanged for coffee, tinned milk and sugar, all of which were also in short supply.

11 OCTOBER

Log Book: To Naples main. Capodichino.

ORB: The Adjutant Flt Lt Race and Medical Officer Flt Lt Griffin and Intelligence Officer Flg Off Brill together with a small party of airmen travelled by road to Naples where they scoured the city for billets for the squadron. Eventually a large suite of well-equipped offices were selected. Some of the other squadrons found well-apportioned villas which had been abandoned by the wealthy and gentry of Naples. Wing and squadrons moved to Capodichino, Naples; 43, 72 and 243 Squadrons from Tusciano and 93 and 111 Squadrons from Battipaglio.

Naples aerodrome was a large grass airport and was much better than the landing strips in what had now become the rainy season. Capodichino became shortened to 'Capo'. With the villas and offices empty, everyone began to scour around to see if anything of any value could be scrounged. It seemed that every squadron had the same idea. Looting was forbidden but most squadrons 'acquired' transport; a few cars and motorcycles ran very well on high octane aircraft fuel until the practice was stopped.

Naples itself was crowded with people begging for food and cigarettes, and made movement around the city difficult. The city had suffered badly from the bombing. Street fighting between Germans and Italians had added to the damage, and the docks had been totally destroyed with sunken ships alongside almost every pier and dockside; it would take some considerable time for the docks to be made serviceable again.

The most serious damage was done by the Germans as they withdrew from the city. They had cut the sewer mains allowing them to run into the water mains and cause contamination. The city was quite literally without water apart from a few scattered wells around which women and children queued for hours to get a few pints of precious liquid. Despite the crowds and wandering vendors selling fruit, ices and wines, the city appeared more dead than liberated. The smell of the broken sewers was overpowering, and filth and rot lined the streets. The shops on the other hand appeared well stocked with perfumes, silks and art objects. The city was also infested with booby traps and time bombs, and planted with prostitutes ridden with disease who were only too glad to ply their trade on the very willing Allied soldiers. Dirt was everywhere, people were lice-ridden and typhus, because of the broken sewers, was a real threat. Much of it was contained by the introduction of a new insecticide called DDT.

A patrol over Naples to the Volturno river by 111 Squadron encountered six Me109s with top cover of four Me109s off the river. Sgt Adams got one Me109G as a probable. Some of the aircraft had a cannon under their wings, but none appeared to be carrying bombs.

12 OCTOBER

ORB: Six aircraft patrol Naples area, 0555–0710. Ten aircraft patrol Volturno river 0920–1100.

93 Squadron came across sixteen Me109s over the Volturno river. Flt Lt Kennedy two destroyed. Sgt Johnson one damaged, and Flg Off Davidson one probable. Some enemy aircraft had Italian markings.

Six aircraft patrol Naples area 1350–1520.

Capodichino was a big improvement on the landing strips and tents they had been used to. Naples also had its attractions though the men rarely went into town. The place was steeped in history. Within sight of the aerodrome, about 8 miles away, was the volcano of Mount Vesuvius with Pompeii at its base. About 50 miles north was Monte Cassino, a great abbey built by Saint Benedict, and a further 70 or so miles north of Monte Cassino was Rome itself.

After the Salerno beachhead had been established and the Allied ground forces had driven north to capture Naples and the surrounding area, it became clear that Kesselring would provide stern resistance across what became known as the Gustav Line, which hinged on Monte Cassino and would later prove almost impossible to take.

First, however, the 5th Army had to establish bridgeheads across the Volturno river, about 20 miles north of Naples, and it was the job of the RAF to support the army's push to secure this bridgehead. When not escorting bombers they patrolled the skies over the river to ensure the army was not harassed.

By this time the Volturno river was a natural obstacle, the rain had swelled it so that it was between 150–300ft wide and anything up to 6ft deep in mid-stream. The current was swift and the water icy cold, and in such circumstances, and against battle-hardened troops, it took a good ten days of ferocious fighting to cross the river and the Volturno line.

During the night Wellington bombers had hit railway bridges to prevent German reinforcements reaching the battle area, supplemented in daylight by the Kittyhawks, Bostons and Marauders hitting anything that moved. The Spitfires continued to provide escort duties as well as standing patrols, and Allied air strength and superiority cleared all resistance. It was only when clouds and the rain clamped down that effective flying stopped. The foul weather was a double hit; it made the advance by the army even harder over an already difficult terrain, and it often rendered the Allied air superiority irrelevant.

Lloyd Snell with 43 Squadron, which was still part of 324 Wing, recalled: 'Our next move was to Naples, within sight of Vesuvius. We slept on the airfield for some time in our two-man pup tents. Early one morning we [were] woken up by locals picking mushrooms around us.'

13 OCTOBER

Log Book: Patrol battle area. Flak!

ORB: Six aircraft patrol Volturno river. For the first time the whole squadron personnel were accommodated under one roof in the five-storey offices. The CO, who had been sick and convalescent since 29/9, returned to the squadron to assume command, in place of Flt Lt Jupp who had deputised for him. 'Polly' Parrott – Flt Lt Peter Parrott DFC, replaced Sqn Ldr Horbaczewski as squadron leader of 43 'Fighting Cocks' but was immediately hospitalised with malaria.

14 OCTOBER

Log Book: Patrol Naples.

ORB: Four aircraft shipping protection. A rainy day, not at all the sort of day to be finding new working quarters in the airfields, wrecked hangars and other buildings. AM Sir Arthur Coningham KCB, DSO, MC, DFC and AFC, visited the airfield and talked to the pilots.

15 OCTOBER

Log Book: Sweep Rome area.

ORB: Six aircraft patrol Volturno river. One Spit IX damaged by flak. Four aircraft shipping protection. Two Me109s encountered. Earlier on Volturno river patrol, six Spits from 243 came across two Me109s, Sqn Ldr Mackie damaged one though three Spitfires were damaged by flak, all pilots uninjured.

Four aircraft shipping protection. Six aircraft 72 Squadron armed recce of landing grounds south of Rome, ten Spits from 93 Squadron patrolled Volturno river as well and came across eight Me109s.

Wg Cdr Dundas flew with the squadron. One Mark IX and one Mark V returned early before combat.

Victories: Flg Off Davidson, Flg Off Hockey, a Canadian, Flg Off Browne, a New Zealander, and Flt Lt Kennedy, also a Canadian, all destroyed one Me109 each. Sgt Downer one Me109 damaged. One Spit Mark V hit by flak but pilot okay. These patrols continued while the 5th Army tried to establish the bridgehead over the Volturno river. They continued to run into Me109s intermittently, they were invariably there but it might be other squadrons that engaged them or they missed them altogether.

16 OCTOBER

Log Book: Sweep Rome area. Thirty plus 190s and 109s. Bombing north of river. Wizard Doggers, Ho! CO two 190s destroyed. Clarky one 190 and one 109 destroyed. Kingy one 109 destroyed. Self one 109 destroyed. Bruce and Con got a damaged each.

ORB: Ten aircraft sweep forward area:

Spit VC, JK944 – Flt Lt M. Johnston (Canadian)
Spit VC, EF640 – Flg Off F. Musgrove

Spit IX, MA637 – Plt Off B.J. Ingalls (Canadian)
Spit IX, EN258 – Flt Sgt J.W. Larlee (Canadian)
Spit IX, JF513 – Sqn Ldr S.W.F. Daniel
Spit IX, MA462 – Flt Sgt J.T. Connolly (Australian)
Spit IX, MA444 – Flg Off R.R. Barnfather
Spit IX, JG722 – Flg Off K. Smith
Spit VC, EF656 – Flt Sgt K.E. Clarkson (Australian)
Spit VC, JK132 – Flt Sgt K.C. Weller

Twenty Fw190s and twelve Me109s seen and attacked.

Victories: Sqn Ldr Daniel two Me109s destroyed, Flg Off Barnfather one Me109 destroyed, Flt Sgt Clarkson two Fw190s destroyed, Flg Off King one Me109 destroyed, Sgt Weller one Me109 damaged and Sgt Connolly one Me109 damaged. One Spit IX hit by flak but there were no casualties in the squadron.

Twelve aircraft 72 Squadron patrol Volturno river 1300–1435. Flt Lt Bamberger from 93 Squadron got one Me109 destroyed. One Spit V returned due to engine trouble.

Barney's Combat Report for the day records:

Spitfire IX, RN-B
Up 1300 hours and down 1435 hours
Nil Cloud, visibility good and general weather good
Sweep Rome Area and Patrol

At 1400 hours thirty plus aircraft were sighted north of river just south of Rome going south-west at 17,000ft. We chased them and identified aircraft as hostile Me109s and Fw190s. In general mêlée and as I went round to get on the tail of one Me109, I closed to within 200yd and I gave it two bursts of rather more than one second each. Strikes were seen all over the enemy aircraft and he crashed into the hillside, the pilot still inside.
Claim: One Me109 destroyed

---

17 OCTOBER

Log Book: Patrol battle area.

ORB: Twelve aircraft patrol Volturno river. Due to have been bomber escort along with 243 Squadron but cloud prevented location of bombers.

Six aircraft 72 Squadron 'Delouse H.2033' and patrol Naples.

The Allied air superiority allowed them to introduce a new system of close air support for the army. To provide quicker and closer support than had been previously possible, mobile observation posts with the forward troops and Brigade HQ were linked by direct radio contact with aircraft in the air. Both the controller and pilots were issued with photographic maps of the area on which there were reference grids to help both the controller and pilots identify target areas. From the patrols maintained overhead by the fighter-bombers, in formation, in line astern, that became known as 'Cab Rank', they were directed to target areas by radio and by using the grid maps. Known as 'Rover David', the system was widely and successfully used, but only because Allied air superiority allowed them to.

18 OCTOBER

Log Book: Patrol battle area.

ORB: Eight aircraft sweep G.2020 and G.7030. Bomber escort for Bostons. Eight aircraft patrol Volturno river and two aircraft patrol Naples.

19 OCTOBER

Log Book: 1. Escort Bostons felt the flak!!! 2. Sweep north of area – chased reported bandits. No see.

ORB: Two aircraft patrol Naples area. Bandits reported not seen. Eight aircraft patrol Volturno river. One Spit IX hit by flak. Twelve aircraft fighter sweep Gulf of Gaeta. Offensive north of the Volturno had come to a standstill.

20 OCTOBER

ORB: Eight aircraft patrol Volturno river and delousing H.0803.

News was filtering through of continued delayed action bombs going off in Naples and the surrounding areas laid by the retreating Germans. Several hundred mines had been laid, under principal buildings. One had gone off near the Central Post Office, killing many innocent Italian civilians, but the prospect of other large municipal buildings being mined meant they were evacuated temporarily.

Engineers trained in bomb disposal could not cope with the number of alarms and suspicious wires running everywhere. The situation was not helped that evening by the first German air raid back on Naples itself with further damage caused to the port area.

21 OCTOBER

Log Book: Patrol Volturno.

ORB: Eight aircraft patrol Volturno river.

During the evening an enemy air raid came in lasting about ¾ hour. Two pilots, Flt Sgt Scott and Flt Sgt Gridley, were caught outside and received injuries from either bomb or shell fragments.

Flg Off Scrase returned to the squadron after spending a short period with 74 Squadron.

22 OCTOBER

ORB: Six aircraft sweep SE of Rome.

Noticeable that squadron aircraft taking part in sweep flew over Rome for the first time.

The British 8th Army managed to force its way across the Trigno despite the appalling weather. Torrential rain, icy mountain storms, almost impassable mud and the lack of billets, that had been destroyed by the retreating Germans, all combined to lower the morale of the Allied units.

23 OCTOBER

Log Book: Sweep north of area. G/C found my flak battery!

ORB: Twelve aircraft patrol forward area.

26 OCTOBER

Log Book: Patrol army push. Flak-happy Smith collects again.

ORB: Twelve aircraft patrol battle area. Provided aircraft to cover an army attack against a hill north of Volturno. No enemy aircraft were observed but formations of Mitchells and Kittyhawks were seen dive-bombing. It was later learnt that the important hill position had been taken. Whole operation carried out by light and medium bombers with squadron providing escort. No ground artillery in use. One Spit VC piloted by Flg Off Smith was hit in various places by flak though the pilot was unhurt. Damage Cat. 1.

The 5th Army, having managed to get across the Volturno river, had continued their push north towards the Garigliano river from where the valley of the Liri led past Monte Cassino towards Rome. It was this valley that was dominated by almost impregnable mountain peaks, including Cassino itself, which had to be bombed before the army could consider any sort of assault. The patrols changed to bomber escorts of Fortresses, Baltimores and Bostons, sometimes three squadrons at a time, or alterntatively up to nine squadrons of Mustangs or Kittyhawk fighter-bombers against the German mountain positions. Strafing transport north of the line became their role as well though there was not much to see in daylight.

Flying in mountain valleys was exhilarating and dangerous. On more than one occasion inexperienced pilots were lost because they got too close to the hills or the ground. The trick was to concentrate on the strafing rather than the perspective of the hills and mountains, but this invariably led to mistakes from those less-experienced pilots.

It also became clear that chasing Me109s was all right in the Spitfire Vs, which were a match in performance terms, but it was no good trying to catch a Fw190 in a Spitfire V because it would be outrun. The introduction of the Spitfire IX gave them the performance again to compete with the Fw190s.

27–8 OCTOBER

ORB: No flying either day due to bad weather. Squadron was actually released for the day under 324 Wing scheme to give each of the five squadrons in turn a completely free day, i.e. each squadron was to have one day's holiday in five.

Liberty runs were arranged and most of the personnel visited the ancient city of Pompeii or the coastal town of Sorrento. Very much liked the idea of the day off!

29 OCTOBER

ORB: Six aircraft sweep to Rome. Ten Fw190s sighted and attacked. Sqn Ldr Daniel destroyed one Fw190.

30 OCTOBER

ORB: Nine aircraft patrol naval vessels. Nothing seen.

31 OCTOBER

ORB: No operational flying. Noticeable that the exodus from the squadron and the wing had increased due to illness.

Before the end of the campaign almost 60 per cent of squadron personnel would be affected by malaria or jaundice. There were severe cases of worms, they all had fleas and many suffered considerable discomfort. The field hospitals were kept busy.

By the end of October the US 5th Army and English 8th Army held a line running from the Garigliano river in the west, across the Abruzzi mountains, along the course of the Sangro river into the Adriatic. The Western Desert Air Force Wings moved forward to the captured airfields around Foggia and then on to all-weather strips prepared for them by airfield construction units close to the front line. Enemy aircraft were seen less frequently.

For the all-weather strips an ingenious 'runway' was laid down with pierced steel plates (PSP), which were pressed metal sections hinged and fitted together to form a continuous landing surface for aircraft, providing a safe strip for landing no matter how wet and muddy the rest of the airfield became. It was a godsend in the damp Italian winter, and without it many airfields would have been rendered unserviceable.

Squadrons from the US 15th Strategic Air Force also moved into the airfields around Foggia and this extended the range of operations to targets deep into Southern Europe and the Balkans. The industrial areas of Silesia, Czechoslovakia and the oilfields in Romania now came within range of these bombers. With long-range tanks, fighters could also provide escort.

Lloyd Snell recalled:

As we were crowded out by heavies we were moved into a school where we stayed until after Christmas. I remember standing under an archway one night when bombs were falling close. A local set up shop one day, across from the school fixing watches. As mine was not working I gave it to him and watched as he took every piece out, brushed each and put it back together, wound it up and handed it back running.

STALEMATE IN ITALY – NOVEMBER 1943

1 NOVEMBER

ORB: Twelve aircraft – cover P-40s over target G.7314.
Six aircraft – low cover to bombers.

On the morning drive from the Mess to the aerodrome, which was actually located on the edge of the plain above the city near the foot of Mount Vesuvius, the squadron personnel had to drive through literally thousands of Italians all walking out of the city. It looked like one continual stream of people choking the road and making movement nigh on impossible. It appeared to be the same all over town, and the reason for it was because the electricity was due to be switched back on that day. There had been rumours that booby traps and mines were set to go off when the electricity was switched back on, as had happened at Salerno. The rumour and gossip had taken such a hold on the Italians that they decided to evacuate, hence all the people on the roads. The squadron escorted thirty-six Kittyhawk bombers which attacked a road junction near Pontecorvino. During a 20-minute period about 200 Allied aircraft flew over the target.

The German defence line beyond the Volturno was generally referred to by the Allies as the Winter Line and actually consisted of three different lines, each progressively tougher than the first. They had all been prepared by Kesselring.

The first one was called the Barbara Line and was a series of strongpoints designed to hold up the 5th Army advance while defences behind it were strengthened and completed. The line stretched across part of the Italian peninsula from Monte Cassino, 7 miles north of the Volturno in the west, to the Matese mountains in the spine of Italy and to the villages of Teano and Presenzano.

Approximately 10 miles behind the Barbara Line was a much stronger line called the Bernhard Line, which ran from the mouth of the Garigliano river to the Matese mountains, again to the west, where the mountains around Monte La Defensa and Monte Camino formed another natural barrier.

Finally there was the most intensely fortified position known as the Gustav Line, which ran along the Garigliano river where the Gustav and Bernhard Lines were one and the same. Inland, however, the Gustav Line snaked some 12 miles to the rear to Monte Cassino.

The German defence of these lines was made all the easier because there were so few well-defined corridors through which a motorised army could advance. There were only two main roads from Naples to Rome and it was along these, and precipitous mountain tracks, that the 5th Army was obliged to attack. One of the main roads was Highway 6, which passed Monte Cassino and then filtered into the Liri Valley, from where the Allies could deploy their tanks and advance quickly across the remaining 80 or so miles to Rome.

First though, the Barbara Line would have to be taken and the Mignano gap negotiated. Cassino would also have to be taken before a crossing could be made across the Rapido river, a natural barrier that ran across the entrance to the Liri Valley. Knowing full well which route the Allies would have to take, the Germans were able to concentrate their defences using the natural barriers of mountains and rivers that blocked their route.

2 NOVEMBER

ORB: 72 not required so stood down all day.
No organised recreation, most personnel went round the shops in Naples.

All personnel were by now in billets and requisitioned cars were the order of the day to get around. Their new surroundings were the lap of luxury compared to the tented accomodation they had been used to on the landing strips. The aerodrome had been Naples city airport and although there had been several days of consecutive rain, it had not, as yet, been unserviceable. It had a large expanse of grass and surrounding it was the concrete perimeter track. Beyond this track were, on three sides, hangars, office blocks and garages and on the far east side, a wood. The airfield itself was surrounded by houses on all sides. Of the fifteen or so hangars, all but one had been destroyed by either the Allied bombing or the Germans when they had pulled out. Overlooking it was Mount Vesuvius, always smoking, changing colour and at night it appeared to glow red at the summit. The rest of the wing and squadron were scattered about all over Naples, so the squadron was actually more widely dispersed than before. The Officers' Mess was in one part of town, a slummy part, but in two quite pleasant houses, and the wing sick quarters was about a half a mile up the road towards the airfield. Pompeii, Sorrento and the Island of Capri were all within easy reach. At times the airfield seemed crowded with Spits everywhere, Dakotas from the Americans' transport, Austers from the Air Observation Corps and more Spits from the Army Co-op Unit.

The 8th Army launched their push against Tuffilo along an 8-mile front. The village had been bombed and strafed by the Kittyhawks but it had been a difficult target to hit from the air and the attack faltered against the German defences.

3 NOVEMBER

ORB: Ten aircraft fighter sweep Venafro. Squadron was to remain over the target for as long as possible in the hope of intercepting dive-bombers but none were seen.

By dusk on the 3rd there had been little progress against heavy German resistance around Tuffilo, but the 8th Army had managed to cross the river in three places, in front of Celenza near Palmoli and north-east of Montenitro, despite being under continuous shell and mortar fire.

4 NOVEMBER

ORB: Twelve aircraft patrol Migrano-Cassino. Two enemy aircraft encountered over Cassino. Flg Off Smith destroyed one Fw190 and Flt Lt Jupp destroyed one Me109.

They made progress around Tuffilo and there were signs that the Germans intended to withdraw, but isolated machine-gun nests kept the British troops pinned down.

5 NOVEMBER

ORB: Twelve aircraft provided escort to two squadrons of Bostons that proved uneventful. However, later in the day enemy bombers attacked the Naples dock area for more than an hour. One bomb fell about 300yd from the squadron billet.

The last German rearguard had left Tuffilo so the Italians apparently raised the white flag to signify that the village was no longer in German hands; British troops could now enter. The Germans had withdrawn, not because of the assault, but because the Trigno Line, as a line of defence, was no longer sustainable as Allied troops elsewhere had broken out and threatened the German flanks. The US 5th Army had also, by now, reached the Garigliano outside Mignano ready to push through the valley.

6 NOVEMBER

ORB: Twelve aircraft on freelance sweep over Rome. One Spitfire shot up by Me109. Aircraft was Cat. E destroyed. Plt Off McIntosh slightly injured.

Other squadrons on the wing were more successful. 43 'Fighting Cocks' and 111 Squadrons encountered thirty plus Me109s and Fw190s on their morning patrols.

Victories: 43 Squadron Flt Lt Turlington one Me109 destroyed, Flg Off Reid one Me109 destroyed, WO Johnson one Fw190 probable, Flg Off Craig one Me109 damaged.

111 Squadron Flt Sgt Plumridge one Me109 destroyed and Flt Sgt Gray one Me109 probable.

The Americans tried to capture the Mignano gap, the forward position on the German defense known as the Reinhard Line, a stretch of ground about 6 miles long over which the Via Casilina ran through the mountains before reaching the open valley of the Rapido. Despite tough German resistance some progress was made, but by taking advantage of the difficult mountainous terrain the Germans were able to set up a dogged defence on the Garigliano, the strategically important river line between central and southern Italy.

7 NOVEMBER

ORB: No flying all day. It was supposed to be the third release day for the squadron but operational demands meant that one Flight was required on duty all day, though no flying was done.

8 NOVEMBER

ORB: No flying all day. Some of the airmen went again into Naples .If they were prepared to pay on the black market some decent meals could be had, but it did not sit comfortably with many because most of the city's population was starving. It was possible to sit in a restaurant overlooking the bay, watch the fishing boats that had now been allowed out with Vesuvius smoking in the background. Clams, fried octopus, boiled fish and the local delicacy, roast veal with fried potatoes with bags of olive oil and a delicate white wine could be obtained, and then it was possible to dance at local night clubs that the nurses also frequented. By the same token, driving through some parts of Naples remained difficult because of the starving population, dirt and disease. Traffic was sometimes appalling and the streets were crammed with lorries, jeeps, Italian taxis, ambulances, carts, let alone the crowds of people. Shops of luxury goods had been well-stocked when they had first entered the city but were now running out of supplies because of the influx of the military. Nurses and local beauties were regularly entertained!

The 78th Division of the 8th Army reached the Sangro river in the east, but attempts to cross it ended in failure as it remained flooded from the heavy rains.

9 NOVEMBER

ORB: Ten aircraft, shipping patrol, covering minesweepers near the mouth of the Volturno river.

10 NOVEMBER

ORB: Eight aircraft, bomb line patrol. 43 Squadron again encountered Me109s, about twelve in all on their patrol over bomb line as well.
   Victories: Flt Lt Laing Meason one Me109 destroyed, Flt Lt Turlington one Me109 destroyed, Flt Sgt Leighton one Me109 probable, Flg Off Brodie one Me109 damaged.
   The wing said goodbye to 243 Squadron who completed move to 322 Wing in the east of Italy. 324 Wing was reduced to four squadrons 72, 93, 111 and 43.

11 NOVEMBER

ORB: Eight aircraft naval patrol over the mouth of the Volturno river again. Ten aircraft bomb line patrol.
   43 Squadron again encountered nine enemy aircraft with Flt Lt Turlington claiming one Ju88 destroyed.

Six aircraft bomb line patrol.

As it was Armistice Day the squadron had poppies on sale in the Mess and contributed £1.5s 0d to the Earl Haig fund and the Officers' Mess £1.7s 0d.

12 NOVEMBER

ORB: Eight aircraft bomb line patrol.

43 Squadron again came across twenty plus enemy aircraft including Me109s and Fw190s on their patrol.

Victories: WO Hedderwick one Me109 destroyed, Flt Sgt Booth one Me109 destroyed, Flt Sgt Leighton one Me109 destroyed and Flt Sgt Smith one Me109 probable.

Twelve aircraft bomb line patrol 1110–1220.

Twelve aircraft minesweeper patrol 1350–1515.

Flt Lt Arthur Jupp, OC 'A' Flight, was tour-expired and left the squadron on posting to take over 324 Wing Training Flight. Flt Lt Hussey DFM, a former sergeant pilot in the squadron, succeeded him in charge of 'A' Flight.

A vacancy had occurred within 43 Squadron for a Flight Commander. Of all those available Tom Hughes, by reputation, was the obvious choice. No. 43 was a crack squadron led by the Polish ace Sqn Ldr Eugeniusz Horbaczewski, or 'Horby'. Horby became Tom's idol. It did not take him long to work out that Tom had not been allowing enough lead time for the bullets to leave the guns and reach the target and soon his score began to mount. Lloyd Snell recalled:

Horby was liked by everyone on the Flights. At one time we were sleeping under mosquito nets between rows of grapes and Horby bought us a large battery-operated consol radio and we set it up in the vineyard. At night we would listen to the news from the BBC and after that the Forces Program with Vera Lynn.

13 NOVEMBER

ORB: Eight aircraft minesweeper patrol, nine aircraft sweep. Fifteen Fw190s encountered. Flt Sgt Morris one Fw190 destroyed and one damaged.

14 NOVEMBER

ORB: Ten aircraft naval patrol, two aircraft calibration escort, four aircraft bomb line patrol and came across four Me109s.

Victories: Plt Off McLeod one Me109 destroyed, Sqn Ldr Daniel one Me109 destroyed, Flt Sgt Larlee two Me109s destroyed without firing a shot.

Larlee had pursued the aircraft in a dive at terrific speed but had pulled out at about 10,000ft. The two enemy aircraft failed to pull out of their dive and crashed within several yards of each other. The speed of the dive had also damaged Larlee's aircraft causing him to crash on landing when his undercarriage failed to lower, but he was unhurt. The Me109s were reported to have had long-range tanks fitted.

15 NOVEMBER

ORB: Four aircraft bomb line patrol.

Despite a few localised successes, the attempt to push the Germans back from the Reinhard Line was halted by Gen Mark Clark who realised that his troops were on the verge of exhaustion. Rest and refit were required for a renewed attack, but the lull in the fighting also allowed the Germans to strengthen the Gustav Line even further.

16 NOVEMBER

ORB: 72 Squadron stood down – no flying.

17 NOVEMBER

ORB: 72 Squadron stood down – no flying. Flt Lt Tom Hughes posted back to take over 'B' Flight.

18 NOVEMBER

Log Book: 1. Spit IX – coded A. Patrol battle area; 2. Spit V – coded M. Patrol battle area.

ORB: Six aircraft minsweeper patrol over the mouth of the Volturno river, six aircraft minesweeper patrol, four aircraft bomb line patrol.

19 NOVEMBER

Log Book: 1. Spit V – coded J. Patrol nautics.

ORB: Eight aircraft bomb line patrol 0930–1100. Flt Lt Johnston was tour-expired and left the squadron for No. 2 BPD [Base Personnel Depot] to await disposal instructions.

The problem now facing the Allied Chiefs of Staff was the issue of how to get to Rome other than through the mountains. There was a school of thought, which included Gen Eisenhower, that believed an amphibious landing around the German lines to threaten their rear would cause them to abandon their positions south of Rome.

For this landing to have any effect, however, at least one or two divisions would have to be landed and this would require a large number of tank landing craft or LSTs. These were now in short supply as most were scheduled to be withdrawn to England in preparation for the proposed landings in north-west Europe the following year. Any landing would have to be close enough to the battlefront so the landing forces could link up with the troops advancing overland, otherwise they could be pinned down on the beachhead and may be pushed back into the sea.

The plan was for Montgomery's 8th Army to attack along the east coast, break through the defences of the Sangro river and drive north-west to the Winter Line at Pescara and threaten Rome from the east. As the rivers were flooded, roads poor and the German defences strong, this was a tall order.

In the meantime, Clark's 5th Army was to break through the Mignano gap, advance and cross the Rapido river and capture Monte Cassino before driving up the Liri Valley to Frosinone about 50 miles south-east of Rome. When they reached Frosinone, two divisions of the 5th Army would be landed at Anzio, about 35 miles south of Rome, would link up and push towards Rome. It was anticipated that the Germans, fearful that their supply and escape routes could be cut, would retreat beyond Rome.

20 NOVEMBER

ORB: 43 Squadron again encountered Me109s on their morning patrol north of Cassino. Flg Off Reid and WO Hedderwick each claimed one Me109 destroyed and Flg Off James one Me109 damaged. One Spit crashed but pilot was unhurt.

Six aircraft naval patrol, six aircraft minesweeper patrol.

The fresh push by the US 5th Army towards the Rapido river began but progress was extremely slow. A simultaneous attack by the British 8th Army had to be postponed because the Sangro river was still overflowing.

21 NOVEMBER

ORB: 72 Squadron stood down – no flying due to poor weather.

Field Marshal Kesselring was appointed commander of 14th Army Group and took over defence of Italy. Field Marshal Rommel was posted to France to prepare for the expected invasion there.

22 NOVEMBER

Log Book: 1. Spit IX – coded B. Patrol battle area; 2. Spit IX – coded A. Sweep to Rome. Flak!!

ORB: Eight aircraft bomb line patrol, ten aircraft sweep to Rome.

23 NOVEMBER

ORB: 72 Squadron stood down – no flying again due to weather.

24 NOVEMBER

Log Book: 1. Spit IX – coded A. Patrol battle area.

ORB: Twice, eight aircraft were sent out on bomb line patrol, five aircraft bomb line patrol, four aircraft minesweeper patrol.

25 NOVEMBER

ORB: One patrol by 43 Squadron in the morning.

26 NOVEMBER

ORB: Four aircraft minesweeper patrol. 43 Squadron on their morning bomb line patrol reported one Ju88 and this was attacked and shot down with all six pilots in the section claiming a share.

 Five aircraft – sweep to Rome. Seven aircraft bomb line patrol. 111 Squadron came across eight plus Me109s, Flg Off Whitney claimed one probable.

27 NOVEMBER

ORB: Six aircraft patrol south of bomb line.

The British 8th Army began to attack across the Sangro river. This had been postponed from the week before due to the rain and the overflowing river. Very heavy fighting followed and the Germans were again pushed back so that a few bridgeheads over the Sangro were established. Mozzagrogna, the kingpin of the German defensive line, was captured.

28 NOVEMBER

Log Book: 1. Spit IX – coded A. Patrol battle area; 2. Spit V – coded J. Patrol battle area. Felt the Flak!!

ORB: Six aircraft sweep Rome area. Two aircraft Naples patrol, eight aircraft bomb line patrol. 93 Squadron whilst ground strafing targets lost Flg Off Swain as missing when his aircraft hit a tree and he crashed in flames. San Maria and Fossacesia fell to the Allies and the 78th Division continued to advance up the coastal road. Canadians were on hand to relieve them.

29 NOVEMBER

Log Book: 1. Spit IX – coded A. Patrol battle area.

ORB: Eight aircraft bomb line patrol.

30 NOVEMBER

ORB: Two aircraft Naples patrol and several aircraft detailed for convoy patrol had to be recalled because of bad weather.

It is interesting to note that Barney recorded the following in his summary for November 1943:

Aircraft types: 1. Spitfire V – 3.15 hours; 2. Spitfire IX – 8 hours; Total Monthly Ops – 11.15 hours. Total Ops – 174.10 hours. Total Spitfire – 399.05 hours.

Following Barney's promotion to flight lieutenant and OC of 'A' Flight, his log book was signed by Flt Lt Roy Hussey DFM, and then in turn by his squadron leader, S.W.J. Daniel DFC and Bar.

STALEMATE IN ITALY – DECEMBER 1943

1 DECEMBER

Log Book: News of Sarah's birth arrived today so we had a party. Good grief what a shambles!! A wizard show all round.

ORB: Twelve aircraft gave cover to medium bombers over the South Apollinare district. No enemy aircraft or flak reported.

The US 5th Army, after waiting for Monty's drive to pull German troops across to the Adriatic, and to thin the defences at the Mignano Gap, launched their main attack. The initial objectives were to take the rugged mountains at the left of the entrance to the gap: Monte Camino and Monte de la Defensa, hence the cover to the medium bombers.

2 DECEMBER

ORB: Eight aircraft bomb line patrol and a further twelve gave cover to Bostons which bombed Trocchia. Flak positions strafed and two guns were destroyed.

Bari, on the Adriatic coast, was attacked by about 100 German bombers. The city was being used to unload vital supplies for the Allied push and, to help save time, all the lights had been switched on around the harbour area so that work unloading the ships could carry on at night. The attacks lasted only about 20 minutes but no Allied fighters were scrambled and the Germans were able to bomb without opposition. Nineteen transport ships were destroyed and a further seven seriously damaged. There were about 1,000 casualties and the harbour was put out of action for several weeks.

Lloyd Snell recalled:

We had left most of our kit in Africa but around the first of December heard that it had arrived in Bari. A truck was sent to pick it up but he arrived late so waited until the next day. That night there was a raid that sank about nineteen ships so we never did get our kit! We could buy eggs on the street and we would sometimes buy a couple and give them to the cooks to fry for us in the inch or two of grease they had in their large frying pans. We found a shop in Naples where they were making fold-up camp cots and they were reasonably priced so quite a few of us bought them as they kept us off the damp ground.

3 DECEMBER

Log Book: Attempted patrol, weather u/s.

ORB: Bad weather meant bomb line patrol aircraft were recalled.

4 DECEMBER

ORB: No operational flying due to weather.

5 DECEMBER

ORB: No operational flying due to weather and notice received that kit in transit had been destroyed after the attacks on Bari three nights before.
  US 5th Army managed to take the strategic summit of Monte Camino.

6 DECEMBER

ORB: No operational flying due to weather.

7 DECEMBER

Log Book: Escort bombers north of Rome. Wizard bombing by Mitchells.

ORB: Ten aircraft bomber escort to Civitavecchia where the Mitchells bombed with excellent results.

8 DECEMBER

Log Book: Delouse bomb area. Flak!!!!

ORB: Major A.C. Bosman DFC, a South African, was posted supernumerary to the squadron with a view to his taking over from Sqn Ldr Daniel DFC and Bar, who is tour-expired. WO Turglon, a French Canadian, also posted in for flying duties.

Eight aircraft bomb line patrol. Twelve aircraft over Frosinone escorted Mustangs which bombed the town.

German defence now centred around the Gustav Line, the heights on either side of the Liri river and behind the Rapido and Garigliano. US artillery was within range of Monte Cassino. Radio brought news of the declarations following the conference between Roosevelt, Churchill and Stalin at Tehran.

9 DECEMBER

Log Book: Strafing Rome area. Good results. Jack and Tom missing. No Reason (came back to squadron May 1944!!).

ORB: Flt Lt Pearson and WO Larlee both posted missing after an armed sweep over the Rome area in the afternoon. Flt Lt Pearson was last seen going down to strafe enemy motor transport and WO Tom Larlee called up on the radio transmitter when 12–15 miles south of Rome saying that he had engine trouble and would have to bale out, but he was not seen by the rest of the squadron.

(Although Larlee was reported missing, Barney later wrote in his Log Book that he evaded capture and returned to the unit on 26 May 1944.)

ORB: Six aircraft escorted Mustangs bombing Civitavecchia and a further six patrolled the bomb line.

10 DECEMBER

Log Book: Bomb line patrol. Transferred to 'B' Flight.

ORB: Eight aircraft patrolled bomb line in bad weather and on their return WO Turglon had to crash-land his Spitfire VC near Garigliano. Crash-landing was exceptionally good, the pilot miraculously put his aircraft down in a small clearing in an apple orchard. The apple orchard sorters were obviously very shaken as they gave Sqn Ldr Daniel a large quantity of their best apples when he went to collect his pilot!

11 DECEMBER

Log Book: Bomb line patrol. Found twelve 190s but my caution stopped clobber. Poor!

ORB: Two aircraft on a bomb line patrol at first light. Six aircraft later escorted Mustangs to Ostia but due to poor visibility no bombs were dropped.

12 DECEMBER

Log Book: Escort Mustangs. NW Rome but weather duff.

ORB: Weather again poor but six aircraft flew as bomber escort north of Rome, uneventful.

---

13 DECEMBER

Log Book: Bomb line patrol.

ORB: Six aircraft sweep over Rome. Eight aircraft bomb line patrol, both uneventful.

---

14 DECEMBER

ORB: Escort to Mitchells dropping leaflets over Ceccano.

---

15 DECEMBER

ORB: Escort Bostons on two bomb line patrols.

---

16 DECEMBER

Log Book: Bomb line patrol.

ORB: Ten aircraft bomb line patrol and escorted Bostons in the afternoon.

---

17 DECEMBER

Log Book: Attempted escort. Returned generator u/s.

ORB: Escort Mustangs to Civitavecchia and patrol over Pontecorno. Sweep over Orte but aircraft again recalled due to bad weather.

---

18 DECEMBER

Log Book: Escort Mustangs. Tom [Hughes] missing. Pretty bloody! POW. Later air test. Search for Tom, no bloody good.

ORB: Sadly marked by the loss of Flt Lt Hughes posted missing who turned back from an escort mission when he was near Capua. Called up on radio transmitter 'that he was going back to see the controller' but was not seen again.

Tom Hughes recalled the incident years later in correspondence:

We were flying together over the Bay of Naples on 17 December when I suspected that I had engine trouble with my Spitfire IX. As I was leading the flight and we were waiting for some American bombers, who were late, I handed over to 'Barney' and dived back towards Naples airport. The Merlin engine immediately picked up as I got down to 2,000ft and I thought I would have a look at the great battle which was raging at Monte Cassino. I flew very low and very fast around the ruined monastery and engaged a flak gun in a duel! I was hit. My engine stopped, my trousers were alight and I crashed into a hillside! I woke up on the operating table of a German field hospital.

Tom had said something pretty strange to Barney before their flight as they were walking out to their aircraft, so strange that Barney recalled the conversation to the intelligence officer when Tom failed to return. He had said to him, 'Look, if I don't come back, you'll take over won't you?' Of course Barney just acknowledged him, but they seemed to be prophetic words.

ORB: Later eleven aircraft patrolled the bomb line without incident.

19 DECEMBER

Log Book: Scramble. Phooey!!

ORB: Squadron provided bomber escort to Arce. Seven went up, all Spitfire Vs, one extra by mistake, and there then appeared to be a mad panic to find more pilots because there was a further sweep due to take off later that morning. Plt Off McLeod destroyed a Fw190, Flt Sgt Coles a Me109G and Flt Sgt Connolly another Me109G as well. On later afternoon bomb line patrol, Flt Lt Hussey DFM destroyed a further Fw190 and Sgt Pullen damaged a Me109.
   Unfortunately, Flt Sgt Bouchier was hit by flak when chasing a Me109 and it was believed that his aircraft crashed south of Ceccano, well behind enemy lines. Major A.C. Bosman assumed command of the squadron today.

20 DECEMBER

Log Book: Attempted patrol. Weather duff. Back to 'A' Flight.

ORB: Squadron patrolled bomb line twice but weather again was poor so the second patrol was recalled. Flt Sgt Wood was posted from 324 Wing Training Flight for flying duties.

21 DECEMBER

ORB: Squadron armed sweep. Bomb line patrol and one bomber escort over Ortona.
   Canadian 1st Division began assault on Ortona, a small port on the Adriatic coast. Lots of fighter-bombers, twelve Baltimores and twelve Bostons were up, with the mountains visible all day, the first day with decent visibility for a while.

22 DECEMBER

ORB: No operational flying. Bad weather meant recall from only patrol.

24 DECEMBER

ORB: No operational flying. Squadron released at 1200 – Let Xmas begin! Sqn Ldr Daniel DFC and Bar left the squadron with their best wishes for the future.

25 DECEMBER

ORB: One bomb line patrol on Xmas day. Flt Sgt Weller was hit by flak over enemy lines and had to bale out but a kindly wind blew him just within our lines, where he was sheltered by Italians and later brought back to the base by Americans just in time for Xmas dinner. Xmas dinner was a tremendous success. The officers and NCOs waited upon the airmen, who had food such that one could not wish to better at home in the most prosperous days. A concert held in the airmen's dining hall after dinner was a fitting end to the day.

26 DECEMBER

ORB: No operational flying due to bad weather which got worse and worse. Cold, windy and lots of rain.

27 DECEMBER

Log Book: Bomb line patrol.

ORB: Two bomb line patrols.

Ortona was captured by the Canadians after fierce fighting but the 8th Army was forced to a halt. It snowed and rained almost ceaselessly and the roads had turned into a quagmire making transportation impossible. While Monty had managed to cross the Sangro river, his plan to push on to Chieta and then to Rome was hampered by a determined and dug-in enemy. Weather that detained tanks and transport made supply impossible and grounded the RAF, or at least made them ineffective in their bombing and ground support roles. For the army, with trucks bogged down and supplies difficult, morale was at an all-time low. Clothes became encrusted with mud and tent areas were surrounded by water. Men rarely washed because it was so cold and most of what food they were able to get was canned and dreary. Also, the small iron stoves used for heat had a tendency to blow up!

28 DECEMBER

Log Book: Bomb line patrol.

ORB: Air Vice-Marshal Broadhurst DSO, DFC, AFC gave an interesting talk to the pilots at dispersal this afternoon. Squadron patrolled bomb line in the morning and in the afternoon deloused the Rome area for the Mitchells to bomb.

29 DECEMBER

ORB: No operational flying due to bad weather.

30 DECEMBER

Log Book: Bomb line patrol. Found eight 190s bombing. Roy damaged one. Oh for a Mark IX!
   Bomb line patrol. Returned u/s.

ORB: Squadron patrolled the bomb line three times and on the second eight Fw190s were seen near the Gulf of Gaeta. Flt Lt Hussey managed to damage one.

31 DECEMBER

ORB: Covered Frosinone in very poor weather. New Year's Eve – a happy time had by all.

Gen Montgomery did not have the strength to force his way through to Pescara and on to Rome through the winter, so he advised Gen Alexander to halt the 8th Army offensive amid almost incessant rain and snow. Meanwhile, news filtered through that Monty had left Italy to assume command of troops in England for the preparation of the invasion of France under the codename Overlord.

   The US 5th Army assault on the Bernhard Line towards Cassino now included plans of a seaborne assault by at least one division at Anzio, about 25 miles south of Rome. This meant the retention of vital landing craft that had been earmarked for the proposed invasion in Normandy and southern France. These landing craft were in short supply but the planned offensive near Anzio was considered vital because it would cut the German lines of communication and threaten the rear of the crack German 14th Division.

CHAPTER 10

The Landings at Anzio

The Anzio landings soon developed into a major operation planned as a giant pincer movement. The invasion itself would be preceded by a strong feint attack against Pescara on the Adriatic coast while, at the same time, the US 5th Army would launch a series of attacks along the Rapido and Garigliano rivers in an attempt to pierce the Gustav Line and break into the Liri Valley. The amphibious landings at Anzio would follow this about ten days later. Their aim was to force two fronts against the Germans and threaten their supply lines and route of retreat. The beaches chosen for the landings seemed ideal. The harbour at Anzio, although not large, was suitable for putting further troops ashore and was reasonably well protected by a mole.

About an hour's drive from Rome, on the western Italian coastline, lie the towns of Anzio and Nettuno with their long fine white-sand beaches, famous for bathing pre-war. About 10 miles north lies the Moletta river and man-made Mussolini canal, and about 20 miles inland are the vineyard-covered Alban Hills which rise to about 3,000ft from the plains. The two main routes into Rome, the historic Appian Way, otherwise known as Highway 7, and the Via Cailina or Highway 6, that bisect the Alban Hills, were the key strategic approaches.

---

1 JANUARY 1944

ORB: No operational flying and in view of the bad weather squadron stayed in billets. New Year celebrated in a quiet and sober fashion.

The weather the previous day meant the mountains were covered in a thick blanket of snow with most road communications cut. A gale blew and there was now driving rain and further freezing conditions.

Lloyd Snell recalled:

New Years Day 1944 and we were in tents north-west of Naples, less than a mile from the Mediterranean. We were close enough to Naples to see ack-ack when they were bombed and see the smoke from Vesuvius when it erupted a little later. We could also hear the artillery at Cassino. We had a marquee for a dining tent and we had eight-man tents rather than our pup tents. We had a kerosene stove in our tent workshop, the wireless personnel were in three different tents so we could take turns using the stove in our sleeping tents, each tent getting it every third night. The other nights we would use a charcoal burner that was actually a two-gallon tin punched full of holes with a long wire handle. The charcoal we made during the day. Some large trees had been bulldozed down so we would start a fire with the drier wood and any that had been charred through we would rake out and extinguish. The charcoal warmed us twice, once when we made it and then at night. There must have been a party somewhere. We had turned in when we heard a couple singing, a little the worse for wear, and so we pretended to be asleep so that they would leave us alone. No such luck, they piled into the tent and were joined by a couple of others also singing. They seemed to stay for ages but it wasn't until the guy next to me suddenly jumped up, put a magazine in his Sten gun and shouted 'I'll get rid of these buggers' and pulled the bolt back that they left for a more appreciative audience!

2 JANUARY

Log Book: Bomb line patrol. Saw 43 collect – pretty bloody.

ORB: Twelve aircraft patrolled the bomb line without any incident apart from the intense flak.

The reference to '43 collect' was in relation to their sister squadron on the wing being able to exchange all their Spitfire Vs for the newer Mark IXs. This meant that they no longer needed the Mark Vs to fly at low altitude with the Mark IXs flying as top cover high above them. However, just before the change, two of 43 Squadron's Mark IXs were lost when they collided as they came into land. Dickie Brodie was unfortunately killed in the accident.

3 JANUARY

Log Book: 1. Bomb line patrol; 2. Escort Mitchells – Nickelling.

ORB: There were two shows of twelve aircraft patrolling the bomb line without incident. Major A.C. Bosman DFC posted to the squadron from No. 7 SAAF Wing as Wingco Flying. Flt Lt John M.V. Carpenter DFC and Bar assumed command with Major A.C. Bosman.

'Chips' Carpenter had been one of the few survivors of the ill-fated Norwegian campaign when outdated Gladiators had been sent to try and fend off the Luftwaffe. He had also flown during the Battle of Britain but had been shot down and badly wounded. Having recovered he had then been posted to Malta and flown there from HMS *Ark Royal* back in 1941 and joined 126 Squadron. After six months of intensive operations he had been awarded the DFC for 'consistently showing great courage and fighting spirit'. After a period instructing fighter pilots in South Africa he had returned to operations with the Western Desert Air Force with Spitfires on 145 and 92 Squadrons before his promotion to squadron leader. Barney recalled he had a wicked sense of humour, and a light-hearted approach to most things. He was extremely popular.

It was noticeable that something was afoot in respect of the plans for the landings at Anzio. The squadron operations largely consisted of escort missions to bombers that pounded the communications, military installations and airfields north and south of Rome. These operations were typical of the build-up to a land offensive and were designed to soften up the targeted area for the prospective battleground. In between there were still fighter sweeps to try and lure the Luftwaffe into the air and standing patrols over the army's forward positions.

4 JANUARY

Log Book: Escort Mitchells but weather duff.

ORB: Twelve aircraft were employed delousing the Frosinone area. Flt Lt Graham J. Cox DFC was posted to the squadron from 111 Squadron for flying duties.

5 JANUARY

ORB: No operational flying. US 5th Army made another push on the approaches to the Gustav Line.

6 JANUARY

Log Book: Bomb line patrol, had a look at Rome.

ORB: Two patrols of twelve aircraft over the bomb line. Flt Lt J.A. Gray was posted to the squadron for flying duties.

7 JANUARY

Log Book: 1. Bomb line patrol. Two recce 190s went past!!! 2. Bomb line patrol. New IXs arrived so once again we're all IXs.

ORB: Weather recce by two Mark IXs during the morning and there were two bomb line patrols of eleven aircraft each.

8 JANUARY

Log Book: Bomb line patrol.

ORB: One bomber escort of six aircraft with a further twelve from 43 Squadron and one bomb line patrol of eight aircraft.

9 JANUARY

ORB: No operations. Sgt Piper and Flt Sgt Clarkson were this day posted OTE [Operationally Tour Expired] to No. 2 Base Personnel Depot. Flg Off J. Howarth RCAF was posted to the squadron.

Again torrential rain did its worst playing havoc with operations and morale and the gloom was deepened by the departure of squadron stalwarts such as Piper and Clarkson.

10 JANUARY

ORB: No operational flying. News that the squadron, along with 43 Squadron, was to move to Lago airfield and into tents. With the rain and the weather bitterly cold and the enemy about 12 miles away this was not an exciting prospect. The Italian name for Lake was Lago - it was to be an apt description.

11 JANUARY

Log Book: 1. Weather recce, my new kite, very nice; 2. Bomb line patrol.

ORB: Weather recce by two aircraft during the morning and there were two bomb line patrols of twelve aircraft each.

12 JANUARY

Log Book: Delousing bomb area.

ORB: There were twelve aircraft which engaged in delousing Arce area. Leave for aircrew personnel was introduced to the squadron today. One medium bomber was seen to break into two pieces after being hit by flak.

In atrocious conditions of blinding snow and freezing slashing rain, units of the French Expeditionary Corps broke through the Gustav Line and reached Sant Elia, occupying Monte Santa Groce. US troops had also taken Monte Trocchia by storming it so the Allied forces were now along the entire length of the Gustav Line. Artillery began to shell the monastery at Cassino and forward troops reached the Rapido river.

13 JANUARY

Log Book: Bomb line patrol but 'J' misbehaving.

ORB: Twelve aircraft patrolled the bomb line and eleven aircraft gave area cover over the south of Rome. News received today of the following awards. A DFC to Flt Lt Roy Hussey DFM, and DFMs to Flt Sgt Keith Clarkson and Flg Off K. Smith.

14 JANUARY

Log Book: Bomb line patrol.

ORB: Two bomb line patrols of two aircraft and one bomb line patrol of ten aircraft were operations for the day. News received of the pending movement of the squadron from Naples Capodichino aerodrome to Lago airfield.

15 JANUARY

ORB: Weather recce by two IXs in the morning. One bomb line patrol of ten aircraft and an area cover over the south of Rome by eight aircraft with 90-gallon tanks. 'A' Party moved from Naples to Lago.

'Capo' – as pilots and squadron personnel regularly called Capodichino – had become their home but they were on the move to allow the build-up of further Allied aircraft in the preparations for Anzio. They were to be replaced by the USAAF's 79th Fighter Group with their P-40 Warhawks, but Capo was also crowded with the Bostons of a medium bomber group, another P-40 outfit, three squadrons of B-25s, an air transport section and an air-sea rescue unit. The US II Corps took Monte Trocchia in the centre of the Gustav Line and were pushing up to the Rapido river.

16 JANUARY

ORB: A bomb line patrol of two aircraft and two bomb line patrols of six aircraft were carried out today. 'B' Party moved to Lago today. Flg Off Smith was posted OTE to No. 2 Base Personnel Depot.

17 JANUARY

Log Book: Naples patrol. New strip. Quite pleasant.

ORB: Six aircraft with six aircraft from 43 Squadron and six from 111 Squadron gave area cover over the north of Rome with 90-gallon tanks attached. Two patrols of two aircraft at high altitude were operated over the Gaeta and four aircraft patrolled over Naples harbour.

Lago airfield was a little wooded island strip along the north bank of the Volturno river, by the sea. Barney's comments did not do the conditions justice, which in reality were quite shocking. With water and mud everywhere, the conditions could only be described as miserable for all. One joker repainted the famous cock of the 'fighting cocks' on the 43 Squadron motto with a duck outside their Flight office.

The British X Corps attacked across the rain-swollen Garigliano to capture the town of Minturno on the extreme left flank of the Gustav Line.

18 JANUARY

Log Book: Escort Mitchells Terni.

ORB: Seven aircraft patrolled the Terni area. Two IXs and four IXs of 43 Squadron patrolled Gaeta at high altitude. Eight IXs patrolled the bomb line and two IXs patrolled the Gaeta area at high altitude later in the afternoon.

19 JANUARY

Log Book: 1. Delouse for bombers north of Rome; 2. Air test – OK.

ORB: One bomb line patrol of seven aircraft and one patrol over Gaeta consisting of two aircraft and nine aircraft were employed delousing the north of Rome. Eight aircraft escorted Bostons to Collefero.

20 JANUARY

Log Book: 1. Escort Bostons Formia; 2. Bomb line patrol.

ORB: Four IXs and six from 93 Squadron and six from 111 Squadron escorted Bostons to Mount Scauri. Two IXs patrolled Gaeta at 25,000ft and eight IXs escorted Mitchells to Viterbo. Four South African pilots were posted to the squadron and these were ex-324 Wing Training Flight Lt J. Franks, Lt P.J. Van Schalkwyk, Lt J.M. Jackson and Lt S.V. Richardson.

21 JANUARY

Log Book: Convoy patrol. Landings south of Rome. Anzio and Co. More to come?

ORB: There was one bomb line patrol of eight aircraft and three convoy patrols. Two of four and one of three aircraft and two high-altitude patrols.

A disastrous dress rehearsal for the landings wasted men and materials, but there was no time for further practice. That night the invasion convoys sailed out from Naples harbour en route for the landing beaches at Anzio.

22 JANUARY

ORB: Despite the rain and mud the squadrons had to cover the Anzio landings. The squadron was detailed to escort Bostons to Pondi with four aircraft and Velletu with nine aircraft.

Codenamed Operation Shingle, the Anzio landings began under cover of darkness, with the 6th US Corps consisting of the 3rd US and 1st British Divisions. The plan also included standing patrols over the beachhead from dawn until dusk. Intelligence reckoned that there could be at least 300 German fighters within striking distance of the beachhead, so standing patrols of Spitfires and Warhawks were kept over the beaches and approaches. Spitfires from 244 Wing and the USAAF's 31st Fighter Group patrolled between 12,000 and 25,000ft while the Warhawks cruised at lower altitudes, but it was not until the afternoon that the Luftwaffe reacted to the presence of the Allied invasion force.

The spectacle of the invasion forces was awesome, hundreds of ships with barrage balloons above them, countless landing craft plying back and forth, everywhere troops, vehicles, bulldozers, artillery, and tanks – and, overhead, protected by the RAF and USAAF.

Over the beachhead, Gp Capt Duncan Smith (Smithy) leading the squadron spotted about six Me109s at about the same height flying in a long line astern formation. Before he could get the squadron into a good attacking position, the Me109s avoided combat by rolling on their backs and diving inland. Other squadrons had better luck. No. 43 Squadron in the morning flew a twelve-ship escort to B-25s returning from their target. They came across about twenty Me109s and one was destroyed by Plt Off T.E. Johnson. The CO of 324 Wing, Wg Cdr M.J. Loudon also claimed a Me109 damaged, and Flg Off R.W. James damaged another. However, the action was not without loss as they lost Flg Off P.J. Richards during the engagement. The USAAF's 79th Fighter Group Warhawks were even more successful, accounting for six Fw190s over the beaches when the Luftwaffe had ventured out. The Spitfire pilots, generally at higher altitude, came across little action and a common view was that they were being made to fly too high for effective interception and would never have any joy, especially as it seemed that the Luftwaffe usually ran in from the sea at about 12,000ft, delivered their dive-bombing attacks and escaped inland at low level.

The landings appeared to have caught the enemy completely by surprise. Almost inconceivably the invasion ships had sailed into the Anzio area undetected. It appeared that the German radar had failed at a critical moment. The bombing of Perugia on the 19th had taken out the German long-range reconnaissance aircraft on the ground while Allied air superiority over German aerodromes on D-Day rendered the rest of the Luftwaffe ineffective. By nightfall on the first day, VI Corps had about 3,000 vehicles and most of the assault force ashore. It had gone almost too well. While every effort had been made to keep the actual landing point secret, the plans allowed for some resistance and to dig in, allowing the beachhead to be consolidated in anticipation of a German counter-attack from the hills. Caught off guard by the lack of resistance, the plan was not revised and they dug in anyway. With hindsight, if they had pushed on, the route to Rome was actually wide open.

---

23 JANUARY

ORB: Squadron patrols over Anzio beaches. There were four patrols over the beaches, two of ten aircraft and two of eight aircraft.

For a typical mission, an RAF pilot was now dressed in helmet and goggles, oxygen mask, gloves, shirt, sweater, trousers and jacket (for protection against fire as well as the cold), and he was advised to wear boots that he would be able to walk in, should he have to bale out. A Mae West with a fluorescent dye marker was worn over the jacket and he sat on a parachute pack that contained a dinghy, paddle, water bottle, emergency rations for three days, a first-aid kit with morphine and either a flare pistol or smoke grenade.

24 JANUARY

ORB: Eight aircraft patrolled the Shingles beaches and later, ten aircraft patrolled the beaches when four Fw190s were seen to dive-bomb the convoy without effect. Flt Lt Hussey and Flg Off King between them destroyed one of them.

25 JANUARY

ORB: One bomber escort of twelve aircraft today.

The US 34th Division succeeded in getting across the Rapido river with strong artillery support, but had to retreat after robust German counter-attacks because the Americans had no tanks supporting them. The Scottish and Irish battalions of the British 24th Guards Brigade were beaten back as they attacked Campoleone on the road to Rome and their HQ staff were captured. A landing ground had been made in the beachhead at Nettuno for emergency landings and the use of casualty evacuation and communications aircraft.

26 JANUARY

ORB: No operational flying.

Attacks continued on the ground in the Cassino sector but with limited success. The Tunisian 2nd Battalion captured Colle Abate and closed in on Terelle, but was running short of ammunition and had its supply lines cut by a counter-attack by German Panzer Grenadiers. Fierce hand-to-hand fighting was the order of the day.

27 JANUARY

Log Book: 1. Cover beaches; 2. Cover beaches – squadron got four today but nothing seen on either trip.

ORB: There were four patrols over the beaches, two of ten aircraft and one of seven aircraft and the last of eight aircraft. On the third patrol, enemy aircraft were intercepted at the beaches area. Led again by Gp Capt Smith, the mixed formation consisted of Me109s and Fw190s with the 109s stepped above.

Smithy turned behind one, opened fire and saw strikes on the Me109's wing root and it started streaming smoke. Smithy followed him down but was then engaged by another Me109 at about 10,000ft and he had to break off. The rest of the squadron was completely split up and it was everyone for himself. On landing it became apparent that Plt Off McLeod had destroyed one Me109, Flg Off Ingalls had destroyed one Fw190 and Sgt Leach had destroyed a further Me109 and, with WO Turgeon, damaged a further Fw190.

On the ground the build-up of the beachhead continued. VI Corps had swelled to the equivalent of four divisions of 70,000 men. The plan was after an extensive naval, artillery and air force preparation, the British 1st Division would push down the Albano road towards Highway 7 and the US 3rd Division would advance on Cisterna, cut Highway 7 and then circle the southern edge of the Alban Hills towards Valmontone. However, the attacks on Cisterna and Campoleone were driven back by German reinforcements, and the bridgehead was coming under fire from German railguns which also zeroed in on the captured harbour of Nettuno which the Allies were using.

28 JANUARY

Log Book: Cover north of beaches.

ORB: There was one bomber escort of eight aircraft sweep over the north of Rome led by the Group Captain with nine aircraft, and a beaches patrol with six aircraft. Between Anzio and Nettuno, an area of ground about 15 miles wide had been gained.

29 JANUARY

Log Book: Cover beaches.

ORB: Two beaches patrols with ten aircraft each were operations today.

US engineers on the ground had constructed tank roads on the approaches to Cassino so that stronger armoured forces could advance. The Luftwaffe attacked Anzio itself and sank the British anti-aircraft cruiser *Spartan* and damaged the freighter *Samuel Huntingdon*, which exploded the following morning after fire reached its cargo of ammunition and fuel.

30 JANUARY

Log Book: Attempted patrol but weather u/s.

ORB: Two aircraft provided high cover for the beaches.

The push from the beachhead began. The US 3rd Division was cut to pieces and had very few survivors after trying to get to Cisterna. The British 1st Division and

US 1st Armoured Division had also attacked towards Albano but came to a halt in marshy ground near Campoleone. With the armour stalled and bogged down, the British flank was exposed, so the advance was halted and they went on the defensive again. There was still no link between the US VI Corps which had landed at Anzio and the US 5th Army fighting outside Cassino, but a pause was needed before a full-scale assault could begin and they dug in, preparing for the expected German counter-attack.

---
31 JANUARY

Log Book: Another 30 hours on operations for the month.

ORB: One bomber escort with twelve aircraft.

ITALY, LAGO AIRFIELD – FEBRUARY 1944

---
1 FEBRUARY

ORB: Weather recce was carried out by two aircraft over the Anzio sector. Twelve aircraft patrolled the Anzio beaches at high and medium altitudes and later in the day four aircraft patrolled a convoy approaching Anzio.

Weather was very bad. General House had originally intended to base a large number of fighters close to the beachhead perimeter immediately after the landings. A shortage of shipping, the confinement of the beachhead itself and the proximity of the fighters available to him from Naples – about 15 minutes flying time – curtailed his initial plans. A squadron of the 31st Fighter Group Spitfires provided spot cover from a strip at Nettuno near the beachhead, but the strip almost immediately became a target for German artillery as it was within easy range. The runway was very short but planes were regularly lost due to the shelling and landing or take-off accidents. It would become familiar to 72 Squadron later in the month.

On the ground the invasion force had been increased to about 70,000 troops, but about five German divisions had sealed off the Anzio–Nettuno beachhead, though they were of course without air superiority. In thick fog at daybreak the 34th Division started an attack from Cairo north of Cassino towards Monte Calverio, with further pushes towards Monte Castellone and Sant'Angelo in Colle.

---
2 FEBRUARY

ORB: Patrol carried out by eight aircraft over the beaches. Two Fw190s were observed but no contact was made. A patrol of eleven aircraft gave medium and high cover over the beaches and a further patrol of eight aircraft were over the beaches again when two Me109s broke cloud at 3,500ft about 5 miles offshore of Anzio. They were too far away for our aircraft to make contact.

Four members of Ralph Reader's 'Gang Show' put on a show in the Airmen's Mess.

Meanwhile, in thick fog, the ground troops pushed on to within 2 miles of Highway 6 and the Via Casilina, and the Americans were on the outskirts of Cassino itself, although they were coming up against stiff German resistance in the form of crack paratroops.

3 FEBRUARY

ORB: Ten aircraft fitted with 90-gallon tanks were detailed from 43 Squadron to R/V with 36 Marauders over Civitavecchia. The Marauders did not R/V, probably because of the cloudy weather conditions. One Marauder [was] seen to ditch at F.2545. Our aircraft gave mayday on Channel D and one of our aircraft landed at Nettuno to give further details.

Gp Capt Duncan Smith DSO, DFC, Officer Commanding 324 Wing, visited the squadron to make an appeal for contributions on behalf of the Battle of Britain Memorial to be erected at Westminster Abbey.

The Germans also started their expected counter-attack at Nettuno. German railguns, nicknamed 'the Anzio Express' by troops, opened fire on the harbour at Anzio, and the transport ships and the landing beaches became targets for the German artillery.

4 FEBRUARY

ORB: No operational flying.

On the ground, the newly formed New Zealand XI Corps under Lt Gen Freyberg, with the British 78th Division attached to it, was to take advantage of the expected US breakthrough by capturing Cassino and the monastery, pushing on up the Liri Valley and cutting Highway 6 to stem the German retreat. There was heavy fighting around Cassino itself.

5 FEBRUARY

ORB: Two patrols were carried out of eight aircraft each over the Anzio beaches and Sgt Pullen force-landed at Nettuno with temporary engine trouble. Pilot and aircraft returned to base OK.

No. 43 Squadron were also over the Anzio beachhead that day. Returning from their first mission of the day they apparently shot up a suspected ammunition dump north of Gaeta but encountered heavy flak, and Flt Sgt H.A. Booth was hit. He managed to limp to the coast where he baled out near the Dutch gunboat *Flores*, but by the time the crew were able to pull him from the water he had died. An Aussie, WO C.S. Luke, was also hit by the heavy flak and killed instantly.

6 FEBRUARY

ORB: Twelve aircraft flew to a point 20 miles SE of Civitavecchia to escort Marauders flying west after bombing Orte. R/V was successfully made and our aircraft returned to base after escorting the bombers 30 miles west of Rome without incident.

German ground troops were still holding out on the high ground around Via Casilina and Monte Calvario, but once these were taken the US troops would be able to control Cassino.

7 FEBRUARY

ORB: Patrol of eight aircraft carried out over the beaches. Some bogies reported but no interceptions made, though it became clear that the lower flying Warhawks of the Yank 79th Fighter Group had better luck.

The Fw190s were set upon and one, in an attempt to gain altitude, jettisoned his bombs that unfortunately fell on the 95th Evacuation Hospital killing about thirty patients and seriously wounding another sixty-four. Further successes followed for the 79th Fighter Group; by the end of the day seventeen enemy fighters had been destroyed with a further twelve probables, while the anti-aircraft gunners claimed another seven.

The German raids were still causing considerable damage and destruction, so plans were made to launch retaliatory air strikes by B-24s on the German airfields including attacks against Viterbo, Tarquinia and Orvieto. A patrol of six aircraft, with six from 43 Squadron and six from 111 Squadron, escorted Mitchells to Viterbo. Twenty plus enemy aircraft were encountered, some of which were Fw190s with long noses seen north of Rome. One solitary Fw190 was seen and destroyed by Flg Off Ingalls and Sgt Pullen, but no bombs were seen dropped by the Mitchells. Despite this, the attacks must have been effective because enemy air activity was considerably reduced over the next few days. German counter-attacks reclaimed Monte Calvario and this strategic hill was to change sides again and then remain in German hands until May 1944.

8 FEBRUARY

ORB: Better weather so today three patrols over the beaches were carried out by eight aircraft, and one bomber escort by two aircraft with six from 111 Squadron. R/V with Marauders at Hadispoli. Bombers escorted 50 miles out to sea without incident. Missions appeared to be split between area patrols, covering the fighter bombers strafing German transport, bombers attacking bridges and communication links and C-47s carrying VIPs.

9 FEBRUARY

ORB: Twelve aircraft escorted thirty-six Bostons to F.8137, and this was the only detail for the day. No bombs were seen to drop. News received today that 1387675 Sgt J.B.

King, who had been reported missing on the 12/7/43 and later re-classified as a POW, was now safe in neutral territory.

10 FEBRUARY

ORB: Two beaches patrols were carried out and were flown without intercepting enemy aircraft.

Two US Liberators, who had been flying in company with our aircraft for some 5 minutes or more, then unobligingly fired on the squadron, fortunately without scoring any hits.

The weather had started to deteriorate again and the pilots had to dodge snow and rainsqualls between Lake Albano and the coast. Further German counter-attacks were launched around the beachhead because Kesselring's aim was to seal the beachhead and prevent the Allies from breaking out.

11 FEBRUARY

ORB: No operational flying.

The Americans tried to capture Monte Calvario and Cassino by frontal assaults. In already appalling conditions, a severe blizzard blew up preventing artillery from correctly shelling intended targets and grounding any potential air support. The American troops were decimated by German paratroops who were dug-in on the slopes.

By the evening, when the US XI Corps gave up the fight for Cassino, not only had they suffered huge losses, but those troops who remained were absolutely exhausted. They were to be replaced by Freyberg's New Zealand XI Corps and the 4th Indian Division including the famous Gurkhas. It was to be Freyberg who asked for the monastery at Cassino to be bombed and destroyed, convinced that it was being used to help German artillery accurately shell Allied troops, and this would then assist the second attempt to capture the strategically important site.

12 FEBRUARY

ORB: Two beach patrols, one of nine aircraft and one of seven aircraft. A smoke screen was reported over the railway station at F.8738 and a big explosion seen at Fondi.

13 FEBRUARY

ORB: During the first beach patrol of the day ten Fw190s were contacted, and as a result of the combat WO Morris destroyed one and damaged two more. He had attacked five in all. A further Fw190 was damaged by Plt Off McLeod. Three further patrols were carried out, two of eight aircraft and one of nine aircraft, but both were uneventful.

14 FEBRUARY

ORB: There were four beach patrols today, two each of eight aircraft and two of nine aircraft. The first three were uneventful but the last patrol provided combat with six Fw190s and their top cover of Me109s. Flg Off Scrase destroyed one Me109 and Sgt Leach and Flt Sgt Coles each damaged one Me109 apiece.

15 FEBRUARY

ORB: Two beach patrols by ten aircraft and eight aircraft were duties for today. Shell bursts were seen over the railway station at F.8739 and flak was reported in the area.

By now the wing kept a squadron at Nettuno, the emergency landing ground on the Anzio beachhead, so that standing patrols could be kept up right until dusk and again at dawn the following morning. The squadrons were rotated each day but the ground crews were left there for up to two weeks before being replaced. Conditions were pretty grim: pilots and ground crew had to sleep and eat in dugouts due to the landing ground being regularly shelled by the German guns, which also were dug into the hillsides overlooking the beachhead.

Lloyd Snell with 43 Squadron recalled:

About the middle of Feb we moved up to Nettuno, part of the Anzio beachhead, by small landing craft at night. It was quieter then although a few shells would be lobbed over from some railway guns that spent their days in a tunnel. We were advised to dig down inside our tent but that would have been a mess if it had rained. At night when we were woken up by shellfire we always said that we would dig down the following day but we never did. The most exciting thing that happened was a visit by an American fighter that landed amongst our tents when everyone was there. We had just eaten. I was standing in front of one tent with my head ducked down, talking to the fellows inside. I straightened up at once and there was the fighter going at right angles, silently. His wingtip was nearly touching the tent I was at. The pilot had his oil-covered face outside the cockpit and his windscreen was also covered in oil. As he touched down his guns fired, putting three holes just under the ridge pole of one tent. Not one injury!

At Cassino 140 B-17s from the US 15th Strategic Air Force based at Foggia began the destruction and bombing of the monastery, and a second wave of forty-seven Mitchells and forty Marauders continued the battering. Some Indian troops caught close to the monastery and, unaware of the intended bombardment, were killed, as were many civilians still in the monastery itself. The bombing was not entirely accurate and some American casualties were sustained when bombs were inadvertantly dropped on the HQ of the US 5th Army at Presenzano, which was 15 miles from Cassino. Most of the monastery and the basilica were reduced to piles of rubble, only the strong outer walls of the west wing and entrance steps managed to defy the bombs. Any survivors from the first wave were slaughtered by the second. In hindsight, the bombing of the monastery acted against the Allies' interests, because it was transformed into an impregnable fortress with bomb and artillery-proof subterranean passages and cellars. The Germans would become masters of using the rubble and ruins in defence.

16 FEBRUARY

ORB: Four beach patrols again stirred up some enemy aircraft. The first of eight aircraft observed some twenty plus Fw190s approaching Anzio from the south-west diving from 13,000ft to 4,000ft. As a result of the combat Flg Off Ingalls destroyed a Fw190. The second patrol of the day of six aircraft was uneventful. The third patrol of eight aircraft came across fifteen Me109s over the Anzio sector and as a result one Me109 was damaged by Lt Richardson SA. On the fourth patrol of the day, a further fifteen Fw190s were seen over the beaches area. Plt Off McLeod damaged a Fw190 after a chase which took him 8 miles south-east of Rome.

After a heavy barrage the Germans counter-attacked across both sides of the Aprilia–Anzio road against the Anzio–Nettuno beachhead. Supported by artillery and tanks the Germans came up against stiff Allied resistance and against very boggy conditions off-road. As a result they had to use the few roads available. This made them easy targets for the Allied fighter-bombers and artillery, so the German infantry divisions were left without support and made only slow progress.

ORB: Judy Shirley, a radio star, and four other members of the Gang Show visited the wing and two shows were arranged in the Airmen's Mess, one for the squadron and one for the other units in the wing. The awards of Mentioned in Despatches were made to Flt Lt Hussey and Flt Lt Prytherch (missing in Sicily) today.

17 FEBRUARY

On the ground, after some probing the previous night, the Germans renewed their assault along the shell-cratered Albano–Anzio road and had penetrated about 4 miles into the Anzio–Nettuno beachhead, with air-support provided by about thirty-five German fighter-bombers. The Americans fell back under the onslaught and after another push supported by Fw190 fighter-bombers, the Germans again succeeded in driving a wedge 2 miles wide and about 4 miles deep into the US positions.

The Allies' last-ditch lines of defence were under threat and the landings at Anzio were on the brink of disaster. It was all in the balance. Reserves were poured into the battle and a plea was made for all available aircraft to support them. The Allied air forces responded with about 800 sorties alone that day. Nearly 1,000 tons of bombs were dropped on the German positions, most of it on the roads between Carroceta and Campoleone. Warhawks, Spitfires and Mustangs strafed the German guns, tanks, troops and battle lines as well and continued to harry them with RAF Baltimores and Bostons, which came down low to bomb within 400yd or so of the US positions in an attempt to stem the push. The overwhelming Allied air superiority provided such a weight of support to the hard-pressed troops on the ground, together with naval bombardment and artillery, that the German push faltered. The Indian Corps at Cassino attempted to storm Monastery Hill and Monte Calvario but they were caught in heavy German cross-fire and pushed back.

ORB: On the first patrol of the day over the beaches we saw Kittyhawks bombing a viaduct at F.8843, but all the bombs dropped south of the target area. Very heavy and intense flak at Genzano. On the second patrol of the day ten aircraft flew over the beaches with nothing to report. An incident on the runway at Lago by one aircraft from 43 Squadron made it necessary for six of our aircraft to land at Castel Volturno until such time as the runway at Lago was repaired. A further patrol over the beaches provided nothing of interest. 43 Squadon also came across fifty plus enemy aircraft on their patrols with Sqn Ldr 'Polly' Parrott able to claim a Me109 damaged, but in the same combat the squadron lost Flt Sgt Williams who had only been with them about a week.

[Flg] Off Barnfather left today on posting to No. 2 BFD as tour-expired. He had been acting adjutant this month owing to the illness of Flt Lt D.K. Rice.

An amazing story, with 'Spanner' Farrish, the Chief Engineer Officer, at the centre of it, then unfolded. No. 111 Squadron had been equipped with new Spitfire IXs powered by Rolls-Royce Merlin 66 engines. The engines had been developed by Rolls to give a better performance bewteen 13,000 and 20,000ft, but the first few operations carried out with them were a disaster because of continued engine failure. Some Spitfires were lucky to get down at Lago or Nettuno, some pilots bailed out and some crash-landed. No. 111 Squadron was grounded as a result. Spanner was not popular.

A team was called out from Rolls-Royce to investigate but it turned out to be nothing to do with the engines. It was the petrol that had been used, which apparently had been taken from drums and had rust or something else mixed in with it. This meant that the spark plug points became smeared with muck and meant that at maximum power, the complete bank of cylinders had a tendency to cut out.

Spanner was mortified and decided that in an effort to get all the Spitfires back in the air again, including those grounded at Nettuno, he would have to sort the problems himself and get up to Nettuno. The problem was how he was going to get there. Nettuno was still being shelled and there were four Spits grounded there. Being an engineer officer Spanner had never piloted an aircraft before, other than with a qualified pilot in a dual-control aircraft like the 'Pisser', but he apparently took it upon himself. Armed with a manual he planned to fly another Spitfire up to Nettuno to see if he could get the rest back in the air again. Spanner going solo in a Spit without his pilot's wings had immediate repercussions.

Merlyn Rees, the Ops Officer, immediately got on to Smithy (Gp Capt Duncan Smith) who took off in another Spit to cover Spanner or to persuade him back to Lago where he thought he would have to bale out rather than try and land the Spitfire. However, around Nettuno he apparently found that Spanner had already landed amid the shelling of the airfield, so he managed to land as well and let Spanner continue with what he had set out to do, namely to get the other Spits back in the air. A remarkable story, but it did not end there. Rumour has it that Spanner was court-martialled.

The weather on the 18th turned bad again, grounding most Allied aircraft apart from a few sorties by A-36s and P-40s. The Germans tried to take advantage again by massing a large number of troops and tanks near Campoleone, but they came under heavy artillery fire and, after several hours of fierce fighting, the last serious bid by the Germans to push through to the sea was halted and they were beaten back. The counter-attack had cost the Germans about 5,000 men; the beachhead had been saved and the crisis at Anzio was over.

After a further push against the Anzio beachhead at the end of February, both sides, exhausted, began to settle down and wait for drier weather. Although there were constant patrols and skirmishes there were no major ground operations on the Italian peninsula for the next two months, with the exception of Clark's 5th Army assault on Cassino in March. The Germans worked to strengthen the Gustav Line, while at Anzio the Allies continued to pour materials and supplies ashore. Cassino would not be taken until May.

Barney was posted back to an OTU in Egypt.

20 FEBRUARY

Log Book: Dakota USAAC as passengers. Naples–Palermo–Tunis 5 hours.

CHAPTER 11

Troubles in Egypt

February–September 1944

26 FEBRUARY

Log Book: Dakota RAF as passengers. Tunis–Castel Benito–Cairo 8 hours.

Barney had been warned on the health hazards of an area like the Middle East before: malaria, sand fly fever, 'gippo tummy', VD, and a disease many had never even heard of – bilharzia. Blood flukes that entered the body, usually by bathing or drinking contaminated water, caused the bilharzia. The flukes were parasitic to a small water snail that lived, for example, in the Sweet Water canal in Egypt. When the flukes infested the human body they laid their eggs in the bladder. These eggs were equipped with a sharp hook that lacerated the bladder and the urinary channels causing haemorrhage. This became apparent when the victim (predominantly men) passed water. It used to be the sign that the Egyptian peasant had attained manhood. Bilharzia was a very debilitating disease and was one of the reasons for the short life expectancy of the Egyptian fellaheen. The men were told that if they ever fell into one of the canals they had to report immediately to the MO. The treatment was a course of several extremely unpleasant injections.

In Cairo they were free to search out any amusements that suited them. There were shops where one could buy all kinds of novelties and souvenirs of Egypt, very much like the seaside shops at home; there were canteens and bars and, the most novel thing of all, outdoor cinemas showing both old and current films, some of which they had seen at home and others that had only recently been released. It was a new experience, sitting under the star-filled Egyptian night sky watching American musicals and comedies.

Barney was very eager to see Cairo having read so much about it, and was quite impressed with what he saw. There was no blackout because by now the war had moved a long way westwards into Europe. He was surprised to find out, too, how many forces canteens there were in the city and sampled many of them over the months. Among his favourites was Music for All, where he could eat to the sound of classical music and which had a marvellous lending library. Money came via Thomas Cook, not far from the famous Shepherds Hotel.

One afternoon he went out to Giza to see the pyramids and the Sphinx, and was escorted by one of the inevitable dragomen who were very amusing, their English vocabulary having been enriched by contact with many clients from the services. One, in particular, was very knowledgeable and in contrast to the normal run of guides his charges were reasonable, so for once Barney did not feel that he had been rooked. One evening he had supper at the Empire Services Club after which he stayed for the cinema show, watching Mickey Rooney and Judy Garland in *Babes on Broadway*. The Empire Club had been an Officers' Club in the pre-First World War days when Britain had been closely involved in administering Egyptian affairs, and it had retained its Victorian-Edwardian appearance and the atmosphere of a gentleman's club. This club had an extensive library and its books were only for reading on the premises.

Cairo offered a wide variety of entertainment and cultural facilities, and it was a dull fellow who could not find something in the city and its surroundings to interest and amuse him. The service clubs were first-class, not only for the food they offered, but for all kinds of amenities – music, games, cinemas, baths, laundries, barber shops, writing rooms and libraries of good books.

The city had its dangers, however, and it was not wise to frequent some of the sleazier bars and cabarets down the darker alleys for all manner of reasons. Barney recalled that the most common source of danger was from the 'shoe-shine' wallahs whose persistence and aggressive tactics was a by-word in the Middle East:

> You might be walking from the station towards the city centre with your nostrils full of the diverse and pungent smells of the Orient, and your ears almost deafened by the sound of Arabic music blasting out from hundreds of loudspeakers when suddenly, around a corner, you came face to face with a band of shoe-shine boys. You tried to ignore them but, in a flash, they had you surrounded and one of them was saying 'Wanna shoe shine, George?'

After a few days off in Cairo, Barney boarded a train for Ismailia. Occasionally they saw camels toiling in the fields and asses carrying huge loads on their weak-looking backs. There were oxen turning the age-old water wheels which irrigated the precious soil. Most views, however, consisted of bare sand and the pear-shaped cacti lining the rail side. After about 2 hours they came to Ismailia. Barney remembered very little of Ismailia itself except for tall tumble-down tenements and mud-walled slums. It was an uninspiring place.

NO. 71 OTU, ISMAILIA, MARCH 1944

No. 71 OTU was formed at Ismailia under the control of 202 Group on 1 June 1941 from the fighter element of 70 OTU. Its task was to acclimatise fighter and army cooperation pilots to desert conditions. From June to September it had been tasked with providing night defence of the Canal Zone, but in the latter month it moved to Gordon's Tree in the Sudan. In October, C Flight was detached to form

74 OTU and with it the commitment to train army cooperation pilots. Further moves occurred on 1 May 1942 to Carthage and on 5 May 1943 back to Ismailia with control passing to 203 Group.

6 MARCH

ORB: No. 57 Course and No. 14 Conversion Course commenced training today with fifty-one pupils in the former and seven on the latter. Three SAAF pupils are expected to bring up the quota on the Conversion Course to ten.

7 MARCH

ORB: Category 1 damage was caused to a Hurricane aircraft today when Sgt M. Boucher, a pupil of No. 56 Course, taxied his aircraft into soft sand, thereby causing it to tip up onto its nose and damaging its propeller. The pilot was held responsible for the accident and his log book endorsed 'gross negligence' by the Commanding Officer. The three remaining SAAF officers reported for the No. 14 Conversion Course.

8 MARCH

ORB: Category 11 damage was caused to a Harvard today when Flg Off J.F. Davies, a pupil of No. 57 Course, swung on landing. The aircraft first swung to starboard, which he managed to correct, but then swung to port and eventually ended up doing a ground loop with resultant damage to the centre section, undercarriage and wing-tip.

Flg Off R.R. Barnfather reported from No. 72 Squadron for Instructor Duties.

9 MARCH

ORB: Normal activity and nothing of interest to report.

10 MARCH

ORB: Two accidents occurred today involving damage to two Spitfires and one Hurricane. The first occurred when Sgt P.A.K. Brumby, a pupil of No. 56 Course, was carrying out a low-flying exercise. His engine cut and in view of the reduced flying speed was forced to land. Category 11 damage caused to the airframe and engine. No blame was attached to the pilot and an investigation is being held into the cause of the engine failure. The other accident was a taxiing accident for which 2/Lt D.A.H. Clarke of No. 14 Conversion Course was held responsible. Both aircraft were being taxied at the time, the Spitfire by Lt Kelly, a pupil of No. 56 Course, who on seeing the Hurricane approach immediately stopped his aircraft. The Hurricane, however, continued on its way and collided with the Spitfire thereby causing Cat. 1 damage to engines and airframe on both aircraft.

Flt Lt J.W. Hicks and Flg Off T. Percival returned from the Engine Handling Course at Heliopolis.

11 MARCH

Log Book: Spitfire air test.

ORB: Owing to early morning mist, flying was not possible until 0730 hours.

12 MARCH

ORB: It was decided to fly the Spitfires today in order to increase the pupils' flying hours on this type of aircraft but bad weather caused flying to be abandoned at 1230 hours.

13 MARCH

ORB: Normal activity, but the unit continues to break flying records with a magnificent total of 258 hours flying time achieved which earned the CO's congratulations, who thanked all personnel for their efforts.

14 MARCH

Log Book: Spitfire air test.

ORB: A dust storm restricted flying to approx. an hour in the afternoon.

15 MARCH

ORB: Another fatal accident brought the total to thirty-four today when Sgt L.F. Pepper, a pupil of No. 57 Course, was killed in a Hurricane. It appears that the pilot called up to say that his engine was on fire and that he intended to land. The airfield was cleared to allow him to land, and the aircraft was seen to make its approach for the runway, carrying out a steep turn, but the aircraft stalled and spun in and was completely destroyed by fire.

It is thought that what the pilot considered to be a fire was in fact a bad glycol leak and that a court martial would serve no useful purpose.

16 MARCH

Log Book: Spitfire formation flying.

ORB: Two pupil pilots, Sgt M. Boucher and Sgt S.J. Williamson, were taken off No. 56 Course today and left for Aircrew Reselection Board at 22 PTC. The funeral of the late Sgt Pepper was also held this afternoon.

17 MARCH

Log Book: Spitfire air test.

ORB: Two pupils of the Royal Egyptian Air Force were removed from No. 56 Course and were posted back to HQ REAF Almaza.

---

18 MARCH

ORB: Flg Off R.R. Barnfather admitted to No. 1 General Hospital Helwan suffering from jaundice.

MARCH–JUNE 1944

No. 1 General Hospital, Helwan, was the main base hospital in Egypt. It had been invaluable when conditions in the Western Desert became critical in 1942 after El Alamein, when the number of casualties had risen to nearly 900. Convoys regularly brought in fresh casualties by sea, or smaller batches by air. Patients brought in by air were admitted to the hospital within 48 hours of being wounded after passing through the field medical units. The advantage of using Helwan was that the airfield was close by. Later, planes reverted to using Heliopolis airfield on the other side of Cairo.

The hospital had been used to dealing with serious jaundice in the latter part of 1942, when an epidemic had stretched its resources to the limit and there were over 1,000 patients being treated. Extra tents had to be erected in fields around Helwan itself to cope with the patients and many were admitted direct to these makeshift facilities. Large numbers of less seriously ill cases were transferred to Maadi Camp Hospital.

The majority of the sick and wounded from the desert came by ambulance through Alexandria to Cairo main station, from where they were taken the 17 miles to Helwan by motor ambulance cars sent from No. 1 General Hospital. There they were quickly transferred from the ambulance cars to the wards where the nursing staff saw that they were washed and put to bed between clean sheets. After their journeys many were so tired that they soon dropped off to sleep, and then the treatment to restore them to health would begin, a long and slow process that might take weeks or months.

Such were the conditions that Barney found when admitted to the hospital on the 18 March 1944 suffering from jaundice. Jaundice itself was not strictly a disease *per se*, though curiously it was sometimes referred to as infective hepatitis. It produced a collection of symptoms resulting from the presence of bile in the blood, either from it not being secreted, or from some impediment to its excretion so that it entered the blood stream again. The signs that marked its condition were a yellowness to the skin, coloured urine and white stools due to the presence of bile.

Barney recalled that he had no appetite, which was common, as the digestive function was more or less impaired, and many patients complained of depression, low spirits and a feeling of general discomfort. He also complained of a bitter unpleasant taste in his mouth, bad breath and was always thirsty. In extreme cases jaundice could result in a high temperature and delirium before death. During its treatment it was important to ascertain the cause and if possible remove it. Gentle laxitives to remove constipation with a simple easily digestible diet were favoured, and plenty of fresh fruit and gentle exercise during convalescence were encouraged. In the ward, each patient had a fly swat, and any fly to alight on a bed was quickly dispatched and a count taken at the end of each day; it helped to pass the time. It would be a long drawn-out process and almost three months before Barney was fit enough to return to duty.

---

12 JUNE

ORB: Flt Lt Barnfather reported back for Instructor Duties from No. 203 Group after his spell in hospital. News had reached the OTU of the landings by the Allies in Normandy, France, on the 6th.

---

13 JUNE

Log Book: 1. Harvard – Self and Flg Off Rounds local flying; 2. Hurricane – air test; 3. Argus – Flg Off Young and self – Helwan and return.

ORB: Sgt N.A. Dyer, ex-pupil of No. 60 Course, who was withdrawn from flying a short time ago, departed for No. 22 PTC for interview by the Aircrew Reselection Board.

What became clear to Barney (and the other instructors) was the number of accidents, and the tragic loss of life, that could have been prevented. Extracts from the ORB for the rest of June make this clear.

---

15 JUNE

Log Book: 1. Hurricane – air test; 2. Hurricane – air test; 3. Hurricane – air test; 4. Harvard – Self and Sqn Ldr Ashton – Ballah and return.

ORB: A heavy landing resulted in a damaged oleo leg and a subsequent crash-landing at 132 MU caused Cat. B2 damage to a Hurricane piloted by Sgt T. Daniel, a pupil of No. 61 Course. The pilot was held responsible and his log book endorsed 'Carelessness' by the Station Commander. The termination of courses marked the return of a number of instructors, Sqn Ldr J.H. Ashton DFC from the Pilots' Gunnery Course at Ballah, and Flg Off J.F. King and Flg Off F.T. Craig from the Engine Handling Course at Heliopolis. There was one departure, Flt Lt F. Bosworth departed on posting to a Yugoslav Holding Unit.

---

24 JUNE

Log Book: Hurricane – air test.

ORB: There were two movements of Training Wing personnel. Flt Lt R.D. Scrase returned to the unit on completion of the Pilots' Gunnery Course at Ballah.

Rod Scrase had been with Barney in 72 Squadron, which Barney had joined in the final days of the Tunisian campaign in May 1943, and Barney was pleased to see his old friend.

27 JUNE

Log Book: Havard, self and Sqn Ldr Daniel – Mariyat and return.

ORB: Undercarriage difficulty was the cause of an accident to a Hurricane when the pilot, Sgt B.S. Hunt of No. 63 Course, experienced trouble when trying to lower it for almost an hour. He tried to land, was forced to go around again, but his engine cut due to fuel shortage. Inexperience again was blamed.

28 JUNE

Log Book: 1. Harvard – air test; 2. Spitfire – air test.

ORB: The first solo flights on the new course produced the usual crop of accidents and today another pupil of 63 Course, Sgt W.C. Clarkson, broke the oleo leg of a Hurricane aircraft as the pilot had failed to allow for drift. Pilot's navigation also sadly lacking as he had been instructed to land at Helwan but was unable to locate it and eventually turned up at Heliopolis. It was also the WAAF's red letter day which caused for some celebration. It was the fifth birthday of the Women's Auxiliary Air Force and they celebrated the occasion by holding a dance.

29 JUNE

Log Book: Hurricane – air test.

ORB: 63 Course maintained their rather dismal record of the past few days by adding another two accidents to their score. The first involved Sgt G.A. Sims in a Hurricane, when he was landing, stalled, opened up again too late and the prop hit the ground. Pilot was held to blame and was withdrawn from flying. The second accident occurred in the course of an oxygen climb and involved Sgt F.J. Richardson. Failure of the R/T caused the pilot to get hopelessly lost and, after flying around in all directions following canals and railways, he was forced to land due to lack of fuel at Benhay in the Delta.

30 JUNE

Log Book: 1. Hurricane – air test; 2. Hurricane – air test; 3. Hurricane – air test; 4. Harvard – Self and Plt Off Schules – Fayid and return.

ORB: Recent spate of accidents maintained when Sgt J.T. Lawrence bounced heavily on landing and crashed causing Cat. 2 damage to his Hurricane, again the pilot was withdrawn from flying.

Plt Offs Tilston and J.T. Connolly from the Royal Australian Air Force returned to
the unit on completion of their FIS Course at Shallufa. 'Con' had been with Barney
in 72 Squadron in North Africa, right through Sicily and Italy before his operational
tour had ended in February. He had been posted to become a test pilot at HQ RAF
Middle East before he joined the OTU at Ismailia on similar duties. There was
much catching up to do as there now seemed to be a '72 Squadron reunion going
on' with Danny Daniel, Rod Scrase, Barney and Con all back together again.

---

1 JULY

Log Book: Hurricane – air test.

ORB: The month started rather inauspiciously with two flying accidents first day. The first
caused Cat. B damage to a Spitfire when WO Greenwood saw black and white smoke
escaping from the engine which was also making an unhealthy grating noise, so he belly-
landed near Quantara. The other involved Sgt P.J. Addis, a pupil of No. 63 Course, when
he stalled the engine in his Hurricane and caused Cat. A damage. The pupil seemed to be
incapable of judging his circuits and landings and was withdrawn from flying.

---

3 JULY

Log Book: Hurricane – air test.

ORB: Ground-looping was the cause of an accident when a Spitfire piloted by Sgt H.A.
Firminger, a pupil on No. 62 Course, suffered Cat. B2 damage. This was the pilot's first
solo on type. A Hurricane was also involved in an accident when it suffered Cat. A
damage when the pilot, Sgt C.W. Riley, coming into land, touched down off the runway
and damaged the oleo leg. Although he became airborne again he had to belly-land
because of the damage to the oleo leg.

---

6 JULY

ORB: Noteworthy for the number of visitors. Wg Cdr Stan B. Grant of 203 Group
collaborated with the Chief Instructor in connection with training matters while the
visits of Sqn Ldrs Deuchas and Smith of HQME concentrated on the siting of the MF-DF
station. The WAAF accomodation was the reason for the Flg Off J.M.E. Adams visit from
the Middle East and Flg Off Moore visited to attend the signals section.

---

8 JULY

Log Book: Hurricane – air test.

ORB: Still another course passed through their hands and today pupils of No. 61 Course
and No. 19 Conversion Course successfully completed their training and were now ready
to take their places in operational squadrons on the various fronts.

11 JULY

Log Book: Hurricane - 4 air tests.

ORB: Inexperience on type was considered the reason for the accident today when Sgt P.S. Mayne, a pupil of No. 63 Course, swung on landing in a Spitfire causing Cat. A damage.

12 JULY

Log Book: Hurricane – air test.

ORB: The lull in the posting of instructors was interrupted today when Flg Off P.D. Jones and Flg Off Fakhry, both of the Royal Australian Air Force, reported from 203 Group for Instructor Duties.

16 JULY

ORB: Two Flying Instructors, Flg Off G. Garnham and Flg Off D.L.S. Wood, both of whom had put in a considerable amount of time on the unit, left today for 22 PTC to wait for air passage to HQ Mediterranean Allied Air Force.

17 JULY

Log Book: 1. Harvard – air test; 2. Harvard – L106 and return; 3. Hurricane – air test; 4. Hurricane – air test; 5. Harvard – Sgt Marshall Fayid and return.

ORB: The Station Commander and Chief Instructor had every reason to be happy over the progress of the courses as we had gone through a complete week without an accident.

However, this amazing state of affairs was short lived. The good record was spoilt and the inevitable happened, and there were two accidents.

The first resulted in Cat. B2 damage to a Spitfire piloted by Sgt A. Marshall who carried out a forced landing near Fayid. The pilot had just completed an aerobatics exercise when he noticed smoke pouring from the engine, which immediately cut and as he was unable to restart it. He had no alternative other than to carry out a forced landing.

The second accident involved a Hurricane piloted by Sgt R.A. Golding who came in to land with a certain amount of drift which caused the undercarriage to collapse, the damage being assessed as Cat. B2.

Two officers, Flt Lt J.B. Orr and Flt Lt J.A. Gray, were attached to the Engine Handling Course at Heliopolis.

21 JULY

Log Book: Argus – Flg Off Young, Hoot, Joe and me to Maryat.

A few days leave, rest and recuperation were in order, happy times sunning and swimming on the Aboukir beach. The station at Aboukir was also peaceful, there was a slight hill surrounded by night-scented stock and Barney remembered that when they used to walk in the evening the scent was one that he never forgot.

22 JULY

ORB: Another accident, this time to a Spitfire which resulted in Cat. B2 damage. The pilot, Sgt D.S. Armitage, Royal Canadian Air Force, a pupil of No. 63 Course, was carrying out a normal landing until he hit a bad patch on the runway that caused the aircraft to swing and ultimately ground-loop.

23 JULY

ORB: The formation of the Air Firing Squadron called for further qualified gunnery instructors and Flt Lt W.E. Schrader, Royal New Zealand Air Force, and Plt Off R.S. Gray, Royal Canadian Air Force, left for this course at RAF Ballah.

24 JULY

Log Book: Spitfire from Aboukir.

29 JULY

Log Book: Harvard – air test.

ORB: The unit's 36th fatal accident occurred this morning when Sgt S. Mountzis, Royal Hellenic Air Force, was killed in a Hurricane aircraft. The pilot was carrying out a pinpointing exercise and was due back at base at 0815 hours. As he was overdue a search was instituted and the remains of the crashed aircraft and his body were found about 7.5 miles from base. It is believed that the accident occurred because at the time there was 10/10 cloud at 2,000ft with its base at 200ft, and the pilot may have broken cloud cover at high speed and low level and, unable to pull out, went straight in. A Court of Inquiry has been convened.

No. 62 Course and No. 20 Conversion Course departed for seven days leave prior to reporting to their respective PTCs. The record of No. 62 Course during their stay is worthy of commendation, they were involved in only one accident, one Cat. B in a Spitfire, and the good standard was maintained by No. 20 Conversion Course who also left with a clean record.

All the pilots of both courses successfully completed them and no one was withdrawn from training.

31 JULY

Log Book: 1. Spitfire – air test; 2. Hurricane – air test.

ORB: The month ended again on a sad note with another accident, this time involving Sgt Green of No. 63 Course who was piloting a Hurricane. He was proceeding on a cine exercise and as the engine was running a bit rough, switched over to the reserve tank, but forgot to switch back over to the main tank, and when the engine stopped he was under the impression that it had seized. He eventually switched back to the main tank but the engine would not start and he force-landed about 13 miles east of the base near the Palestinian Road, with Cat. B damage.

Statistically the month of July showed a high standard of achievement, two OTU Courses and two Conversion Courses successfully completed their training, representing an output of approximately 115 pilots, all of whom were ready to take their places on various operational fronts. The general health of the station remained satisfactory in spite of the apparent increase in the malaria mosquito, precautionary measures preventing an epidemic.

2 AUGUST

Log Book: 1. Hurricane – air test; 2. Hurricane – air test.

ORB: The month started badly with another accident which caused damage to two aircraft.

It appeared that a Harvard piloted by Flg Off T.A. Jowett, Flying Instructor, with Sgt T.E. Bladun, a pupil of No. 65 Course, had touched down and run approx 50yd along the runway when a Spitfire piloted by Sgt F. Yates, a pupil of No. 64 Course, collided with it, the wing striking the cockpit cover of the Harvard. Damage was assessed as Cat. B2 for the Spitfire and the Harvard. Sgt Bladun was admitted to hospital suffering from amnesia.

3 AUGUST

Log Book: 1. Hurricane – air test; 2. Spitfire – air test.

ORB: The immunity from fatal accidents recently enjoyed by the unit came to an end when Sgt D.S. Shircore, a pupil of No. 64 Course, was killed, the unit's 37th fatal accident. He was flying as No. 2 in a line-astern chase and failed to pull out of the dive from 9,000ft. The aircraft exploded on hitting the ground.

7 AUGUST

ORB: Another fatal accident when Sgt R.A. Culver, a pupil of No. 63 Course, flying a Hurricane, spun in out of clouds causing Cat. 2 damage to the aircraft. A Court of Inquiry was convened to investigate the cause of the accident.

8 AUGUST

Log Book: 1. Spitfire – air test; 2. Spitfire – air test.

ORB: An influx of new personnel to the station, Flt Lt N.L. McCulloch, Flg Off W. Raybould and Flg Off H.S. Smith arrived from 203 Group for Instructor Duties and Flt Lt W.H. Foster from RAF Ballah for Engineer Duties.

12 AUGUST

Log Book: 1. Harvard – air test.

ORB: Cat. A damage was caused to a Hurricane piloted by Sgt T.C. Austin, a pupil of No. 65 Course. The undercarriage collapsed at the end of the runway but as no technical failure could be found, it was presumed that the pilot failed to check with the hand pump.

14 AUGUST

Log Book: Argus – Sqn Ldr Daniel – Helwan and return.

15 AUGUST

Log Book: Hurricane – air tests x 3.

ORB: The discovery of a crashed aircraft confirmed what had been feared for some time from a long-overdue Fairchild [Argus] aircraft, which had left Heliopolis carrying Sqn Ldr J.H.P. Gauvain and Flg Off Terry DFC on board. It crashed 4 miles south of Abu Sueir and both had been killed, but the predatory instincts of the natives had been satisfied because the bodies had been stripped of all personal effects.

16 AUGUST

Log Book: 1. Hurricane – air test; 2. Harvard – Flg Off Jackson Fayid and return.

ORB: There was a further influx of Flying Instructors with Flt Lt D. Fisher RAAF, Flg Off J.L. Houle and Plt Off W. Wheatley, both of the RCAF, arriving from 203 Group. There was one departure, Sqn Ldr S.W. 'Danny' Daniel left for 22 PTC to await air passage for HQ MAAF. The funerals of Sqn Ldr J.H.P. Gauvain and Flg Off Terry took place today.

19 AUGUST

Log Book: 1. Spitfire – air test.

ORB: No. 63 Course and No. 22 Conversion Course, having completed their training, departed on seven days leave prior to reporting to their various PTCs. Only three pupils of No. 63 Course were considered unsuitable and had been withdrawn from training and were posted eventually for reselection. The OTU Course was involved in twelve accidents but the Conversion Course left with a clean record. With the departure of these, course preparations were made to receive No. 66 and No. 23 Courses, the pupils of which were assembled today. The termination of the Gunnery Course also meant that Flt Lt W.E. Schrader, RNZAF, and Plt Off R.S. Gray, RCAF, both returned to the unit. Two airwomen were admitted to No. 1 General Hospital yesterday suffering from typhoid fever and a full investigation was at once instigated.

20 AUGUST

ORB: Tour-expired personnel of the Royal Canadian Air Force: Flt Lt D.B. Rodgers, Flg Off J.S. Bushe, Flt Lt R.L. Hazell, Flg Off T. Percival and Flg Off F.H. Reid, all left for 22 PTC to wait for a sea passage back to the UK and repatriation to Canada.

21 AUGUST

Log Book: Hurricane – air tests x 2.

ORB: Two further airwomen were admitted to No. 1 General Hospital reported to be suffering from typhoid and, with the cause still unknown, all the usual precautions are being taken.

24 AUGUST

Log Book: 1. Argus – Flt Lt Young – to Helwan; 2. Spitfire – from Helwan.

ORB: The elimination of taxiing accidents, which at one time had reached epidemic proportions, reared its head again when Sgt D.J. Cable, a pupil of No. 64 Course, piloting a Hurricane, taxied into a Harvard. The latter had been stationary at a marshalling point waiting for permission to take off.

25 AUGUST

Log Book: Hurricane – air tests x 2. Harvard – air test.

ORB: Flt Lt M.L. Burke RAAF arrived from 203 Group to take up Instructor Duties.

27 AUGUST

ORB: There was some movement among the Training Wing personnel. Flt Lt R.R. Barnfather departed on posting to AHQ [Air Headquarters] Eastern Mediterranean, and Flg Off W. Raybould and Flg Off H.R. Hall for the Engine Handling Course at Heliopolis. Wg Cdr W.M. Sizer DFC and Bar assumed command of the station during the absence of Gp Capt R.E. Bain on leave.

29 AUGUST

Log Book: Baltimore, Flt Lt Crouch as pilot – five passengers: Maryat–Gambut, 3 hours.

5 SEPTEMBER

Log Book: Dakota – Gp Capt Cox – eight passengers – El Adem–Heliopolis, 4 hours.

A few days' rest and recuperation in Heliopolis were just what Barney needed. There he was accommodated in modern, light and airy barracks with verandahs, showers and toilets. If he was not resting or sleeping he could go from Heliopolis to Cairo by metro tram and in due course went again to Giza and saw the pyramids and the Sphinx. During one such tour around a pyramid, he recalled that the guide lit a piece of magnesium tape so that they could see the walls of the chamber.

The trams became famous and a favoured mode of transport. They had been restricted to 45mph in wartime to prevent accidents, but in pre-war years they had touched 60mph!

The men could also go swimming at the local pool, although care had to be taken not to get sunburned. In the evening, being sub-tropical, it was dark by 8 p.m. and they had the open-air cinema in Heliopolis. There was also a huge hotel, the Heliopolis Palace, which sounded very posh but residents there complained they had just bare rooms. The hotel did have one thing going for it: in the basement there was a row of shops where you could get anything from a haircut to a Persian rug. Also, across the street was a patisserie where they went for morning coffee and the most delicious sticky cream cakes.

In Cairo they could have supper in the Tedder Club. For 9 Piastres they could enjoy three eggs and chips and iced fruit salad, and afterwards they would wander around the town, occasionally coming across a shop in which sundry workers were making leather belts and similar goods. Barney recalled that the front of the shop was open and some of the work was actually being done on the pavement by workers dressed in nothing but a few rags.

18 SEPTEMBER

Log Book: Mitchell – Flt Lt Cross and Sqn Ldr Boddington. Heliopolis–Benghazi–Hal Far–Cannes, 8 hours.

21 SEPTEMBER

Log Book: Dakota, USAAC – Cannes–Lyons, 1 hour.

23 SEPTEMBER

Log Book: Dakota, USAAC – two 1-star generals as passengers as well – Lyons–Verdun–Paris, 3 hours.

24 SEPTEMBER

Log Book: Dakota, USAAC – Flt Lt Smith and RCAF crew – Paris–Northolt–Swindon, 2 hours.

Barney, who since August had been with 94 Squadron, was given nearly a month's leave before being posted back to Italy, where he had a brief spell with 43 Squadron, the famous 'Fighting Cocks', in Florence. His trip back was via Brussels and Lyon over a period of two weeks in October.

CHAPTER 12

Counter-Attack in Italy

Back in Italy the Germans had launched another counter-attack at Anzio in March, and once again the whole might of the Allied air forces was called upon to help meet the threat. Monte Cassino was heavily bombed, but the rubble and disruption it had caused actually delayed the advance because the Germans were able to hold on for a couple more months, fighting for every yard of ground from the deep holes created by the bombs. It was not taken until May. In a new all-out effort to try and help the Allied armies make more headway, the air forces launched Operation Strangle, which was an attempt to destroy all lines of enemy communication. Allied bombers had attacked railway targets of all types and bridges in a line drawn roughly between Pisa and Rimini. The Spits and other Allied fighters were used in fighter-bomber roles against German transport and communications, too. The Monte Cassino offensive had seen increased activity from the Luftwaffe and 324 Wing had continued their successes with, notably, at least nine claimed by Barney's ex-colleagues at 72 Squadron on 7 May.

With Cassino taken, the British 8th and US 5th Armies continued to advance on Rome, entering the Holy City on 4 June. No sooner had news of its capture reached the British press and public, than the story got put in the background by the events in Normandy and the Allied invasion of 6 June.

From Rome the Allied armies pressed forward, but they were checked by Kesselring, first at the Trasimene Line and then, as he withdrew his forces, the famous Gothic Line in the northern Appenines. The Luftwaffe was quiet, principally because many units had been withdrawn to France to meet the perceived greater threat in Normandy following the landings there.

The US 5th and British 8th Armies continued their advances, the 5th up the western coast and the 8th towards the centre of Italy, Florence in particular. XII Air Support Command retained sole responsibility for support of the US 5th Army, and from Corsica began a series of operations in support of the army between Leghorn and Genoa.

In June, Barney's ex-colleagues in 324 Wing, including 43, 72, 93 and 111 Squadrons, had moved to Corsica in support of these operations. By the end of June the British 8th Army had cleared most of the Germans from around Trasimene and were closing in on Florence. The Germans withdrew up the line of the Arno river fighting frequent rearguard actions. By 11 July Arno itself had been taken by the Americans; by the 18th Ancona had been taken by the Poles; and on the 19th Leghorn was taken, again by the Americans. The advance slowed further at this point because several US 5th Army divisions were withdrawn for the planned invasion of southern France. Despite this, units of the US 5th Army entered Florence on 5 August after support from Western Desert Air Force units.

The planned invasion of Southern France, known initially as Operation Anvil, had its name changed to Operation Dragoon and was to be supported by the DAF units including 324 Wing based on Corsica. The invasion itself was planned for August, at the same time as the British 8th Army began a further assault on the Gothic Line.

For the first two weeks of August, heavy bombers of the Strategic Air Force, with support from the medium bombers of the Tactical Bomber Force, bombed targets around the Marseilles and Toulouse areas with the Spitfires of 324 Wing, and those of 251, 322 and the Free French Wings, providing fighter cover.

During the night of 14/15 August, American C-47s dropped paratroops along the coastal belt and, at dawn, a heavy attack by aircraft of all forces was directed at the sea defences and the landings were made between Cannes and St Tropez. The Allied air forces' strategic bombing had held up German reinforcements, so the landings were met with little resistance. Marseilles soon fell and by the end of the month a line from Grenoble to Bordeaux had been captured.

By 12 September the US 7th Army had made contact with General Patton's 3rd Army, which had pushed down from Normandy, and all Allied forces in France fell under the command of Gen Eisenhower. At this point all RAF squadrons in France, including those of 324 Wing, flew back to Italy and were based around Florence for the push against the Gothic Line.

By early September Kesselring had withdrawn his troops around the Gothic Line. Gen Alexander, now in charge of the Allied armies, decided to pitch the US 5th Army against the central positions while the British 8th Army attacked strong positions across the Coriano Ridge. The new attacks were launched on 13 September and met some of the heaviest fighting and resistance yet encountered. Most air support was directed towards road and rail targets, supply dumps, gun positions and troop concentrations, with strategic bridges blown to prevent troop movements between the Po river, Turin and the sea.

By the end of September, the rains that had been a feature of the previous winter returned and rapidly brought any advance to a halt. Most airfields were reduced to either lakes or quagmires and became unserviceable, and there was a general acceptance that the push would need to be postponed until the following spring.

It was into this stalemate that Barney returned to operations with 43 Squadron at Florence after his rest and instruction period with 71 OTU.

43 SQUADRON, ITALY – OCTOBER 1944

The British 8th Army had continued to try and push on towards the next German defence lines along the Savio river, despite the rains. Bridges across the river became the main target for the Allied bombing campaign. Fighter-bombers also cut railway lines between Ferrara, Bologna and Ravenna, while light and medium bombers attacked the railway marshalling yards around Bologna.

Most of 324 Wing's sorties were flown in support of the US 5th Army thrust towards Bologna, where there was hope that a breakthrough could still be achieved. Although there was massive air support for the US 5th Army offensive for the first two weeks of October, the dogged German defence held and the Americans were stopped short of Bologna as Kesselring moved German divisions away from the Adriatic coast to reinforce the centre.

No. 43 Squadron's arrival back in Italy, to Florence from France on 1 October, was horrifically tragic and possibly the reason for Barney's transfer to the squadron. The base at Florence, known locally as Peretola, did have a concrete runway and adequate dispersals, but little else. There was another squadron already there, a SAAF fighter recce squadron, but there was no flying control or night flying facilities.

The flight back from France had been scheduled to stop at Bastia in Corsica for refuelling, despite having the range to do the hop in one go. No. 43 Squadron landed at Bastia and was being fuelled up (although progress was painfully slow) when it became clear that unless they took off soon there would not be sufficient daylight to allow them to land safely at Florence. The sensible decision may have been to stay overnight at Bastia and fly to Florence the following morning. That said, they took off from Bastia without all the planes being refuelled and arrived over Florence at dusk, short of fuel. Another squadron, 111, was ordered to land immediately leaving 43 still in the air and running out of fuel and daylight.

To help them, petrol bowsers, jeeps and other vehicles were lined up along either side of the runway with their headlights panned to light the runway. Several got down in one piece but Lt M. Duchen from South Africa struck the cab of one of the bowsers and somersaulted beyond the vehicle. The next Spitfire, piloted by Flt Lt J.L. Lowther, did not see the wreckage of Duchen's plane and smashed into it, bursting into flames. Lowther ran from the fireball but Duchen died in the inferno, as did Plt Off Ainslee, another 111 pilot, who had tried to rescue him. Another South African, Lt Dalton, also tried to land and he too struck the wreckage and was badly burnt.

The rest of the Spits were ordered to circle and abandon their aircraft once their fuel was exhausted, which was a little disconcerting to say the least, but after intervention from the USAAF they were diverted to Pisa where they landed safely. Perhaps due to the horrific events that night, but certainly because new pilots were required, there was no operational flying until 16 October.

On 12 October the Allied air forces had carried out devastating attacks against the German defences under Operation Pancake, which, as the name implied, was the intended flattening of the German ground defences. Nearly 700 heavy bombers, 300 medium bombers and 300 fighter-bombers dropped their bombs on German positions. The effects were devastating: damaged roads tied up engineers, traffic jams were everywhere and troop and traffic movements delayed, command posts were hit, supply chains choked, artillery damaged and gun crews dispersed, strong points hit and the German defence softened. Panic ensued, but the Germans, completely without air support, hung on.

14 OCTOBER

ORB: Florence – a sweep in the afternoon cancelled.

15 OCTOBER

Log Book: Dakota, Flt Lt Roper RCAF – Swindon–Northholt–Brussels.

ORB: Florence – Lt J.C. Mentz SAF arrived from 154 Squadron.

16 OCTOBER

Log Book: Beechcraft, Sqn Ldr Smart – Brussels–Le Bourget.

ORB: Two Spit IXs were received from 357 MU.

17 OCTOBER

ORB: Six aircraft airborne set out to sweep the Bergano–Verona area. 10/10 cloud cover experienced from the mountains to the north of Florence in layers of continuous cloud right up to 26,000ft. Aircraft did not penetrate cloud layer. Three more Spit IXs from 357 MU.

18 OCTOBER

ORB: Weather and aerodrome conditions remained bad and a sweep of the Turin area was cancelled. In the evening the officers entertained the sergeants in the Officers' Mess.

19 OCTOBER

ORB: Another sweep due to take off at 1400 hours was cancelled owing to weather and aerodrome conditions.

20 OCTOBER

Log Book: Dakota, USAAC Lyon–Sienna, Italy.

ORB: Six aircraft airborne took off on a sweep of the Verona–Bergano area. Two fires with black smoke rising to a height of 15,000ft were seen south-west of Milan. Scant heavy accurate flak was experienced and two aircraft returned.
  Flt Lt Barnfather arrived from 94 Squadron.

21 OCTOBER

ORB: Six aircraft airborne and took off to provide cover for B-25s bombing various targets. They flew to Lodi but saw no bombers. Weather conditions in target area west of Adda river were 10/10 clouds at 7,000ft. The aircraft therefore flew north-east to Brescia and Verona but the weather there in the valley was 10/10 cloud at 11,000ft. Medium accurate AA was experienced and what appeared to be two uncamouflaged aircraft were seen on the runway at Ghodi.

22 OCTOBER

ORB: Weather again overcast with area cover in the afternoon for P-47s cancelled.

23 OCTOBER

Log Book: Spitfire IX air test.

ORB: Further mission cancelled due to weather conditions in the Po Valley.

24 OCTOBER

ORB: Six aircraft took off on a sweep over the Verona–Bergano area but owing to cloud cover over Bergano, they only flew to Brescia and Verona. Weather was 10/10 clouds at varying heights over the mountains between 6,000 and 14,000ft. It was clear over Cremona and Brescia eastwards.

Heavy AA was experienced and one aircraft was hit. The pilot, Flt Lt I.G. Thompson, stayed in his aircraft for a while losing height, but when he saw both the ailerons flapping upwards and the rudders locked, he hit the silk. He returned to the Mess within 2 hours, the worse only for a few splinters in his thigh.

26 OCTOBER

ORB: Weather prevented aircraft taking off for a sweep. Flg Off D.S. Reid admitted to hospital and Flg Off R. King took over as Intelligence Officer.

27 OCTOBER

ORB: A sweep by six aircraft postponed and then cancelled. Three new pilots from 5 RFU arrived: Flg Off G.W. Edwards, Flg Off G.C. Hollingworth and Flt Sgt G.R. Leigh.

28 OCTOBER

Log Book: Spitfire IX air test and practice.

ORB: WO R.P. Tutill welcomed into the Officers' Mess as a pilot officer.

29 OCTOBER

Log Book: Spitfire VIII – air test and practice.

ORB: Air tests were very popular now, the only opportunity and offering these days to the flying minded!

Organised exercise for all pilots was received in a grudging manner by those gentle-minded, but nevertheless hundreds turned out in a great soccer match between A Flight and B Flight. Battle was also joined on a nearby steeplechase track.

30 OCTOBER

ORB: Weather was bad, low cloud, poor visibility and a succession of rainstorms. A lecture on 'Spit-bombing' bomb carriers was given on the aerodrome by Flt Lt Perry, the Wing Armament Officer.

The reaction of some of the pilots was utter amazement – after all, whoever heard of a Spitfire carrying bombs? But it was clear that their role was to change to that of dive-bombers in support of ground troops. One wag was heard to comment that they ought to rename the Spitfires to 'Bomb-phires' and this name was evidently widely recorded in the press of the time.

Lt H.P.Anderson SAAF from 243 Squadron was also posted in to join the squadron.

31 OCTOBER

ORB: Six aircraft airborne from 1330–1445 hours took off in an area cover over Venice. One section returned after 20 minutes as the leader had developed low oil pressure. At 1345 about fifty to sixty aircraft were reported but they were not in the target area. The weather was fair over the valley with 6/10 clouds at 11,000ft. On the return flight heavy AA was encountered.

Flt Lt E.W. Creed and Plt Off P.J. Hedderwick returned to the squadron after being attached to 244 Wing for a week to accumulate bombing experience.

In summary for the month, Sqn Ldr Arthur Jupp recorded:

> The move from the South of France back to Italy taken well. Due to the nature of the move the squadron was unable to operate for the first part of the month. When the unit re-assembled, the weather deteriorated and was so poor no extensive operational flying was done.

By now, despite the air support provided to the US 5th Army, the Allies were too weakened against the reinforced German defence to exploit any advantage gained from the air superiority.

They were halted 9 miles short of Bologna and there would be a stalemate again for the winter.

1 NOVEMBER

ORB: A dawn sweep brought six pilots out of bed with added keenness after reports from yesterday, but fog quickly formed and the show was cancelled. Three more Spit IXs received from 357 MU.

2 NOVEMBER

ORB: An early release today after a night of continuous rain. Gp Capt Duncan Smith talked to the whole wing on its hard and successful work of the past few months, and of its forthcoming return to the 8th Army where the conditions would be less comfortable and the bombing work more active and harder.

3–4 NOVEMBER

ORB: Weather bad, no flying.

5 NOVEMBER

ORB: After a foggy morning Flt Lt E.W. Creed took off with a flight of three and was sent after a bandit north of La Spezia on the deck. No contact was made but they were greeted with some heavy concentrated flak about 2 miles out to sea from La Spezia. Landed at 1340 after stooging over Genoa.

6 NOVEMBER

Log Book: Spitfire IX sweep Verona area.

ORB: CO led a flight of eight Spits just south of Lake Garda but nothing to report.

7–10 NOVEMBER

ORB: Weather u/s, no flying except for a few air tests.

11 NOVEMBER

Log Book: Spitfire IX sweep Lake Garda area.

ORB: Wg Cdr Ernie Wootton DFC, who had taken over 324 Wing in October, led a flight of six Spits on an area cover over Padua. Unfortunately, Flt Lts Creed and Cummings were shot up by American P-51 Mustangs and broke off their attack before more damage was done. Later in the day the squadron was glad to hear that Creed had crash-landed near Rimini with cannon splinters in his arm and chest, but there was no word about Flt Lt A.M. Cummings whose Spitfire was not observed after it dived out of formation. It was later learned that he had been killed.

The squadron was well represented in the RAF vs Army game at Florence stadium and had five players in the team.

12 NOVEMBER

ORB: No flying early release. 'A' Party sent out under Adjutant Flt Lt Fisher for Rimini. Rumours of flooded streams and slippery roads made us wish for a safe journey for all concerned.

13 NOVEMBER

ORB: Area cover for B-25s bombing railway route into northern Italy. Plenty of cloud cover and haze about and, after climbing up through 10/10 ceiling, they experienced the great joy of flying smooth gleaming Spitfires, streaking along the peaks of an unbroken sea of rolling cumulus clouds under a dazzling sun. They all returned without incident.

After a short stay Flt Lt Barnfather was posted [back] to 94 Squadron.

16 NOVEMBER

ORB: New base at Rimini and back under the operational control of the Western Desert Air Force. Many were glad to see the back of Florence, the mud, the mist and the rain that swelled the Arno river to an even dirtier brown than it was normally.

Using pierced steel plates (PSP) for runways had become essential to mobile air operations as the war moved across Europe. New runways could be rolled out and airfields created wherever they were required, as was the case at Rimini, the squadron's new base. Intensive training for their dive-bombing future would begin the following day and would follow the Western Desert Air Force system of close air support that had been so successful in the past. The system came under the name 'Rover David Cab Rank', where a controller on the ground called up close air support for targets of selection by using a grid system on maps that had been especially prepared for joint use. It proved to be remarkably accurate and successful.

17 NOVEMBER

Log Book: Dakota, USAAC – Pisa–Rome–Naples, 3 hours.

19 NOVEMBER

Log Book: Dakota, SAAF – Naples–Bari–Athens, 4 hours.

CHAPTER 13

Civil War in Greece

94 Squadron, Kalamaki, Greece

No. 94 Squadron had been formed from 55 Training Unit at Gosport in 1917 and had re-formed for the air defence of Aden in March 1939 when it was equipped with Gloster Gladiators. In 1941 it had moved to Egypt and was re-equipped with Hurricanes, then with Kittyhawks in May 1942, only to be replaced again with Hurricanes for coastal convoy protection in the advance following El Alamein, and interceptor duties around the Delta region in Egypt. As the Germans were pushed west by the Allied armies, the squadron followed to various bases around the coast of Egypt and Libya.

The squadron eventually got Spitfires and the later version Mark IXs in February 1944. Unlike many other squadrons, it had remained in North Africa after the German collapse and from there had carried out fighter sweeps over Crete, bomber escort duties for South African Bostons and Marauders attacking Crete, before relocating to Greece in September 1944. The squadron was taken off operations, bomb-racks were fitted and dive-bombing practice was the order of the day, in preparation for their move into this sphere of operations at Kalamaki near Athens.

Some days earlier the Germans had begun a general withdrawal. No. 94 and other squadrons began reconnaissance, strafing and bombing operations as they retreated through Greece and Yugoslavia. By mid-November operations ceased because the Germans had retreated out of range of the 94 Squadron Spitfires, and also because of the confused situation on the ground. Russian troops were also pressing forward their own advance across the Danube river.

No. 94 Squadron, therefore, turned its attention to Crete again where the Germans had consolidated their positions on the western end of the island. Their role initially was to monitor troop movements, the practice being to send out a section of two aircraft to reconnoitre the island and note the troop positions.

November was the squadron's most successful month to date as they were fortunate in having a large number of targets available. In the previous month, most operations had been against motor transport sections, but the Germans' increased use of rail transport to evacuate their troops and equipment from Greece meant the squadron turned its attention to train-busting.

By 2 November Greece was considered clear of Germans and the squadron started to operate over the border into Yugoslavia. Very soon the Germans were out of range of Kalamaki so Sedes aerodrome at Salonica was used as a refuelling and re-arming base. A small ground party was flown there by 221 Squadron Wellingtons for this purpose. Within a few days the squadron were bombing as far as Skopje, with success.

21 NOVEMBER

Log Book: Spit V, sector recce.

ORB: Section carried out a recce over Lakkoi and Meskla areas on Crete. Nothing seen. Weather and visibility good. Section also carried out recce along north coast road of Crete with several staff cars seen going towards Iraklion.

22 NOVEMBER

ORB: Section carried out low-level recce along north coast of Crete, weather was very bad with rain and 10/10 cloud over the island and 8/10 cloud over the sea. Work was being carried out on the airfield at Iraklion.

23 NOVEMBER

Log Book: Spit V, air test.

ORB: Section carried out a recce along north coast road of Crete. Weather was very bad with 10/10 cloud so nothing was seen. Another section carried out a recce along the north coast of Crete from Rethimnon to Iraklion and then onto Kastellion. Nothing was seen.

24 NOVEMBER

ORB: Section carried out a recce over Maleme and Khania – nothing observed but considerable amount of 88 flak was seen. Section carried out a recce along north coast of Crete to Iraklion and again there was 10/10 cloud from 6–8,000ft. Section saw nothing, only a few staff cars on the roads. Section carried out a recce over north coast road of Crete. Apart from 8/10 clouds over western end, weather and visibility good.

25 NOVEMBER

ORB: Carried out a recce over the north coast of Crete, two staff cars were seen. There was accurate flak and No. 2 of the section, Flg Off Tolkowsky, had his tail section damaged.

26 NOVEMBER

Log Book: Spit V, attempted recce.

ORB: Airborne to carry out a recce along the north coast of Crete, nothing was seen. Visibility was good, returned to base without incident.

27 NOVEMBER

Log Book: Spit V, Crete recce.

ORB: Barney and WO Bill Dorman flew a recce of Kastellion–Pedhiadhos over Crete and although visibility was good, nothing of interest was seen and they returned to base without incident.

Section flew to Crete and landed at Iraklion airfield. Airborne from there and carried out a further recce on the way back to base, without incident. Further section carried out strafing attacks of motor transport in Crete. No targets were seen but 88mm flak was encountered around Suda Bay. All aircraft returned to base without damage.

28 NOVEMBER

ORB: Section took off for Iraklion to stand by for further operations and then carried out recce from Iraklion to Suda Bay and Maleme. Aircraft returned to Iraklion after an uneventful trip.

In April 1941, after German troops had invaded Greece, the Germans rapidly overran the Greek armies and the British forces that had been sent to their aid. After an attempt to hold the island of Crete, King George II and his government, headed by Emmanouil Tsouderos, fled to Egypt and a collaborationist government controlled by Germany was established in Athens. Greece was then divided up among the Italians, Germans, and Bulgarians. The harshness of the occupation regime led to terrible famine and spiralling inflation. More than 100,000 Greeks died as a result of the famine and, in 1943, most of the country's Jews were deported to Nazi death camps in Poland.

Despite the hardships of the occupation, the Greek people maintained the will to withstand it, and a number of resistance groups were formed. By far the largest of these was the National Liberation Front (known by its Greek acronym, EAM). Along with its military arm, the National People's Liberation Army (ELAS), the EAM was under communist control, although its membership was far from being exclusively communist. Of the smaller organisations, the most significant was the National Republican Greek League (EDES), which held to a more conservative political programme than the EAM. Virtually all resistance groups opposed the return of George II, whom most Greeks identified with the repression of the Metaxas dictatorship. In 1942 the British began parachuting in arms and personnel to aid the Greek resistance.

In September 1943 the Italians surrendered following the Allied invasion of Italy. The prospect of the liberation of Greece led to rivalry and a power struggle between the EAM/ELAS and the EDES. The ELAS attacked the EDES in October 1943, and the two resistance groups fought actively through the winter before reaching an uneasy truce in February 1944. In August, representatives of all the resistance organisations joined together in support of a government-in-exile established in Cairo, Egypt, under the premiership of Georgios Papandreou. In October Greece had been liberated from the Nazis and the National Unity Government returned from abroad with Georgios Papandreou as prime minister. The situation in the country was critical.

The British, who had been given military control of the area by the Allies, demanded the disbanding of the ELAS guerilla army and the surrender of its weapons. After the German withdrawal, this principal Greek resistance movement, which was controlled by the communists, refused to disarm. A banned demonstration by resistance forces in Athens in December 1944 ended in battles with the Greek government and British forces.

At the beginning of the month sections were standing by for operations against the Germans who were still isolated on Crete. However, on 3 December, the precipitation of the Greek internal crisis by the violent ELAS demonstration in Athens brought an entirely new job to the squadron. At first, when it did not appear probable that the armed revolt of the ELAS against the Greek government would be serious, the squadron made several 'showing the flag' flights over Athens. Later, as the position became more critical, sections flew on patrol to disperse bands of armed rebels approaching the city. In order to avoid unnecessary bloodshed pilots were carefully briefed to 'beat up' parties first, then if they did not disperse, to fire warning shots in front of them. As a last resort, the parties were to be strafed.

The idea of fighting Greeks was at first distasteful but later, as it became apparent that ELAS meant trouble and were entirely ruthless in their treatment of both civilians and prisoners, the attitude changed. This was particularly after ELAS had opened fire on some British troops in Piraeus. From then onwards the squadron operated in close support of the army, and were directed by them, via VHF and while in the air, from one target to another.

There was a good deal of strafing of motor transport outside Athens and Piraeus, and of ELAS troops entrenched in the hills outside Athens. Specific houses were strafed and possible gun points neutralised. On the night of 17 December AHQ Greece was attacked and all day on the 18th the squadron was active in its defence, beating up gun positions. In the early morning of 19 December AHQ was captured and about 600 prisoners taken. An armoured relief column, which the squadron had escorted arrived too late but managed to rescue about 100 men.

After the fall of the AHQ, sections of the squadron operated for several days shadowing parties of RAF prisoners being marched north over the mountains. In addition, sections carrying special containers of food and clothing on their bomb-racks made continual reconnaissance over all the areas, looking for possible escapees, none of which were found. Meanwhile, large army reinforcements had arrived and the squadron continued giving close support in Athens and Piraeus. When parties of prisoners were later located they were kept supplied by the squadron dropping containers.

Medical supplies were dropped at Levagnia where RAF personnel were in hospital. Supplies of food, cigarettes, news sheets, soap and anti-louse powder were also dropped to further parties at Khifisikori and Amphiklia. At Khifisikori the party signalled their needs in writing using white stones on the grass, and on one occasion wrote the word 'thanks' after the supplies had been dropped. At the end of the month, close air support was given to an armoured column proceeding to Pallini to rescue a detachment of soldiers who had been isolated.

The late Sqn Ldr R.G. Foskett RAAF, the former Commanding Officer of the squadron, was awarded the OBE for the excellent work he had done in training the Yugoslav officers and airmen who formed a flight of the squadron; and Flt Sgt Goulding was awarded the BEM for his good work also in training Yugolsav airmen.

1 DECEMBER

ORB: Three sections took off for Iraklion, Crete, for operations but had to return because the airfield was unserviceable.

2 DECEMBER

Log Book: Spit V, to Iraklion – recalled.

ORB: Aircraft were airborne heading for Iraklion, Crete, but ran into bad weather after 30 minutes and returned to base.

3 DECEMBER

Log Book: 1. Spit V, to Iraklion; 2. From Iraklion.

ORB: Barney led section which took off for Iraklion for further operations against the garrison. A further section was ordered to beat up a communist meeting in Athens. Later further sections were ordered to beat up a communist meeting in Athens. One aircraft made a forced landing about 20 miles north-east of Athens, but the pilot was unhurt. The section detailed for Iraklion earlier in the day returned from Crete and made a recce for caiques between north-west Crete and Kythera. All aircraft returned to Kalamaki later that day.

Political events now meant a change in operations for 94 Squadron. Since the Allied landings in Greece, the British government had sought to bring the Greek regent back into power, but the Greek Communist Party were against this and it became the root cause of the open confrontation between the communist forces, the Greek government and the Allied forces in and around the Athens area.

Athens was placed out of bounds and the airfield was secured. All personnel carried sidearms at all times. Supplies for the base were either flown in from Italy or arrived in tank-landing craft that beached near the airfield, as the sea formed one of the airfield boundaries. In the event, Kalamaki only came under attack on one or two occasions and these were easily repelled by the ground defence.

4 DECEMBER

The initial RAF operations against the communist army, or ELAS, were by low-flying aircraft in and around the Athens area.

ORB: Two aircraft carried out a recce for any communist gatherings in and around Athens. One section flew to Iraklion for further operations and returned later after carrying out an anti-caique recce on the north-west of the island. A few caiques were seen.

5 DECEMBER

Log Book: Spitfire air test, fired over the heads of troops to disperse them.

ORB: Sections flew to Crete for further operations. Sections also carried out a recce for ELAS troops in the Athens area. Troops seen and aircraft fired over their heads to disperse them. The sections at Iraklion took off from the base there to bomb an ammo dump south of Khania. All bombs fell into the target area but results were unobserved, and later they bombed a further suspected fuel dump at Alikianov, again without observed results. Unfortunately, the situation deteriorated and a full-scale civil war ensued.

6 DECEMBER

Log Book: Spitfire strafe rebels Athens.

ORB: Section carried out a recce over Tatoi airfield for any ELAS troops and a further section made a recce along the roads around Athens seeking further ELAS troops. Section carried out a standing patrol over Negara and a recce for troops in the Athens area. A section carried out strafing attacks on guerilla troops that were moving towards Kalamaki but results were not observed.

7 DECEMBER

Log Book: Spitfire recce Athens.

ORB: A section escorted an RAF convoy into Athens from AHQ against any possibility of attacks from ELAS troops. Further section did a road recce south of Lamia for guerilla troops and some were seen. Section carried out a recce around [the outskirts of Athens], but no guerilla activity was seen, and then strafed high positions in the Pireaus area, which were held by ELAS, positions in the Lofos-Strefi area, also held by ELAS, and then positions near to the Olympic stadium in Athens. A section strafing ELAS positions in the Pireaus area encountered small-arms fire and Sqn Ldr Jack Slade's aircraft was hit. In the afternoon further sections strafed ELAS positions in the Filappos and Lofos areas.

8 DECEMBER

ORB: Individual aircraft sorties were the order of the early morning flights, Flg Off Graham Hulse carried out a recce of ELAS HQ, Flg Off E.W. Barber carried out a recce along roads between Athens and Kifisa but nothing was seen and Flg Off N. Watts escorted a road convoy into Athens without incident.

One section was airborne to carry out a recce of the Lamia area but as they reached Thivia they encountered bad weather and had to return to base.

Flg Off L. Duddridge escorted a Wellington into Tatoi airfield and a further section was airborne to strafe ELAS positions in Athens but found no targets. However, a further section came across ELAS motor transport north-east of Athens and destroyed two and damaged a further four transports, and finally one section strafed ELAS forces around Athens stadium.

9 DECEMBER

Log Book: Spitfire strafe Piraeus.

ORB: Section led by Barney strafed ELAS positions in the Piraeus area. Plt Off A. Dixon carried out a recce for a 75mm gun north-east of Athens but could not find it. One section provided escort to an RAF convoy into Athens and Flg Off D. Jackson strafed ELAS positions in the Athens area. A section carried out a strafing attack of ELAS motor transport on Tatoi airfield. Four trucks and all available petrol on the airfield were destroyed and the section then carried out a general recce of Athens. Another section continued the strafing attacks on ELAS motor transport near Tatoi and destroyed one and damaged two more.

10 DECEMBER

Log Book: Spitfire bomb East stadium.

ORB: Sqn Ldr Jack Slade DFC carried out a recce of Athens and Piraeus for movements of guerilla troops. One section went out on a recce for a 2-pdr gun believed to be situated near the powder magazine. No gun was seen but a number of troops were seen taking cover in slit trenches and by the walls of the powder magazine. [Flg] Off Graham Hulse took off to escort a motor transport convoy into Kifisa but the convoy was unable to leave because the road was blocked in several places. He carried out strafing attacks on these roadblocks.

One section, late morning, carried out low-level strafing attacks on high ground south of Athens stadium held by guerilla troops and these were later found to be very successful. A further section, mid-afternoon, carried out bombing and low-level strafing attacks on the same guerilla positions near the stadium. All bombs were seen to fall in the target area. Later on a section carried out a recce in the area around the Grand Bretagne Hotel in Athens for a 75mm gun. Gun flashes were seen but the aircraft were not fired upon.

11 DECEMBER

ORB: One section carried out a recce between Athens and Kifisa for roadblocks, another section carried out a recce between Elevsis and Tripolis, though nothing was seen except a few motor transport trucks and, mid-afternoon, a section strafed motor transport in the Piraeus area. Six were attacked and destroyed while they were being unloaded of their ammunition. Late afternoon, section strafed ELAS position in the north of Athens near Likavittos.

12 DECEMBER

ORB: One section carried out a recce along the road at Liosia north-west of Athens, encountered motor transport and destroyed two and damaged a further three.

A further section carried out strafing attacks from the Athens brewery to the swimming pool. One house was destroyed, several were damaged and one truck was also damaged.

13 DECEMBER

ORB: A section led by Sqn Ldr Jack Slade carried out strafing attacks in the Athenian area and a number of houses were set on fire.

14 DECEMBER

Log Book: Spitfire recce Faliron area.

ORB: A section carried out a recce of Faliron but nothing was reported.

15 DECEMBER

Log Book: Spitfire strafe Singros area.

ORB: Sections took off to bomb gun positions north of Piraeus, bombed target areas but could not see the guns. A further section strafed ELAS positions in the Singros area and then the Lofus-Strefi areas.

16 DECEMBER

ORB: Carried out strafing attacks in the Lofus–Strefi areas and then a quarry in the Pireaus area occupied by ELAS forces.

17 DECEMBER

ORB: Section airborne to strafe a train at Elevsis and engine was destroyed, then moved on to motor transport at Megara.

18 DECEMBER

Log Book: Spitfire recce AHQ.

Air Headquarters for the Greek-based RAF squadrons had been set up some miles outside the city. When the civil war had broken out it was considered safe to leave it there because RAF Command thought that AHQ could defend itself if it came under attack. However, 94 Squadron had to carry out strafing attacks on ELAS troops attacking AHQ and attacks were successful as a number surrendered.

ORB: Further section carried out attacks against gun positions in the Kifisa area. A supply-dropping Halifax to the AHQ was escorted by one section, then a further recce along the Phaleron–Athens road. Supply containers dropped by the Halifax had fallen into ELAS hands so they were strafed, some containers were hit.

19 DECEMBER

Attacks by ELAS troops against AHQ were successful and it fell with a large number of RAF personnel taken prisoner.

ORB: A section carried out a recce on roads and railways at Elevsis, Corinth and Tripolis, further attacks against the containers dropped by the Halifax yesterday. One section escorted tanks travelling from Kalamaki to AHQ and then a further section carried out supply-dropping to the personnel at AHQ and recce near Kifisa.

20 DECEMBER

Log Book: Spitfire recce for prisoners.

ORB: Section took off to drop supplies to AHQ personnel who had escaped, but supplies were returned to base as they could not be found. A further section led by Barney and Ken Collins found them marching north and then carried on to recce ELAS troops north-east of Kalamaki.

21 DECEMBER

ORB: Supply-drop to RAF prisoners escaped but no one was seen so supplies brought back to base. Section took off to recce for guns in the Athens area but returned without seeing anything. One section, early afternoon, strafed ELAS motor transport trucks in the Piraeus area, two trucks and one bus were destroyed. Carried out further recce for ELAS troops in the Piraeus area.

22 DECEMBER

ORB: Carried out a general recce of Athens for ELAS troops.

23 DECEMBER

Log Book: Spitfire strafe motor transport.

ORB: Sections carried out standing patrols and strafed motor transport around the Piraeus area.

24 DECEMBER

ORB: No flying all day.

25 DECEMBER

Log Book: Spitfire armed recce.

ORB: Section took off to recce Elevsis, Corinth and Tripolis but bad weather meant they had to return to base. Further section carried out an armed recce in the Piraeus area and strafed ELAS troops seen. Also dropped supplies to prisoners.

This was the only Christmas Day throughout the war that Barney flew, and to use his own words, 'therefore I did not wish the ELAS Merry Christmas'. Also, Barney's Spitfire was hit and damaged on the ground when another Spitfire ran into it, but this was entirely the fault of the other pilot; Barney was unhurt.

26 DECEMBER

Log Book: Spitfire patrol Athens and Piraeus.

ORB: Carried out patrol over Athens and Piraeus.

27 DECEMBER

ORB: Carried out patrol and armed recce over Athens and Piraeus, then an armed recce of the hills around the base, but nothing was seen.

28 DECEMBER

ORB: No flying all day.

29 DECEMBER

Log Book: Spitfire recce roadblocks.

ORB: Section carried out a recce along the Pallini road for roadblocks, then as escort to an armoured convoy proceeding along the Koropi road. Further section strafed Analipsis monastery in Athens, attacks were successful, as were those carried out against ELAS strongpoints north of Piraeus.

---

30 DECEMBER

ORB: No flying all day.

---

31 DECEMBER

Log Book: Spitfire cover armoured column.

ORB: Section attacked houses which were ELAS strongpoints in Piraeus, attacks were successful as our troops moved in soon after. Further sections dropped supplies to RAF prisoners at Lamia and Amfiklia, and an armed recce to a road convoy proceeding to Pallini.

By now the ELAS troops were being contained and began a general retreat, commandeering all forms of motor transport which kept the squadron busy strafing the vehicles as they moved northwards.

Two very different types of operations characterised the work of the squadron through January, 1945. The first was the destruction of very large numbers of ELAS motor transport, which were successfully strafed when they attempted to evacuate their troops and stores after the army had broken into Feristeri. The rebels were pursued northwards and constantly attacked.

The other type of operation was reconnaissance and supply of British prisoners in the hands of ELAS. This was also very successful and large numbers of prisoners received food and supplies.

---

1 JANUARY

ORB: Section carried out supply-dropping to POWs at Amfiklia without incident. Further section dropped medical supplies to hospital at Lavadia.

---

2 JANUARY

Log Book: Spitfire, supply-dropping.

ORB: Took off to drop supplies to prisoners at Amfiklia and Kifishikori but owing to bad visibility sections were unable to locate the prisoners.

A further section carried out a general reconnaissance of Athens and strafed motor transport. Sqn Ldr Jack Slade led sections that strafed motor transport in the Feristeri area and supplies were dropped at Amfiklia.

3 JANUARY

Log Book: Spitfire, recce caiques Milos.

ORB: Lt Van der Merwe from South Africa took off to drop supplies to POWs at Atalani but no one was seen. Section led by Flt Lt Barnfather carried out a reconnaissance for caiques around Milos island but did not observe any.

4 JANUARY

Log Book: Spitfire, patrol and strafe.

ORB: Flg Off G. Hulse carried out a patrol over armoured cars proceeding towards Feristeri and destroyed one. A further section did a recce for prisoners around Lamia but no one was seen. Further patrols by several sections were carried out over the armoured column proceeding to Feristeri and several more were destroyed.

5 JANUARY

Log Book: Spitfire, strafe M/T.

ORB: Section strafed motor transport at Elevsis destroying three. A further section strafed ELAS motor transport along the road north of Akharnai and about eight were destroyed. Sqn Ldr Jack Slade and Flt Sgt R.J. Andrews, an Australian, took off at lunchtime to strafe the ELAS forces at Megara and Elevsis. Andrews crashed while attacking the motor transport as his plane was unable to pull up without hitting some trees, and he was killed when his plane crashed. Jack Slade later visited the place and found that Andrews had been buried by a Greek shepherd just north of Mandra.

A further section carried out an armed recce north-west of Athens for any movement of ELAS forces, one motor transport destroyed. Flt Lt Barnfather and Sgt K. Collins then strafed motor transport in the Elevsis area and destroyed seven with a further three damaged. Later in the afternoon, further sections carried out recce around Athens for guns but did not see any, but did destroy further motor transport.

6 JANUARY

Log Book: Spitfire, recce POWs.

ORB: Section led by Flt Lt Barnfather carried out a recce for POWs around Atalindi and Amfiklia but did not observe any, could not get as far as Lamia owing to bad weather but did come across motor transport, strafed and destroyed one. Sqn Ldr Slade led a further section to strafe ELAS troops south of Corinth but did not see many to attack, but again observed motor transport with two destroyed and a further six damaged on the way home. Further armed recce of the Elevsis and Koropi areas, with little traffic but M/T was destroyed and several ELAS troops killed.

7 JANUARY

ORB: Sections carried out armed recce of traffic around Kifisa and Koropi but without anything to report.

8 JANUARY

ORB: Covered armoured column 'Flanker' at Elevsis, several trucks were destroyed. One section carried out a further recce for ELAS troops over Levadia but none were observed.

9 JANUARY

ORB: No operational flying.

10 JANUARY

ORB: Sections carried out armed reconnaissance for ELAS movements between Elevsis and Corinth and Larisa and Amfiklia, not much to report.

11 JANUARY

ORB: No operational flying.

12 JANUARY

ORB: Sections carried out a recce for POWs at Lamia, Larisa and Trikkala, provided an escort for an armoured column and staff car to Thive, and then on to Lamia.

13 JANUARY

ORB: Sections carried out a recce for POWs at Lamia again, an armed recce over Eastern Peleponese where some M/T were destroyed. ELAS troops were reported around Patras but none were encountered. A further section dropped supplies at Velvendos and strafed M/T in the Larisa and Agrinon areas, several were destroyed and more damaged.

14 JANUARY

ORB: Section carried out an armed recce around Lamia and Trikkala. Several more M/T destroyed. One section that had taken off for Larisa had to return owing to bad weather. One section took off to strafe ELAS troops north of Konstandinos but did not observe anyone there.

15 JANUARY

ORB: No operational flying.

16 JANUARY

ORB: Carried out an armed recce for POWs at Lazarina.

17 JANUARY

ORB: No operational flying.

18 JANUARY

ORB: Carried out an armed recce for POWs at Lazarina again but only got as far as Volos, weather was very bad with very low clouds. Later, a further section carried out a recce for POWs south of Trikkala but again did not come across any.

19 JANUARY

ORB: Section carried out a recce for POWs south of Trikkala but again did not come across any.

20 JANUARY

ORB: Section carried out a recce for POWs south of Trikkala but had to turn back because of further bad weather and low cloud.

21 JANUARY

ORB: Section to Volos landing strip.

22 JANUARY

ORB: Carried out an armed recce for POWs at Lazarina but did not observe any.

23 JANUARY

ORB: Sections carried out recce for POWs around Trikkala and Volos but did not observe any, but came across about 100 POWs at Lazarina.

24 JANUARY

ORB: Sections carried out recce for POWs around Lamia and Rendina and then an armed recce around Trikkala and Volos, observed a lot of activity around Volos.

25 JANUARY

ORB: Recce for hostages around Lamia but none seen.

26 JANUARY

ORB: Again a further recce for hostages around Lamia but none seen, and a further section carried out a shipping recce south of Volos and observed one ship and two escort vessels going south.

27 JANUARY

ORB: Recce for hostages around Lamia but none seen.

28 JANUARY

Log Book: Spitfire IX, local flying.

29–31 JANUARY

ORB: No operational flying.

On 1 February 1945, instructions were received from 337 Wing that the squadron was to stand by to move to Sedes in Salonika, but after numerous false alarms and cancellations the aircrew finally proceeded on the 14th. The ground party embarked on the 17th and arrived on the 18th. In view of the uncertainty, the squadron carried out little operational flying: One bombing sortie against Milos was carried out and several reconnaissance flights. After the move to Sedes, and the aircraft became serviceable, recces throughout Greece were made to note conditions of roads, railways and any traffic.

7 FEBRUARY

ORB: Section bombed German army camp in Milos, bombs were dropped in target area but results not observed. One aircraft returned early after jettisoning his bombs.

A squadron concert party was formed and rehearsals were in full swing with the first show planned for the following month.

A meeting of all photography enthusiasts was held with a view to forming a camera club, and with over twenty people attending, and with the promise of a few more, it was considered such a hearty response that the formation of the camera club was definitely approved. The club arranged facilities for members to do their own developing and printing.

8 FEBRUARY

ORB: Weather recce to Crete was aborted due to bad weather.

10 FEBRUARY

Log Book: Spitfire local air test.

ORB: Weather recce to Crete and Milos.

14 FEBRUARY

ORB: The aircrew from the squadron moved to Sedes near Salonika and took over the Mark VIII and Mark IX Spitfires of 32 Squadron. As the army was also moving north to take control of the country they had to open up lines of communication, a task hampered by the Germans who had blown bridges during their earlier retreat.

18 FEBRUARY

Log Book: Fairchild, local air test.

ORB: Recce in Peloponese for conditions of and movements on roads and railway system.

19 FEBRUARY

Log Book: Fairchild with Flg Off Anderson recce roads Xanthe.

ORB: Recce for conditions and movements in Thrace paying special attention to bridges.

With a soccer field available, games were soon in full swing and an inter-section league was formed. Other sports would be introduced once the squadron had settled down following its move. The squadron sick quarters had been established in one wing of the main building of the farm school that lay about a mile off the main road from Salonika and Sedes. One four-bedroom ward had been set up and four more beds could be used in another room in an emergency. Electric light and running water were laid on and the sewage system appeared to be working satisfactorily.

20 FEBRUARY

Log Book: Auster, Colonel Peters, Sedes to Volos.

The squadron had also taken on charge about three Austers and Barney had been made responsible for organising and flying the army officers to the outlying areas.

22 FEBRUARY

Log Book: Auster, Colonel Peters, Volos to Sedes.

27 FEBRUARY

Log Book: Spitfire 1. Recce; 2. Abortive recce.

ORB: Sections led by Flt Lt Barnfather were airborne to recce conditions of road and rail and report on movements in an area near Thrace. Barney in his aircraft returned early with engine trouble.

A Greek pilot was treated for facial injuries in the hospital after a collision in mid-air. Wg Cdr Woodruff of 337 Wing had been in the other aircraft and his body was brought to the sick quarters later that evening after it had been recovered from the sea.

There were very few opportunities for operational sorties during March. The first few days were spent keeping a watch on army columns moving out into the surrounding countryside to disarm ELAS troops, but very few incidents occurred. During the latter part of the month an intensive training programme was undertaken so that the squadron would be fit if it were called back into action.

The squadron concert party put on two shows which were well received by the squadron but were too topical to be of much interest to other units. An ENSA concert party, 'We Three', was presented on 23 March, again much appreciated. The Camera Club appeared to be in full swing, especially with the printing and developing that was being done, and a competition was held with many excellent snaps entered. Soccer was played almost every day, a few hockey trials were held and games with other units were arranged.

A quiet month overall, but the ground crews were generally busy getting the aircraft serviceability record improved. There were now no enemy attacks in the area; Crete and other islands were being attacked by Greek squadrons based at Hassani.

2 MARCH

ORB: Recce for road and rail movements in the Epirus and Thrace areas.

5 MARCH

ORB: Recce for road and rail movements, Florina and Xanthe areas.

6 MARCH

Log Book: Spitfire IX, battle formation.

7 MARCH

ORB: Recce for army column in Drama. Saw forty assorted vehicles in north-west suburbs with many people around. All peaceful. Further vehicles were seen approaching Kavalla.

9 MARCH

ORB: Recce for road and rail movements in the Thrace area and central Greece but no incidents.

10 MARCH

ORB: Recce for road and rail movements again in the Thrace area and central Greece.

14 MARCH

Log Book: Spitfire IX, air test.

17 MARCH

Log Book: Spitfire IX, to Hassani.

18 MARCH

Log Book: Spitfire IX, Hassani to base.

21 MARCH

Log Book: Spitfire IX: 1. Squadron formation; 2. Search, landed Hassani; 3. Hassani to base.

For the rest of March and into April, 1945, Barney and his colleagues had few opportunities for operational flying until 94 Squadron was formally disbanded on 16 April. Barney was posted back to 72 Squadron where he rejoined his old colleagues at Klagenfurt in Austria.

CHAPTER 14

The Final Days

By the end of March 1945, on both the eastern and western fronts, the Allied armies were pushing up against the borders of Germany. France and Belgium had been liberated but fighting continued in northern Italy, Yugoslavia and Hungary. Holland, Denmark and Norway remained under German occupation. The threat of Hitler's secret weapons had ended – the terror of the V1 flying bombs and V2 rockets had ceased, and a renewed U-boat offensive had been crushed, but the German Army would not suddenly collapse as it had done in 1918.

At the beginning of April, fighting on German soil continued on both fronts. The American 3rd and 9th Armies had been trying for several weeks to encircle Germany's industrial heartland of the Ruhr when, on 1 April, a pincer movement met at Lippstadt, severing the Ruhr from the rest of Germany. On 4 April American troops reached the first Nazi death camp, a sight that was to shock the Western world. More than 3,000 emaciated corpses lay in and around the slave labour camp named Ohrdruf. On 11 April the camps at Nordhausen and Buchenwald were liberated and the full horror of what the Germans had done began to be revealed, and then on 15 April the hell hole that was Belsen was liberated, followed by Dachau at the end of the month.

Back in Italy, Barney's old squadron, No. 72, had been re-equipped with the Spitfire Mk IX in its LF version, that was configured as a bomber and could carry two 250lb bombs. The squadron had been operating in a close tactical support role, hitting enemy strong points, roads, railways and canals, flying as many as 500 sorties a month. Targets were usually pre-selected, but once their bomb loads had been released the pilots were free to go hunting targets of opportunity. It was a tight-knit, happy squadron once again; there was no division into Officers' and Sergeants' Messes and the pilots flew together and messed together. It was clear that the war was drawing to a close, but the dive-bombing continued and the flak was just as dangerous.

---

9 APRIL

This day marked the beginning of the final assault in Italy. After an initial softening up by some 800 medium and heavy bombers, the squadron and the rest of 324 Wing with forty-eight aircraft in total were detailed to attack enemy gun positions on the banks of the River Senio with blaze bombs (or fire bombs as they became known). Everybody was excited to know that this could be the final push. In support of the Polish Corps along the Senio river, the aim was to drive the Germans out of Italy. Throughout March and right up to the final drive, the overwhelming Allied air superiority had concentrated on severing German lines of communication to deny them supplies and prevent their escape. By 9 April every major railway line north of the River Po was cut at multiple points. The Germans were isolated.

At about 1520 hours the heavy artillery opened up all along the front line, the shells pounding into the banks of the River Senio from all angles. For a while the guns fell silent only to be replaced by the roar of Thunderbolts, Kittyhawks and Spitfires (including those from 324 Wing) as they flew up and down the river with their own bombs, rockets and machine guns. After the sound of aircraft had died away, the ground artillery opened up again and continued to pound the river bank. In all, there were five gun bombardments and four air attacks until, at just after 1900 hours, a sudden silence marked H-hour. Aircraft returned on a dummy run to keep the Germans' heads down, but their noise also disguised the roar of the amphibious vehicles which crossed the river and clambered up the banks on the far side, followed closely by the assault troops which struggled forward in the gathering dusk. The final assault had begun and the attacks against specific target areas opposite the British V Corps and the Polish II Corps along the Senio had started.

10 APRIL

ORB: Four missions of four aircraft each against enemy targets and a further four aircraft completed and armed recce. WO Williams' aircraft caught fire in his bomb dive and crashed and burned out. No parachute was seen. Later, Flt Lt King made a 'wheels-up' landing after experiencing trouble through enemy action but his aircraft crashed into a tree and caught fire and he died in the fire. A very sad day for the squadron as they lost two experienced pilots, one of whom had been a flight commander.

No. 324 Wing continued to be employed in a close support role, directing their attentions at enemy-occupied houses, strongpoints, gun positions and troop concentrations which were bombed and strafed consistently, while the heavies carpet-bombed the crossing of the Santerno river. Operations were hampered by unprecedented strong winds and a few targets along the river were obscured by cloud cover. With such a large number of aircraft over the target at once, and in difficult flying conditions, there were the inevitable losses to flak and collisions. On the ground the Allied armies' advance could have been held up by natural obstacles such as the river banks, which had taken a pounding, or the German artillery, which had also suffered, but Allied air superiority meant that attacks against the artillery continued without interference and the troops on the ground mopped up the German infantry and light weapons. At times it seemed the whole countryside was enveloped in a mass of yellow smoke.

11 APRIL

ORB: Another heavy day with five missions of four aircraft each on close support army targets, and two armed recce of four aircraft each. Flt Lt Rayner was re-posted as Flight Commander and appointed to command A Flight.

Allied medium bombers continued to pound the Brenner Line to prevent the Germans from restoring it to use. On the ground the 8th Army had reached the general line of the Santerno and its New Zealand elements were soon across the river.

12 APRIL

ORB: D-Day for the 5th Army but bad weather caused a postponement for two days. Fog in the morning caused a delay to proceedings, but the army provided two close-support targets, each of four aircraft, and in the afternoon Gp Capt Beresford DSO, DFC led the squadron of twelve aircraft together with a further twelve from the rest of the wing, equipped with blaze bombs again to attack the western flood banks of the Santerno river. Several very successful attacks were made on enemy headquarters and POW evidence confirmed the accuracy of the attacks. Flt Sgt Williams from 43 Squadron, who was part of the 324 Wing show that day, was wounded in the shoulder by small-arms fire and did well to get his flak-damaged Spit back to base.

13 APRIL

ORB: Another very heavy day when the squadron flew five missions of four aircraft each on 'Rover Tom Cab Ranks' and four aircraft each on 'Pineapple Sundae' and finished off with all twelve aircraft on a 'Timothy'. WO Pete Schneider, an Aussie, was believed hit by flak and he baled out behind enemy lines. His aircraft burnt out but he was seen to escape from the aircraft and step out of his parachute so was posted missing, not yet returned.

14 APRIL

ORB: D-Day for the 5th Army postponed from two days earlier but fog shrouded the airfield first thing in the morning. By 9 a.m. the fog began to lift and H-hour was reset. Still flying hard, the squadron completed twenty-eight missions mainly against enemy gun positions and their headquarters. US Thunderbolts joined the RAF Spitfires and Kittyhawks in fighter-bomber operations that were designed to ease the way for the ground assault. No. 43 Squadron lost WO A.G. Edwards when his Spit took hits after strafing a staff car and he baled out and was captured.

15 APRIL

ORB: A further twenty-eight sorties, this time mainly in support of the heavy bombers that targeted Praduro and Bologna. In the evening the DAF Dance Orchestra played in the wing cinema, which was a most welcome break to everybody because the demands of the previous seven days, since the new offensive started, had left everybody tired.

USAAF B-25s flew sorties against Praduro and then against possible escape routes around Bologna, before expanding their operations to cover the reserve areas facing the 8th Army and keep pressure on the Brenner Line. Air support continued on a massive scale.

16 APRIL

ORB: Hampered by low cloud again in the morning but the army provided seven targets which were made up of four aircraft each and targets 5 and 6 were 'Rover Paddy'. A strong cross-wind had rendered the Ravenna landing ground unserviceable so the wing laid on a pre-arranged plan that had been established for just such an emergency. The Ravenna main airfield, that was manned as a crash-landing strip, was pressed into service. Personnel, bombs, ammunition and fuel were carried over to the strip and a full day's operations were carried out from there. That the plan was successful was proved by the fact that the wing as a whole put up the highest day total of all fighter-bomber sorties – 136. The plan went without a hitch and was a supreme example of complete cooperation between all sections of the wing.

Although hampered by low cloud, the Bologna area was again hit by almost 750 heavy bombers while the fighter–bombers maintained round-the-clock pressure on the German forces facing the 5th Army.

17 APRIL

ORB: This was the heaviest day yet. The squadron had nine missions, eight of which were close support army targets, the final one being an attack on a pontoon bridge across the River Po. It was very noticeable that the pilots, especially the leaders, were very tired indeed. Working continually at full pressure was certainly showing its mark. The Group Captain asked the Intelligence Officer how many times the pilots had flown and was told that Capt W. E. Colahan and Flg Off F.T. Craig had led three shows. He decided that in future no pilot would be allowed to fly more than twice a day and that a return would be made up each night of all the missions and the shows completed by each pilot.

News of the liberation of the concentration camps at Nordhausen, Buchenwald and Belsen had reached the Allied forces and the squadron in particular. As a result their attitude towards the Germans hardened.

18 APRIL

ORB: US B-24s and B-17s heavily bombed the Bologna area and there were three close-support targets for four aircraft each and two maximum efforts, twelve aircraft on a 'Timothy' making a total of thirty-six sorties for the day. Pete Schneider, reported missing on the 13th, was now believed to be a POW. Apparently one of his captors had been, in turn, taken prisoner by our boys and he informed the Army Intelligence Officers of Schneider's capture.

US B-24s and B-17s again attacked the Bologna area and dropped nearly 1,000 tons of bombs. This aerial effort coupled with the advance of the US 5th Army meant Bologna was soon to fall.

19 APRIL

ORB: Another big day when we flew nine missions of four aircraft each, of which six were 'Rover Jack Cab Ranks'. In addition there were two armed recces and one army target to hit.

German lines of communication were now in ruins and the 5th and 8th Armies had linked up and were ready for the final push up the Po Valley. The Germans had tried to increase the problems faced by the 8th Army's V Corps in the Argenta Gap by flooding the land, but the intensive Allied air attacks had softened up the defences and the battle had developed into an infantry slog. By pulling back the infantry it allowed the RAF fighter-bombers room to attack further; the weight of the flame throwers, artillery assault and fighter-bomber attacks meant that the German defences crumbled.

20 APRIL

ORB: The day opened up with four aircraft on an armed recce of the battle area when unfortunately the CO, Maj H.E. Wells, crash-landed 3½ miles south of Argenta. He was quite badly hurt and taken to hospital and then moved from one to the other until he finally reached 66th General Hospital at Ricciche at midnight the same day. He was visited by the Gp Capt, Medical Officer and Intelligence Officer but lying on a stretcher in the operations room he was severely dazed and had head and shoulder injuries so was in no fit state to answer any questions as to whether his crash was due to enemy action or not. There were two more missions of 'Rover Jack Cabs', of four aircraft each and four on a barge route, and later on four aircraft carried out a dusk patrol north of the aerodrome.

21 APRIL

ORB: A signal received from 11 Field Ambulance that the CO's injuries did not permit him to return to the squadron, so Capt W.E. Colahan SAAF assumed temporary command.

On the ground the 5th and 8th Armies continued their rapid advance hounding the retreating Germans through the Po Valley. Vast quantities of German transport were destroyed.

22 APRIL

ORB: Three missions of four aircraft each on 'Rover Cab Ranks'.

23 APRIL

ORB: Thirty-two sorties carried out, five missions of four aircraft each were armed recces, two were 'Rover Paddys' and to wind up Lt Col Faure led an attack on bridges with a further four aircraft.

No. 43 Squadron lost their Irish CO, Sqn Ldr John 'Paddy' Hemingway, who collected a packet of German flak and had to bale out. He was unhurt and on landing was chased by German troops, but managed to avoid them for several hours before he was able to hide in a farm. He was later picked up by an armoured column of the 27th Lancers and returned to Ravenna.

24 APRIL

ORB: Twelve aircraft with 90-gallon tanks escorted twenty-four B-26s to Villach. On their return, the tanks were dropped and the aircraft were bombed up ready for two armed recces of four aircraft each and two 'Rover Cab Ranks' against river crossings over the Po. All nine bridges were destroyed, the Germans were trapped and began to surrender.

25 APRIL

ORB: Another busy day with nine missions of four aircraft each, four 'Rover Cab Ranks', four armed recces and an attack on the methane gas station near Monselice.

26 APRIL

ORB: A somewhat easier day when the squadron flew four missions of four aircraft each, two were 'Rover Cab Ranks' with one directed at Nebelwerfers and the other against enemy gun positions.

27 APRIL

Log Book: Dakota, SAAF – Athens to Bari.

ORB: No operational flying.

28 APRIL

Log Book: Dakota, SAAF – Bari to Forli.

ORB: Four aircraft were detailed on a 'Rover Paddy' to recce motor transport north of Monselice. News reached the squadron that Flt Lt Johnny A. Gray, ex-72 Squadron and now a POW, had been awarded the DFC.

29 APRIL

Log Book: Spit IX – Sector recce.

ORB: Squadron flew three missions of twelve sorties on offensive patrols of the battle area. 90-gallon tanks were carried as the retreating Germans were now beyond normal range but these were dropped prior to strafing motor transport.

---

30 APRIL

Log Book: Spit IX, armed recce north of Udine, one flamer and four damaged.

ORB: Continued the offensive patrols with the drop tanks, squadron flew five missions of four sorties each and picked up a huge bag of enemy motor transport destroyed and damaged. 43 Squadron lost Sgt A.S. Crookes when his Spitfire was hit by flak and he was forced to crash-land south-east of Motta.

News had reached the squadron that, in Germany, American troops had entered Munich, the scene of Hitler's pre-war political rallies. Closer to the squadron in Italy, American troops had entered Turin.

Sqn Ldr Ernest Cassidy, Officer Commanding No. 72 (Basutoland) Squadron remarked:

> The grand finale was quite as hectic as we had anticipated and once more the weight of bombs dropped was doubled. There were enough close support targets to satisfy the most ferocious Hun hater and everybody went all-out to have what we all knew to be our last crack at the enemy in Europe. Bombing accuracy was very satisfactory and the squadron dropped blaze bombs for the first time, and very popular they proved. Pilots got a great kick out of seeing the sheets of flame cover the Senio flood banks which were infested with Huns. Casualties during the month were fairly heavy but not so bad as might have been expected considering the effort put up.

---

1 MAY

News was received on the squadron that confirmed the rumours that Hitler had killed himself. The death of Hitler, and American troops fighting in the streets of Berlin, were two significant steps that marked the beginning of the end of the war.

ORB: Four aircraft carried out an uneventful armed recce north of Udine but nothing to report. Sqn Ldr Ernest Cassidy DFC officially posted from No. 92 Squadron to take over from Capt W.E. Colahan.

Cassidy had been with 249 Squadron in Malta in 1941, having flown there with the rest of the squadron from HMS *Ark Royal*. He had also been instrumental in setting up the Malta Night Fighter Unit. At the end of the year he had been posted back to England to instruct and was then again posted, after a rest, to command 222 and 64 Squadrons before joining HQ Middle East. He went to 92 Squadron before his posting to 72 Squadron.

The rather sad vestiges of a once proud German army were in a headlong and confused retreat by now. A typical column under attack consisted of horse-drawn vehicles, a couple of old motor trucks and perhaps a bus or two; all headed north.

With such slow-moving traffic, the columns were easy targets for the Spitfires, which flew unopposed creating havoc among the retreating troops.

2 MAY

ORB: Two aircraft on an offensive patrol, nothing to report. Fighting on the Italian front finished at 12 p.m. after the Germans had surrendered.

The newspaper headline around the world was of Hitler's death. The German surrender had been conveyed in a radio message to the American 34th Division at 9.15 a.m. and the last 40,000 Germans laid down their firearms. Down the road, someone had set fire to a German ammunition dump, which lit up the night sky. The celebrations went on for some time and most people nursed heavy hangovers.

3 MAY

ORB: No operational flying. 'A' Party, with Flg Off R.E. Brill in charge, left for the Udine area with the proposed route: Ravenna, Alfonsine, Argenta, Ferrara and Padua.

4 MAY

ORB: No operational flying, sixteen squadron aircraft flown to Rivolto airfield, 'A' Party arrived there at 1800 hours. 'B' Party left Ravenna at 1700 hours for Rivolto but made a stop for the night at Ferrara.

5 MAY

ORB: No operational flying. 'B' Party resumed their journey but road blocks and traffic jams delayed their progress and they did not reach Padua until 2200 hours.

6 MAY

ORB: No operational flying. 'B' Party continued in their slow progress and managed to reach Rivolto at 1730 hours.

7 MAY

ORB: No operational flying – Plt Off Degerland, who had been reported missing on 13 March, was reported safe as a POW.

8 MAY

ORB: No operational flying, hostilities with Germany ceased, Victory in Europe Day. Daily routine on a peacetime basis was brought into action. Wednesday afternoons were to be devoted to sports half day and a day off on Saturday and Sunday.

Barney recalled that the radio they had was tuned in to the Home Forces station and the crackle of the speaker soon drew a small crowd around. They all listened in amazement to an unknown announcer who described the jubilant scenes in Trafalgar Square. He remembered quite clearly that his emotions at the time were mixed. On the one hand it was good to feel that perhaps some of his loved ones back home in Keynsham were taking part in similar scenes of rejoicing. On the other hand he (in hindsight) and most of his comrades felt somehow cheated that they, who had 'risked life and limb', and had been away from home for so many years, were not there in England to share in the triumph.

---
9 MAY

ORB: VE-Day, official holiday by order of Field Marshal H.R. Alexander. On the ground, thousands of Germans were trying to make their way home, some lucky not to be shot and killed by victorious Allied forces. Some had thrown away their uniforms, most were walking but occasionally bus loads, trucks and wagons and carts were used. Guns and ammunition lay everywhere. Burned-out vehicles and clutter littered the routes and the remnants of the once proud Wehrmacht were in disarray.

---
10 MAY

Log Book: Junkers 13 with Sqn Ldr E. Cassidy. Local flying.

ORB: 'A' Party left for Klagenfurt in Austria.

The news of final victory in Europe had produced a measure of euphoria that many could not believe. Klagenfurt saw riotous celebrations, accompanied by Austrian beer and wine in incredible quantities. They had seen nothing like it since the fall of Tunis back in 1943, when wine had run down the gutters in the streets. During May Austria was occupied by American, Soviet, English and French troops. Many Austrians had experienced life in the concentration camps, death marches, being on the verge of collapse from exhaustion and hunger, or facing certain death at the hands of fanatical SS guards.

Command posts were set up to evacuate the camps and hospitals. Many internees were to be sent back to their countries of origin: Poland, Lithuania, Russia etc., but many did not want to go because they knew they would not be wanted there. Many chose not to go, preferring to stay in their displaced persons' camps living on Red Cross parcels, while officials of the United Nations Relief and Rehabilitation Agency (UNRRA) worked to obtain permission for them to enter the country of their choice, which was predominantly the United States.

Many Red Cross parcels which had been sent to POWs had never been distributed by the Germans, and instead had been stored. This was quickly rectified. In large parts of Austria there was very little destruction or signs of the war, apart from in Vienna, which was severely damaged and had been looted by the Russians. Elsewhere, life was close to normal.

Later, in July, Austria was divided into four occupation zones. From August 1945 the Allied Council exercised supreme executive power. The number of occupation troops was reduced from 700,000 to 20,000 of the Western Allies, and 40,000 of the Soviets. Gradually the Austrian government was authorised to act on its own, particularly in the Western zones. Austria was reinstated as a Democratic Federal Republic when the State Treaty was signed on 15 May 1955. However, zoning continued until 25 October 1955, when the last foreign soldier left the country.

Among the RAF units present in Austria for this period were the following from 324 Wing: 43 Squadron, Spitfire VIII, Klagenfurt, 11 May–10 September 1945; 72 Squadron, Spitfire LF IX, Klagenfurt, 11 May–8 September 1945; 93 Squadron, Spitfire IX, Klagenfurt, 16 May–5 September 1945 (when disbanded); 111 Squadron, Spitfire IXe, Klagenfurt, 16 May–12 September 1945.

---

11 MAY

Log Book: Junkers 13 with Lt Harvey. Udine–Klagenfurt.

---

14 MAY

Log Book: Spitfire IX, formation.

The airfield at Klagenfurt was littered with row upon row of abandoned Luftwaffe transports, a sad reflection of the once powerful German air force. There was time now for the ground crews to work on the appearance of the Spitfires, which were given an immaculate finish of beeswax polish, applied to give both a sheen and, allegedly, to improve the performance and increase the flying speed. Klagenfurt was close to the Austrian Alps and several trips were arranged to explore them. Among the picturesque mountain villages were attractive beer gardens with occasionally a small brewery. Needless to say, supplies were bundled into whatever transport could be found and returned to the squadron for everyone to enjoy. The area was also covered with marked walks and remote cafes, and most spare time was spent in the mountains, relaxing, eating and drinking.

---

28 MAY

Log Book: 1. Spitfire IX, to Revolto; 2. DAF fly-past, landed Lavorino for DAF party!

The celebration had been organised by Air Vice-Marshal Robert Foster. The fly-past proved spectacular as squadron after squadron swept across the air base. No. 324 Wing was led by Barney Beresford, and 72 Squadron put up a good show in tight formation. That night the AOC's garden at Brazzaco, near Venice, was turned into a fairyland, the branches of the trees bedecked with coloured lights, a flare path marked the driveway, floodlights pinpointed the various cocktail bars, there were tents full of food and the DAF Band played in the background. Guests from other commands and the army, who had been present at the fly-past, were there to meet the pilots, the squadron commanders and wing leaders. It was the last great occasion where veterans of the fighting in North Africa, Sicily and Italy met up and were appreciated, particularly by the soldiers on the ground who had witnessed the accuracy of the fighter-bomber strikes so close to their own lines, and which had proved fundamental in driving the Germans back.

The extent to which the DAF fighter-bomber attacks had helped to bring about the final capitulation was highlighted by General von Senger, the captured German Commander of XIV Corps:

> The effect of Allied air attacks on the frontier route of Italy made the fuel and ammunition situation very critical. We had no difficulty with food since we bought it locally. The night bombing was very effective and caused heavy losses. We could still move when required at night but could not move at all in the daytime due to air attacks. The fighter-bomber pilots had a genuinely damaging effect. They hindered practically all movement at the focal points; even tanks could not move during the day. The effectiveness of fighter-bombers lay in that their presence alone over the battlefield paralysed every movement. It was the bombing over the River Po crossings that finished us. We could have withdrawn successfully with normal rearguard action despite the heavy pressure, but due to the destruction of the ferries and river crossings we lost all our equipment. North of the river we were no longer an army.

To have been part of the great victory made everyone, including Barney, justifiably proud.

---

29 MAY

Log Book: Spitfire IX, Lavorino–Klagenfurt.

Sailing on the lake, picnicking in the mountains and partying in the Mess were the order of the days. There was no fraternising with Austrian civilians so in the evening they stayed on the airfield and the army remained in their camps.

---

30 MAY

Log Book: Spitfire IX, formation and air test.

CHAPTER 15

After the War

June 1945–January 1946

For Barney, the month of June was very uneventful on the flying front, comprising cross-country flying exercises, aerobatics and formation flying practice. By now parcels had started to arrive from England containing a few of life's little luxuries. There was still snow on the nearby mountain peaks and plenty of rest and recuperation could be had by the squadron. The Velden area on the Wörthersee was one popular billet and about 30 miles west of Klagenfurt; Villach was another popular holiday resort. It was really beautiful in the summer of 1945. When the Austrians dressed up to go out on a Sunday afternoon it was done with style. The men would usually be in leather shorts and decorated hats, and the ladies wore colourful dresses. It was all so different to the heat and dirt of North Africa, and the cold and wet devastation of Italy.

Hotels such as the Mossdacker were frequented, where the food was first class and a swimming pool was available. Velden had been a well-known holiday resort before the war but, despite the ravages of the conflict, its surroundings still remained beautiful. The larger hotels like the Mossdacker were commandeered by the military and turned into rest camps or made available for 48-hour passes. The hotel provided unbelievable luxury: there were proper beds and sheets; knives, forks and tablecloths; and a menu that really *was* first class. Pretty young waitresses were a temptation but by and large everyone behaved like officers and gentlemen.

At the other end of the lake was Klagenfurt and the air base. Occasionally, shows were put on for the benefit of the Allied forces. Barney recalled seeing *Die Fledermaus* and a Beethoven recital by the Klagenfurt Symphony Orchestra. The water in the lake was, he recalled, very cold, but the sun was hot and you could lie on the wooden planking that ran down to the lake's edge and up to the hotel terrace.

Although it was pleasant where they were, not that far away it was a very different story. Flying training 'just in case' continued, for although the war was at an end, units were required to remain fit for further operations if necessary. They were situated in an area that was still under heavy German influence, and not far from Italy or Yugoslavia and the communist world. Unease on the borders, incidents, disappearances and civil clashes maintained a state of tension. The end of the war had left great confusion in the area.

The main military forces in Yugoslavia were commanded by Marshal Tito, who had resisted the Germans and been useful to the Allied cause. During the early stages of the Second World War, the partisan activities had not been directly supported by the Western Allies, but after the Tehran and Yalta conferences in 1943, the partisans were sustained by Allied airdrops to their headquarters. The Balkan Air Force had been formed in June 1944 to control operations that were mainly aimed at helping Tito's forces. Due to his close ties to Stalin, Tito often quarrelled with the British and American staff officers attached to his headquarters.

On 5 April 1945 Tito had signed an agreement with the USSR allowing 'temporary entry of Soviet troops into Yugoslav territory'. Aided by the Red Army, the partisans helped in the liberation. All external forces were ordered off Yugoslav soil after the end of hostilities in Europe. The remaining fascist Ustaša and royalist Checknik troops and their supporters were subject to summary trials and execution en masse, so British troops had to be used to bringing situations under control. There were also odd bands of well-armed partisan and guerilla troops roaming around, as well as refugees and displaced people and, to complicate matters even further, all sorts of political factions were involved. The troops had a tough job because many of the displaced people did not want to return to where they had come from. Some had to be forced at gunpoint because they were in fear of their lives if they returned home.

No. 72 Squadron, as part of 324 Wing, was kept on as a mobile force, and the continued presence of the RAF guaranteed that the Allied Military Government in Austria could operate satisfactorily.

Some of the squadron inspected a deserted POW camp that had been used to hold 100 or so British prisoners of war. Although it was now empty, they recalled there was something quite eerie about the atmosphere of the place. It was as though all the memories were somehow trapped inside the wooden huts. The men from 72 were glad to get out, back into the open air.

---

14 AUGUST

ORB: VJ-Day – it was VE-Day all over again. The announcer back in London described the noisy scene as tens of thousands of jubilant servicemen and civilians swarmed the streets.

As summer filtered into autumn and then into winter, snow began to fall on the mountains so they learned to ski. Their equipment was fairly basic as there were no proper ski boots around – they used their army issue boots that they had got used to wearing while flying (in case they had had to bale out over enemy lines and walk back). They managed to hire some skis and sticks and, since most of the ski lifts were still running, they were able to get in a fair bit of practice. At the hotels they were always looked after. When they returned to their temporary quarters they were invariably greeted with a large tot of brandy to warm them up and fabulous hot meals.

Over the following seven weeks there was very little flying acitivity to speak of, adding up to just fourteen sorties: aerobatics, sector recces, air tests and bombing practice. Barney's final log book entry as an operational Spitfire pilot was on 21 October 1945. It was brief and to the point: 'Spitfire IX to Zeltweg'. Gp Capt Barney Beresford, OC 324 Wing, signed off Barney's log book for October with the following assessment: 'Rated as exceptional as a fighter-bomber pilot and a flight commander.'

Back on Civvy Street

When Barney finally got home to England he remembered quite vividly his homecoming. His wife, Dorothy, was in the garden at 68 High Street hanging the washing out on the line. It was a beautiful crisp midwinter day and she was surprised to see him.

'Oh hello, what are you doing here?' she said.

'Where's my baby?' replied Barney.

'She's upstairs asleep. Don't you go waking her up.'

He had only seen her once since she had been born; welcome home, he thought!

Barney was released from the RAF but was retained on the Reserve List. He attended 12 Reserve Flying School at Filton annually from 1948 until 1952 where he would have a week's refresher course in a Tiger Moth and later a de Havilland Canada Chipmunk after they were introduced into service. He remained on the Reserve until 1956.

He rejoined Gordian Strapping as a salesman. Life returned pretty much to normal and the annual company bash was always a 'good show'. Holidays were taken in Devon and Cornwall and Bournemouth with the children; Jane, and then Pip, had arrived to join Sarah.

Barney did not talk much about the war for some time afterwards, there appeared to be a strong cultural sense of maintaining a 'stiff upper lip', and he lost touch with his friends and colleagues from the RAF days that had survived with him. There were too many that had been lost, and that brought back painful memories, among them his good friend Roy Hussey. The losses of youth and innocence were tragic.

During the school holidays, while the children were growing up, one of them might travel with him to see his customers; he was grateful for the company. There was a spell with Hugh Sutherland as a pension adviser and then as a publican, when the Barnfathers ran the Rose and Crown in the Somerset village of Crosscombe, between Wells and Shepton Mallet. He continued to drink heavily. They had drunk a lot back in the war but the difference then was being able to have a quick blast of oxygen, which was a very good cure for a hangover. There were times when he thought he was still one of the boys, his wife recalled with fondness, but he also drank to forget some of the war experiences.

After the Rose and Crown they lived for a few years in a pretty cottage on the hillside overlooking Crosscombe, but then moved back to Keynsham to be nearer family. He retained his love of football and, for a time, he was secretary of Keynsham

Town Football Club and the local Conservative Club. Manners were important to him. Treat others as you would wish to be treated; that was how he lived, and how he expected his children to follow. It mattered to him that they displayed kindness in another's trouble, and courage in their own.

By now Barney and Dorothy were grandparents, and it was only now that Barney started to recount his war experiences, if his children and grandchildren showed an interest. Very occasionally he would get out his log book as it was full of memories. In his own handwriting he had kept a record of every flight and with it additional comments and small anecdotes. Each month it was signed off by his squadron leader or flight commander.

Then Barney suffered a stroke which left him paralysed down one side. He lived a little longer but was barely able to move. He died in 1984, a kind, fun-loving man who was a caring father and grandfather. He is remembered fondly around Keynsham: 'Mad bugger that Barnfather!'

Appendix

ROBERT 'BARNEY' BARNFATHER'S RAF SERVICE CAREER
1941–45

Training

July–Sept 1941   No. 1 Training Squadron, No. 9 Service Flying Training School, Hullavington

Sept–Nov 1941   No. 57 OTU, Hawarden, Chester

Operations

Nov 1941–April 1942   No. 234 Squadron, Ibsley, Hampshire

May–July 1942   No. 603 Squadron, Malta

Aug 1942–March 1943   No. 52 OTU, Aston Down, Gloucestershire

May 1943   No. 72 Squadron, Tunisia

June–July 1943   Hal Far, Malta

July–Sept 1943   Comiso, Sicily

Sept–Dec 1943   Tusciano, Italy

Jan–Feb 1944   Naples, Italy
Lago, Italy

March–Aug 1944   No. 71 OTU, Ismailia, Egypt

Aug–Oct 1944   No. 94 Squadron, Egypt

Oct–Nov 1944   No. 43 Squadron, Florence, Italy

Nov 1944–April 1945   No. 94 Squadron, Athens and Kalamaki, Greece

April–Nov 1945   No. 72 Squadron, Ravenna, Italy
Klagenfurt, Austria

Index